SAGE was founded in 1965 by Sara Miller McCune to support the dissemination of usable knowledge by publishing innovative and high-quality research and teaching content. Today, we publish over 900 journals, including those of more than 400 learned societies, more than 800 new books per year, and a growing range of library products including archives, data, case studies, reports, and video. SAGE remains majority-owned by our founder, and after Sara's lifetime will become owned by a charitable trust that secures our continued independence.

Los Angeles | London | New Delhi | Singapore | Washington DC | Melbourne

Fiscal Consolidation, Budget Deficits and the Macro Economy

Fiscal Consolidation, Budget Deficits and the Macro Economy

Lekha S. Chakraborty

Los Angeles | London | New Delhi
Singapore | Washington DC | Melbourne

Copyright © Lekha Chakraborty, 2016

All rights reserved. No part of this book may be reproduced or utilised in any form or by any means, electronic or mechanical, including photocopying, recording or by any information storage or retrieval system, without permission in writing from the publisher.

First published in 2016 by

 SAGE Publications India Pvt Ltd
B1/I-1 Mohan Cooperative Industrial Area
Mathura Road, New Delhi 110044, India
www.sagepub.in

SAGE Publications Inc
2455 Teller Road
Thousand Oaks, California 91320, USA

SAGE Publications Ltd
1 Oliver's Yard, 55 City Road
London EC1Y 1SP, United Kingdom

SAGE Publications Asia-Pacific Pte Ltd
3 Church Street
#10-04 Samsung Hub
Singapore 049483

Published by Vivek Mehra for SAGE Publications India Pvt Ltd, typeset in Minion 10.5/12.5 pts by Zaza Eunice, Hosur, Tamil Nadu, India and printed at Chaman Enterprises, New Delhi.

Library of Congress Cataloging-in-Publication Data

Name: Chakraborty, Lekha S., author.
Title: Fiscal consolidation, budget deficits and the macroeconomy : monetary-fiscal links in India / Lekha Chakraborty.
Description: Thousand Oaks, California : SAGE, 2016. | Includes bibliographical references and index.
Identifiers: LCCN 2016003211 | ISBN 9789351509899 (hardback : alk. paper)
Subjects: LCSH: Budget deficits—India. | Fiscal policy—India. | Finance, Public—India.
Classification: LCC HJ2157 .C4287 2016 | DDC 339.5/20954—dc23 LC record available at http://lccn.loc.gov/2016003211

ISBN: 978-93-515-0989-9 (HB)

The SAGE Team: Supriya Das, Sanghamitra Patowary and Rajinder Kaur

TO MY MOTHER 'SALMA'

Thank you for choosing a SAGE product!
If you have any comment, observation or feedback,
I would like to personally hear from you.

Please write to me at **contactceo@sagepub.in**

Vivek Mehra, Managing Director and CEO, SAGE India.

Bulk Sales

SAGE India offers special discounts
for purchase of books in bulk.
We also make available special imprints
and excerpts from our books on demand.

For orders and enquiries, write to us at

Marketing Department
SAGE Publications India Pvt Ltd
B1/I-1, Mohan Cooperative Industrial Area
Mathura Road, Post Bag 7
New Delhi 110044, India

E-mail us at **marketing@sagepub.in**

Get to know more about SAGE

Be invited to SAGE events, get on our mailing list.
Write today to **marketing@sagepub.in**

This book is also available as an e-book.

Contents

List of Tables	ix
List of Figures	xi
List of Abbreviations	xiii
Preface	xv
Acknowledgements	xix

1 Introduction	1
2 Fiscal Deficit and Macroeconomic Activity of Central and Subnational Governments	13
3 Fiscal Deficit, Capital Formation and Crowding Out	43
4 Deficit–Interest Rate Link and Financial Markets	79
5 Monetary–Fiscal Policy Coordination: Fiscal Rules and Testing for Monetary Seigniorage	104
6 Fiscal Seigniorage: Composition of Deficits	121
7 Fiscal Deficit and Seigniorage Link: Monetary Policy Regimes and Empirical Analysis	128
8 Fiscal Deficit and Inflation	153
9 Policy Takeaways: The Revival of Fiscal Activism	163

Bibliography	171
Index	193
About the Author	198

List of Tables

2.1	Trends in Different Concepts of Deficit in India (as Percentage of GDP)	14
2.2	Financing Pattern of Fiscal Deficit (as Percentage of Total)	17
2.3	Composition of Fiscal Deficit: Structural and Cyclical (as Percentage of GDP)	20
2.4	Trends in Central Government Expenditure (as Percentage of GDP)	21
2.5	Gross Fixed Capital Formation in India and Its Major Components (as Percentage of GDP)	23
2.6	Correlation Matrix of Fiscal Deficit and Capital Formation	24
2.7	Correlation Coefficient of Fiscal Deficit and Rates of Interest	26
2.8	Correlation Matrix of Fiscal Deficit, Seigniorage, M3 and Inflation	27
2.9	Money Multipliers of Indian Economy	28
2.10	Combined Deficits of the Central and State Governments (as Percentage of GDP)	42
3.1	Selected Empirical Evidences on Crowding Out	49
3.2	Unit Root Test Results for Private Corporate Investment and Its Apriori Determinants	63
3.3	Public Investment Model	67
3.4	Public Infrastructure Investment Model	70
3.5	Public Non-Infrastructure Model	73
3.6	Fiscal Deficit and Private Corporate Investment Links	74
4.1	Selected Empirical Evidences on Link between Fiscal Deficit and Rate of Interest	83
4.2	Unit Root Test Results for Rate of Interest and Its Apriori Determinants	92
4.3	Real Long-Run Rate of Interest Model	95

4.4 Real Long-Run Rate of Interest Model: Hsiao (1981) Detection of Optimal Lags of the Manipulated Variables and FPE of the Controlled Variable (G-Sec Rate)   96

4.5 High-Frequency Regime: Unit Root Test Results for Ex Ante Real Rate of Interest and Fiscal Deficit   102

4.6 High-Frequency Regime: Detection of Optimal Lags and FPE   103

5.1 Robustness Check of Seigniorage–Inflation Tax Links: Estimates from Maximum Entropy Ensemble of Bootstrapping   114

5.2 High-Frequency Data Estimation of Monetary Seigniorage Laffer Curve: ECM Estimates   118

5.3 Annual Frequency Data Estimation of Monetary Seigniorage Laffer Curve: Error Correction Mechanism Estimates   118

6.1 Fiscal Seigniorage Laffer Curve, Annual Frequency Data (1970–71 to 2012–13): Error Correction Mechanism Estimates   126

7.1 Historical and Empirical Evidences against Central Bank Independence (No Deficit–Money Links)   136

7.2 Historical and Empirical Evidences for Central Bank Independence (Deficit–Money Links)   138

7.3 Unit Root Test Results   143

7.4 Seigniorage Model: Results from Asymmetric VAR   145

7.5 Stability of Money Multipliers: Evidence from Buoyancy Estimates   147

7.6 Money Supply–Deficit–Asymmetric VAR Model   148

7.7 Descriptive Statistics of Money Multipliers   151

7.8 Reserve Money Model in High-Frequency Data Regime   151

8.1 Inflation Model: Detection of Optimal Lags of the Manipulated Variables and FPE   161

8.2 Inflation Model: High-Frequency Regime   161

List of Figures

2.1	Revenue Deficit/Fiscal Deficit (RD/FD) Ratio	16
2.2	Movement of Selected Real and Nominal Rates of Interest in India	25
2.3	Trends in Seigniorage	27
2.4	Trends in M1/M0 and M3/M0	29
2.5	Trends in Revenue Deficit of Subnational Government (as Percentage of GDP)	30
2.6	Trends in Fiscal Deficit of Subnational Government (as Percentage of GDP)	31
2.7	Revenue Deficit of High-Income States: Ex Ante and Ex Post FRBM	32
2.8	Fiscal Deficit of High-Income States: Ex Ante and Ex Post FRBM	33
2.9	Primary Deficit of High-Income States: Ex Ante and Ex Post FRBM	33
2.10	Revenue Deficit of Middle-Income States: Ex Ante and Ex Post FRBM	34
2.11	Fiscal Deficit of Middle-Income States: Ex Ante and Ex Post FRBM	34
2.12	Primary Deficit of Middle-Income States: Ex Ante and Ex Post FRBM	35
2.13	Revenue Deficit of Low-Income States: Ex Ante and Ex Post FRBM	35
2.14	Fiscal Deficit of Low-Income States: Ex Ante and Ex Post FRBM	36
2.15	Primary Deficit of Low-Income States: Ex Ante and Ex Post FRA	37
2.16	Revenue Deficit of Special Category States: Ex Ante and Ex Post FRA	38
2.17	Fiscal Deficit of Special Category States: Ex Ante and Ex Post FRA	39

2.18 Primary Deficit of Special Category States: Ex Ante and
     Ex Post FRA   40
2.19 Subnational Revenue Deficit: Ex Ante and Ex Post FRBM   41

3.1 Movement of Trend and Cyclical GDP in India: 1980–81 to
     2013–14   59
3.2 Trends in Infrastructure and Non-Infrastructure
     Investment in India   69

4.1 Plot of Hodrick–Prescott Filtered Expected Inflation WPI
     Series in India   93
4.2 Intertemporal Variations in 91-Day Treasury Bill:
     2006:03–2015:07   97
4.3 Plot of Actual Rate of Inflation and Hodrick–Prescott
     Filtered Expected Inflation Series in India:
     2006:03–2015:07   98
4.4 Co-Movement of Rate of Interest and WPI Rate of
     Inflation   99
4.5 Co-Movement of Rate of Interest and CPI Rate of
     Inflation   100
4.6 Co-Movement of WPI and CPI Rates of Inflation   101
4.7 Nominal and Ex Ante Real Rate of Interest in India:
     Deregulated Financial Regime   102

5.1 Trends in Deficits   109
5.2 Financing Pattern of Deficits   109
5.3 Two Significant Components of Seigniorage   111
5.4 Seigniorage and Inflation Tax   113
5.5 Seigniorage and Dual Inflation Equilibria   115

6.1 Fiscal Seigniorage in India (in Per Cent)   124
6.2 Co-Movement of Fiscal and Monetary Seigniorage
     (in Per Cent)   124
6.3 Fiscal and Monetary Seigniorage in India (in Per Cent):
     Decadal Averages   125

7.1 Cyclical and Trend Components of Index of Industrial
     Production   149
7.2 Trends in Money Multipliers: High-Frequency Data   150
7.3 Movements of Macrovariables in High-Frequency
     Regime   152

List of Abbreviations

AIC	Akaike information criteria
AVAR	Asymmetric vector auto regression
CBI	Central bank independence
EDP	Excessive deficit procedures
FRBM	Fiscal Responsibility and Budget Management
FPE	Final Prediction Error
FTPL	Fiscal theory of price level
GDP	Gross domestic product
HIS	High-income states
IIP	Index of industrial production
IMF	International Monetary Fund
LIS	Low-income states
MEBOOT	Maximum entropy ensemble of bootstrap
MIS	Middle-income states
NCEUS	National Commission for Enterprises in the Unorganized Sector
NCM	New consensus macroeconomics
NK	New Keynesian
NMC	New macroeconomic consensus
OMO	Open market operations
PSBR	Public sector borrowing requirement
RBI	Reserve Bank of India
RET	Ricardian Equivalence Theorem
SBC	Schwarz Bayesian Criteria
SLR	Statutory liquidity ratio
TTP	Trend through peaks
UMA	Unpleasant monetary arithmetic

Preface

Fiscal consolidation has been the norm of recent macroeconomic policy adjustment in India. Excessive deficits have often been indicated for maintaining low interest rate regime, lack of private capital formation, creation of seigniorage and rise in inflation. However, there is considerable ambiguity about the impacts of fiscal deficits on macroeconomic outcomes. This book empirically takes up these issues against the backdrop of fiscal consolidation package. The fiscal rules at the centre and state level in India—Fiscal Responsibility and Budget Management (FRBM) Acts—were enacted with the aim to eliminate revenue deficit and to reduce the fiscal deficit to three per cent of gross domestic product (GDP). Against the backdrop of New Monetary Framework, the monetary policy has also articulated a regime towards central bank independence (CBI) and inflation targeting in India. It is disquieting to observe the tendency of considering the monetary and fiscal policies in isolation while assessing the impact of macroeconomic institutions on policy outcomes. There is no systematic analysis of the macroeconomic impacts of these macro policy shifts and the weakening of the plausible fiscal–monetary policy coordination. This book tries to fill this gap through applied macroeconometrics, using the annual data as well as the high-frequency data analysis of deregulated financial regime.

I sincerely acknowledge the comments from an anonymous referee who has rightfully highlighted the need to capture the fall out of subnational deficits which also contribute to the macroeconomic impacts. Indeed, I have raised the concern regarding the measurement issues related to deficits and that it would have been ideal to consider public sector borrowing requirement (PSBR) instead of fiscal deficit to study the macroeconomic impacts. But why it could not be done has been explained in Chapter 1 of the book. Though the subnational deficits are addressed in Chapter 2 of the book, it needs to be highlighted that nature of impact of the state level deficit on macro economy will be different than central deficit due to credit market fragmentation for government borrowing between union and states and forced contractual borrowing at the state level. Since the enactment of fiscal rules at the state level during the early 2000, states have managed to keep their fiscal deficit well below the FRBM target. If there are issues related to fiscal imbalance and macro economy, it could be better captured if only union government's fiscal deficit is considered for the purpose of econometric analysis. To capture the impacts, I have used the recent high-frequency data on fiscal deficit and other macroeconomic variables of the deregulated financial regime. Such high-frequency data at the state level is not available and similar exercise with the state deficits or combined deficit cannot be carried out.

As a prelude to the analysis of impacts of deficits, I have undertaken a nostalgic survey in macroeconomics of the existing macroeconomic paradigms, discussing the impact of fiscal deficit. While the Neoclassicals envisioned the detrimental effects of deficits, the Keynesians always argued that an appropriately timed fiscal deficit can have beneficial consequences. These diametrically opposite debates are captured in Chapter 1. This symposium on deficits has also captured the much-debated Ricardian Equivalence Theorem (RET), which envisioned that rational economic agents can see through the intertemporal veil and realised that deficits merely postpone taxes to future generations. The contemporary relevance of the paradigms and the measurement issues related to deficit are discussed in Chapter 1.

What is missing in the design of numeric fiscal rules is the macroeconomic channel through which the deficits affect the output gap. It is not only the levels of deficit but also the financing pattern of deficits that create macroeconomic consequences. This aspect was surpassed in the debates related to fiscal rules and budget management policies. The fiscal rules have taken the deficit financing rules as granted and deal with only numerical targets of deficits. However, excessive use of any financing mode of deficits has macroeconomic repercussions and cannot be tackled by focusing on the fiscal rules alone. In Chapter 2, I have extensively used simple data explorations to analyse the trends in deficits and its financing pattern over the years and also the movement of fiscal deficit in relation to selected macroeconomic

Preface **xvii**

variables including capital formation, rate of interest, seigniorage, money supply and inflation. Intertemporally, the monetisation of fiscal deficit has been brought down through deliberate open market operations (OMO), especially in the deregulated financial regime. It is often argued that a shift in the financing pattern of fiscal deficit from seigniorage financing to bond financing may exert upward pressures on rate of interest, which can affect the interest-sensitive components of private spending.

It is interesting to contextualise this book against 'the rise and fall of fiscal activism'. As recently as till 2007, there was a widespread consensus among macroeconomists that fiscal policy has failed as a countercyclical policy instrument. However, ex post to global financial crisis, with massive fiscal stimulus packages, a wide range of economists in universities, governments and businesses have started rethinking fiscal policy as an active countercyclical policy tool. Prior to financial crisis, there was an increasing consensus among the (new Keynesian) economists to use monetary policy as a countercyclical policy, as they visualised that monetary policy could be adjusted more rapidly through interest rate changes, and could be effective in manoeuvring aggregate demand. But it failed. In this process, they have projected entirely a different view about the efficacy of fiscal policy. Fiscal deficit is often cited as a culprit for all macroeconomic maladies. In Chapter 3, I have looked into the empirical link between fiscal deficit and the capital formation in the economy, against the backdrop of present debates on the taxonomy of real and financial crowding out. The complementary relationship between public and private spending that has occurred irrespective of the mode of financing of fiscal deficit has been analysed and positive evidence in the context of Indian economy have been found. The results from asymmetric vector autoregressive models refuted that public investment, especially the public infrastructure investment, displaces private investment broadly on a dollar-for-dollar basis. The interest rate sensitivity of private investment itself does not indicate financial crowding out either. The evidence for financial crowding out can only be established after checking whether real rates of interest rise is induced by fiscal deficit. In Chapter 4, I found no evidence of financial crowding out for both administered and deregulated interest rate regime, which is quite contrary to the popular belief that increase in fiscal deficit induces the rate of interest. The 91-day treasury bill rate adjusted for inflationary expectations is selected as the reference rate and the link between the two is analysed. The asymmetric vector auto regression (AVAR) results revealed that rate of interest is affected by inflationary expectations and not by deficits.

Ex post to global financial crisis, many economists have argued that the appropriate role of monetary policy in the post-crisis era since 2007 is to seigniorage finance the deficits. However, in India, with the enactment of New Monetary Framework, agreed between Government of India and central bank in February 2015, we have moved towards inflation targeting and an increased CBI. Against this backdrop, the fiscal seigniorage, a relatively new concept, is worked out in the Indian context in Chapter 6, which tries to establish its effect on the central bank autonomy. The fiscal and monetary linkages are analysed in Chapters 5 and 6, using the estimates of monetary and fiscal seigniorage and a plausibility of a Laffer curve. The preliminary evidence for a seigniorage Laffer curve is noted in this book. Unpacking this link further between deficits and seigniorage in Chapter 7, I have found that seigniorage financing per se is not inflationary. However, the plausibility whether fiscal deficit is inflationary cannot be ruled out. It is often argued that fiscal deficit contributes directly to inflationary pressures. The recent fiscal theories of price level determination (FTPL) argued that the problems of price level indeterminacy can be solved if the central bank peg the nominal interest rate at a level consistent with the central bank's desired inflation rate, rather than by controlling the growth of (base) money supply. Fiscal policy has enormous influence on the price level even when the central bank is not forced to accommodate fiscal tendencies. The results from asymmetric vector regressive models in Chapter 8 revealed that supplyside factors exert inflationary pressures in Indian economy more than deficit per se. Given that fiscal deficit per se has less adverse macroeconomic consequences, has the move from 'discretion' to 'rules'—both fiscal rules and inflation targeting rules—been a transformation of macroeconomic policies towards a New Macroeconomic Consensus (NMC) in India? Would the disappearing deficits through fiscal rules have adverse long-run consequences on economic growth? I hope this book would spark such debates in young minds.

Lekha S. Chakraborty

Acknowledgements

Special thanks to Pinaki Chakraborty for his constant inspiration for completing this book. Despite his busy schedule as Chief Economic Adviser at the Fourteenth Finance Commission, he was always energetic to discuss about the progress of my book. I owe him more than I realise.

I am grateful to Rathin Roy, Director of National Institute of Public Finance and Policy (NIPFP), who played a singularly significant role in making this book a reality within a stipulated timeframe by providing me with an enabling environment at NIPFP. I express my sincere thanks to Dimitri Papadimitriou and Rania Antonopoulos of the Levy Economics Institute of Bard College, where I am affiliated to as a Research Associate.

I express my gratitude to Ashok Lahiri, T.M. Thomas Isaac, Chandan Mukherjee, M. Govinda Rao, K.L. Krishna, Kavita Rao Sugato Dasgupta and Sivaramakrishna Sarma for their academic inputs at various stages of my work.

I owe my special gratitude to Unni Nair, Supriya Das and Sanghamitra Patowary SAGE Publishing, to make this book a reality within the tight time frame.

Thanks to Amita Manhas for her diligent secretarial assistance.

Lekha S. Chakraborty

1
Introduction

In recent years, fiscal deficit reduction has become one of the principal objectives of fiscal reforms in both developed and developing countries. The Maastricht Treaty was the commencement of fiscal consolidation reforms across the globe. Two of the Maastricht criteria for entry into the European Monetary Union were that member nations should have a budget deficit of not more than three per cent of GDP and a national debt of not more than 60 per cent of GDP. Also, there were Medium Term Fiscal Consolidation Plans launched in the industrial countries in the 1980s; for instance, Deficit Reduction and Debt Control Act in Canada, the Goria Plan in Italy, the Medium Term Financial Strategy in the United Kingdom, the Gramm-Rudman-Hollings Act in the United States and the Trilogy in Australia (Kopits and Symansky, 1998 and Schaechter et al., 2012). In India, efforts were, thus, made to contain the fiscal deficit by both the central and state governments. The Fiscal Responsibility and Budget Management (FRBM) Act was enacted by the Government of India in 2000 with the aim to eliminate revenue deficit and to reduce the fiscal deficit to three per cent of GDP by 2008–09. All the states in India also have introduced FRBM legislations. The rationale behind the reduction in fiscal deficit emanated from the theoretical paradigms of macroeconomics, which argued that excessive fiscal deficit often triggers inflationary pressures in the economy, increases rate of interest and crowds out private capital formation, creates balance of payment crisis and in turn debt spiraling. However, considerable ambiguity exists about the link between fiscal deficit and macroeconomic activity.

Is fiscal deficit containment a prerequisite for sustained reduction in the rate of inflation in India? If so, would the extent of monetisation of fiscal deficit in India eventually create inflation? Does fiscal deficit crowd out private investment in India and, if so, to what extent? Is the transmission channel for the crowding out via changes in rate of interest? Does fiscal deficit affect rate of interest in India? It is imperative to analyse the macroeconomic consequences of fiscal deficits in India for an informed policy debate on the issue.

1.1 Fiscal Deficit: Relevance of the Concept in Measuring Macroeconomic Impact

Although the nature of relationship between fiscal deficit and real economic activity received enormous attention in the recent years, literature on this subject did not have a definite conclusion regarding the impact of deficit on real economy. The questions that have been frequently addressed are whether deficits (i) are inflationary, (ii) are expansionary, (iii) alter the composition of output away from investment and net exports or (iv) do not have any impact on real economy (Boskin, 1988). Increased attention has also been given to develop an appropriate concept of deficit, which can capture the exact impact of fiscal policy on the macroeconomy. It is argued that unless a correct indicator of government deficit is adopted, there is a possibility of miscalculation of pre-emption of resources by the government.

As for the coverage, the ideal concept of deficit to study the macroeconomic impact is the public sector borrowing requirement (PSBR). In other words, any measurement of government deficit should consider the deficit of the public sector as a whole, instead of sectoral deficit of different public sector entities. But problem lies in covering the public sector as a whole for a comprehensive measurement of public sector deficit, as there are intra-public sector transactions for which data is not readily available. Unless intra-public sector transactions are netted out, estimation of public sector deficit may suffer from the problem of double counting, leading to the over estimation of deficit. Thus, any measurement of government deficit should be defined of a public sector of given coverage, the intersectoral linkage within the public sector has to be delineated and a time horizon should be specified to assess the impact of fiscal deficit (Blejer and Cheasty, 1991).

Various concepts of deficit and their use as indicators to evaluate the budgetary performance of the government is a recent phenomenon in India. This evolution is also a result of the contemporaneous paradigm shift to a series of *purpose-specific* deficit measures worldwide from the conventional approach of *single measure* of budget deficit. Four pioneering surveys on the measurement of *purpose-specific* budgetary deficits deserve mention; there are four International Monetary Fund (IMF) studies by Blinder and Solow (1974), Heller et al. (1986), Blejer and Chu (1988) and Blejer and Cheasty (1993) (for details, see Pattnaik et al., 1999). Traditionally (up to the late 1980s), the concept of *budget deficit* was in prominence in India, and containing of *budget deficit* was the prime objective of fiscal management. *Budget deficit* or the overall deficit of the central government was that part of the deficit covered by 91-day treasury bills and withdrawal of cash balances with Reserve Bank of India (RBI). As *budget deficit* was the borrowing from the central bank, it increased reserve money and created inflation. Thus, emphasis was given to reduce the volume of *budget deficit* (Editorial Note, 1996).[1] As RBI was holding dated government securities,[2] which also increased the reserve money into the system, *budget deficit* could only give a partial picture of the total increase in the reserve money. In order to capture the exact impact of deficits in the creation of reserve money, Chakraborty Committee (RBI, 1985) recommended the concept of *monetised deficit*, which can be defined as the increase of net RBI credit to the central government.[3]

---

[1] Even if the budget deficits as officially defined are controlled, but tax revenues are inadequate to finance current and capital expenditures, the deficit financed through 'open market borrowing' would have to increase. To the extent that such borrowing is not a draft on the private sector savings, it too could result in an increase in money supply, through the mechanism of a refinancing facility on government securities offered by the central bank, for example. Further, to the extent that the budget deficits finance productive capacity in industry and productivity enhancing infrastructure in agriculture, and thereby relax supply constraints in the system, they should result in output increases rather than inflation.

[2] A fraction of the new issue of government securities is taken up by the RBI when the demand for these securities is inadequate among public and financial institution. This also adds to the reserve money into the system.

[3] RBI's holding of ad hocs, dated government securities, 91-day treasury bills and government's currency liabilities constitute the net RBI credit central government, the measure of monetised deficit in India.

4 FISCAL CONSOLIDATION, BUDGET DEFICITS AND THE MACRO ECONOMY

Rakshit (1987) argued that in an open economy, even the monetised deficit is not a proper indicator to rely on to understand the increase in reserve money due to the budgetary operation. According to him,

> If the government borrows from the reserve bank in order to repay some foreign loan, the amount of high-powered money remains unaltered, the fall in foreign exchange reserves being offset by rise in government securities on the asset side of the Reserve Bank's balance sheet. Indeed, when the government takes loans from the domestic market in order to make payments abroad, the reserve money registers a decline; opposite is the effect of financing the domestic expenses of the government through borrowing from external sources. Hence, even apart from the *budget deficit*, the excess of net external borrowing by the government over its payment abroad raises the amount of reserve money into the system.

Apart from this, impact of *budget deficit* also depends on the RBI policy with respect to the maintaining of cash reserve ratio, ceiling on bank credit and distribution of credit.[4]

Traditional measure of *budget deficit* and its expanded form, the *monetised deficit*, excludes part of the resource gap of the government, which is financed through borrowing outside RBI. Thus, in recent years, emphasis has been given to contain the *fiscal deficit*, which is the net borrowing requirement of the government.[5] Conventional measurement of fiscal deficit is defined as the difference between total government receipts (non-debt-creating) and the total government

---

[4] '... diversions of bank loans to sectors where cash transaction predominate tend to reduce the supply of money through a rise in the demand for currency. By the same logic a larger allocation of plan expenditure in favour of Rural Employment Generation or similar programmes will be attended with a smaller money multiplier for a given level of deficit financing'. (Rakshit, 1987)

[5] Along with fiscal deficit, other important deficit indicators introduced to assess the budgetary performance of the government are *primary deficit* and *revenue deficit*. In India, *primary deficit* is an indicator to assess the impact of current year's discretionary fiscal action on indebtedness of the government. *Primary Deficit = Fiscal Deficit – Interest Payments*. *Revenue deficit* as a concept has received immense attention in recent years. Boskin (1988) argued that conventional deficit does not measure government dissavings. Government dissavings are reflected in the revenue deficit. *Revenue deficit* is defined as the difference between the revenue earning of the government and revenue/current expenditure government. In the context of structural adjustment programme, as a policy of demand management, reduction of both fiscal and primary deficit assumed paramount importance. Among the economists, there have been arguments for and against the adoption of these indicators to evaluate the budgetary performance of the government.

expenditure net of repayment of previously incurred debt. The most widely accepted definition of fiscal deficit is the following:

> Fiscal Deficit as conventionally defined on cash basis, measure the difference between total government cash outlays, including interest outlays but excluding amortization payments on the outstanding stock of public debt, and total cash receipts, including tax and nontax revenue and grants but excluding borrowing proceeds. In other words, not all outlays related to public debt servicing is included in the measure of deficit: interest payments are added to non-debt-related expenditures but amortization payments are excluded. On the other hand, current revenues are recorded as government income while proceeds from borrowing are not. In this manner, fiscal deficits reflect the gap to be covered by net government borrowing including direct borrowing from the central bank. (Tanzi et al., 1988)

From the methodological point of view, inclusion of net lending and debt servicing as a part of the government expenditure and foreign grants as a part of the revenue may give an incorrect picture of fiscal stance of the government. With regard to the foreign grants, it can be said that they are discretionary in nature and cannot be considered as a constant and steady source of government revenues. However, grants are included in the government revenue as a constant source of finance on the ground that the current expenditure it finances could not take place if the grants are not forthcoming (Blejer and Cheasty, 1991).

The point to be noted here is that the definition of fiscal deficit considered interest payment as a part of the government expenditure but repayment of principal is not. The economic rationale behind such a classification is that unlike interest payment, repayment of outstanding debt does not represent new income to asset-holders and, therefore, leaves demand pressure unchanged, and thus can be excluded from government expenditure. However, under an unsustainable debt situation, the amortised debt may not be voluntarily reinvested in new government bonds. Under such circumstances, government might have to generate larger tax revenues to finance the deficit or they can consider the amortisation as a part of the government expenditure, and the resulting deficit would correspond to the government's gross borrowing requirement.

Another methodological limitation of the fiscal deficit is that it is cash based, instead of being based on accrual deficits. Cash-based

6 FISCAL CONSOLIDATION, BUDGET DEFICITS AND THE MACRO ECONOMY

deficit shows the disbursement of cash for government outlays and revenue in terms of cash received within a year. The accrual deficit tries to capture the net resource requirement of the government as consequence of its policy announcement within a fiscal year, irrespective of the fact whether the transaction has actually taken place or not. For example, while estimation of accrual deficit makes provision for the depreciation of fixed capital as an outlay. In practice, countries often prolong beyond 365 days, the period over which transaction authorised in a given budget document may be carried out. (The extension is known as a 'complementary period'.) Thus in any fiscal year, transactions that change the measured deficit of the previous year can continue to take place alongside transactions determining the current year's deficit.[6] In India, gross fiscal deficit is defined as the excess of the sum total of revenue expenditure, capital outlay and net lending over revenue receipts and non-debt-creating capital receipts including the proceeds from disinvestment. Thus,

Gross Fiscal Deficit = Revenue Expenditure + Capital Outlay
+ Net Lending – (Revenue Receipts
+ Non-debt-creating Capital Receipts).

This definition of fiscal deficit is also not free from the limitations of measurement as discussed earlier.[7]

---

[6] From the macroeconomy point of view, this measurement of government deficit is argued to have limitation in measuring the excess demand generated from the budgetary operation of the government (Tanzi et al., 1988). It is pointed out that different taxes and expenditure affects demand differently and thus for a given level of deficit composition of budget is important. It is further noted that tax revenue is an endogenous variable and mobilisation of taxes depend on factors affecting the shape of macroeconomy. Finally, excess demand generated from the deficit not only depends on the size of the deficit but also on the manner in which it is financed.

[7] According to Gulati (1994), one has to be very careful in including the items like 'disinvestment proceeds' as a component of non-debt-creating capital receipts and transfer payment and receipts by the government. He argued that in a situation when the government is selling of equity in public sector undertakings and not making any fresh investment in such undertakings, the amount thus realised would legitimately be considered in the nature of government receipts that should be taken to raise not reduce fiscal deficit because such receipts itself takes on the nature of borrowing, in the sense that amount thus received, like other amounts the government borrows, goes towards the financing of current government expenditure (for detailed discussion, see Gulati, 1991 and 1994 and Khundrakpam, 1996).

Apart from methodological limitations, it should be noted that in India, a reliable measure of total public sector deficit[8]—the ideal measurement of deficit to capture the macroeconomic impacts—is not constructed due to paucity of data on intra-public sector transactions and the data at subnational (local) government. Therefore, the second best alternative measure of deficit which can capture the macroeconomic impacts in India is the combined gross fiscal deficit of centre and states, which is around 10 per cent of GDP in the year 1999–2000. But as the market borrowing programmes of state governments is under the control of the central government, fiscal deficit of the subnational governments may not have similar impact on macro variables as that of central government's deficit. Thus, we adhere to the fiscal deficit figure of the central government for our study based on the availability of best possible data, partial nature of other concepts of deficit and the relevance of the measure in analysing the macroeconomic impacts of fiscal policy stance.

1.2 Alternative Paradigms on Macroeconomic Effects of Fiscal Deficit

It is important to recall in this context that diametrically opposite views exist in theoretical literature on the macroeconomic effects of fiscal deficit. Since Adam Smith's *Wealth of Nations* and David Ricardo's *Principles of Political Economy and Taxation*, the macroeconomic effects of the levels of deficit and its alternative modes of financing public expenditure on the economic activity has been a matter of debate. The issue of macroeconomic impacts of tax financing versus bond financing of deficit equally has been re-debated since Barro (1974) published his seminal article titled 'Are bonds net wealth?' There exist three alternative paradigms which analyse the macroeconomic effects of fiscal deficits: Neoclassical, Keynesian and Ricardian. The Neoclassical paradigm envisions the economic agents as far-sighted and rational who make intertemporal decisions with

---

[8] Public sector deficit comprises of the deficits of the central government, state governments, local governments and public sector enterprises. It is to be noted that local governments generally do not have budget deficit as they do not have exclusive borrowing powers.

8 FISCAL CONSOLIDATION, BUDGET DEFICITS AND THE MACRO ECONOMY

respect to consumption and income within a finite horizon (their own life cycle); thus fiscal deficits raise total lifetime consumption by shifting taxes to subsequent generations. A second major assumption of Neoclassicals is that markets are clearing, such that economic resources are typically fully employed. That is, if the economy operates at the full employment level, increased consumption necessarily implies decreased savings and interest rates must then rise to bring capital markets into balance. Thus, persistent fiscal deficits *crowd out* private capital accumulation (Berheim, 1989 and Diamond, 1965).

Diamond (1965) first applied Overlapping Generations Model to analyse the macroeconomic impacts of public debt. His study noted that in a situation of long-run equilibrium path, setting budget deficits shift taxes to future generations. Given the time path of the government expenditure, households will experience a positive net wealth effect that stimulates consumption and private savings. However, as private savings do not rise enough to offset the decline in government savings, national savings decline. In a closed economy context, the study noted that real interest rate would go up and act detrimental to investment. And in a small open economy, capital inflow will be induced and hence, through an appreciation of the exchange rate, a deterioration of the current account deficit, be it through the retardation of domestic capital accumulation or through growing foreign indebtedness, future living standards will be affected adversely. However, Diamond's model did not permit private domestic agents' access to international capital markets, which makes his model more suitable to less developing countries, where government is the sole agent with international creditworthiness than the applicability to developed market economies integrated to an international financial system (Buiter, 1990).

The Keynesian paradigm differs from the Neoclassical paradigm in two fundamental ways. First, it envisions that a significant proportion of economic agents are either myopic and/or liquidity constrained and second, these agents have very high propensity to consume out of their current disposable income. This assumption guarantees that aggregate demand is responsive to changes in disposable income. The assumption allows for the possibility that economic resources are underemployed at the moment of deficit financing. A deficit-financed tax cut will then unreservedly increase consumption and through the multiplier process, national income. As the economy is moving to a higher growth path, investment is activated too. Keynesian paradigm, thus, believes that appropriately timed deficits have beneficial consequences through stimulating consumption and national income, as well as savings and capital formation. (Berheim, 1989 and Eisner and Pieper, 1984). As to the future burden of the debt, Eisner and Pieper (1984) even go to state: 'Extra taxes in the future, if there are to be any, may then readily be paid out of higher future income'. Blanchard (1985) here cautioned that deficits, instead of being suddenly enlarged, increase slowly over time. The initial current fiscal stimulus is small, but then it is anticipated to be larger and thus to lead to high short-term real rate of interest later. As a result, the long-term rate of interest increases, leading to a decrease in aggregate demand, which could more than offset the fiscal expansion, at least initially. Under these circumstances, fiscal expansion temporarily could have perverse effects on output.

Apart from the two diametrically opposite views on the impact of levels and financing modes of deficit on the macroeconomy held by Neoclassicals and Keynesians, Ricardian paradigm envisions that rational economic agents can see through the intertemporal veil and realise that deficits merely postpone taxes to future generations. Berheim (1989) pointed out that this foresight gives rise to a 'Say's law' for deficits, that is, the demands for bonds always rise to match government borrowing. This also implies that economic agents have infinite life span and successive generations are linked through voluntary, altruistically motivated resource transfers. Under these assumptions, consumption is determined as a function of *dynastic resources* (that is, the total resources of a taxpayer and his descendants) and since deficits merely shift the payment of taxes to future generations, they leave dynastic resources unaffected.

Barro (1974) resuscitated Ricardian proposition that an increase in the bond-financed deficit can have no effect on aggregate demand because it will be offset by an equivalent increase in the savings of private sector in anticipation of increased future taxes to be levied by government to repay the borrowing. Thus, Ricardian equivalence theorem (RET) states that it is irrelevant whether a given budget deficit is financed by tax increase or by debt issue (Barro, 1974). In other words, the RET amounts to the statement that government's fiscal impact is summarised by the path of its expenditure. Given its path, rearrangements of the timings of taxes—as implied by budget deficits—have no first order impact on the economy. In this respect, the role of RET in public finance is analogous to that of the Modigliani–Miller (1958) theorem in corporate finance (Barro et al., 1998).

The important restatement of RET theorem under the rubrics of debt neutrality and ultrarationality explained that the effect of public spending is fully measured by the size and content of real public spending, regardless of how this spending is financed (Buiter, 1990). This issue of differential incidence of tax financing and bond financing on macroeconomy has also resurfaced in Vickrey's writings as *public debt illusion* (Vickrey, 1961). The Neoclassical paradigm is viewed as the finite version of Ricardian equivalence model. Keynesian paradigm pays little attention to the intertemporal nature of decision-making by economic agents, which is a point of departure from the other two paradigms. Keynesians were concerned about the 'transitory' budget deficit while other two, the permanent budget deficit (Berheim, 1989).[9] Although the theoretical explanation of the link between fiscal deficit and macroeconomic activity differs across paradigms, it is noted across paradigms that the macroeconomic effects of fiscal deficit depends not only on the levels of deficit but also on the financing pattern of deficit.

1.3 Financing of Deficits: A Theoretical Framework

The macroeconomic impact of fiscal deficit broadly depends on how it is financed. Government can finance deficits by seigniorage and through the creation of debt, both internal and external. Excessive use of any financing mode of fiscal deficit results in macroeconomic imbalances, namely, seigniorage financing leads to inflationary

---

[9] Transitory deficit emanates from the cyclical factors, which is linked to the economic activity, which has got only temporary effects on budget balance while permanent deficit emanates from the structural factors which are permanent in nature. The major structural factors could be compositional shift in the public expenditure, growing revenue deficits, interest payments or the rise in the cost of borrowing in relation to the real rate of growth of the economy.

pressures in the economy; domestic debt financing leads to a credit squeeze through higher interest rates or when interest rates are fixed, through credit allocation and ever more stringent financial repression and the crowding out of private investment and consumption. Excessive financing of deficit through external debt may lead to current account deficit and appreciation of the real exchange rate leading to a balance of payment crisis (if foreign reserves are run down) or an external debt crisis (if debt is too high) (Easterly and Schmidt-Hebbel, 1993).

The fiscal deficit financing identity is the analytical starting point for evaluating the macroeconomic effects of fiscal deficit.[10] This is an essential tool in understanding both the linkage between monetary and fiscal policies and the macroeconomic consequences of fiscal deficits. The fiscal deficit can be defined and linked with changes in government net debt as follows:

$$\Delta D_g = [C_g + I_g - T] + r.D_{g-1} \qquad (1.1)$$

where $\Delta D_g = [D_g - D_{g-1}]$

which is the change in the government debt between current and previous period.

C_g = Government Consumption Spending
I_g = Government Investment Spending
T = Tax revenue and other non-debt-creating receipts
r = Nominal Rate of Interest

The RHS of Equation (1.1) measures the fiscal deficit. To finance the existing fiscal deficit, government can resort to seigniorage financing or bond financing. To start with, let us suppose government resorts to seigniorage to finance the fiscal deficit. The immediate result of this move is captured in the change in the money supply. Effect of deficit on the money supply can be captured from Equation (1.2) for the changes in the monetary base $[M_b]$:

$$\Delta M_b = [\Delta D_{gc}] + e.\Delta FOREX \qquad (1.2)$$

---

[10] The intertemporal government budget constraint is one way of showing the linkage between fiscal deficits and alternative sources of deficit financing.

where $\Delta M_b = M_b - M_{b-1}$

ΔD_{gc} = change in the debt held by central bank
$\Delta FOREX$ = $FOREX - FOREX_{-1}$ [change in foreign exchange reserves]
e = nominal exchange rate measured in terms of domestic currency per unit of foreign currency.

A change in debt held by the central bank (ΔD_{gc}) equals the overall change in debt (ΔD_g) minus the change in the debt held by the public (ΔD_{gp}), which is expressed in Equation (1.3).

$$\Delta D_{gc} = \Delta D_g - \Delta D_{gp} \qquad (1.3)$$

ΔD_g = overall change in debt
ΔD_{gp} = change in the debt held by the public

Substituting the expression for ΔD_{gc}, Equation (1.2) can be rewritten as:

$$\Delta M_b = [\Delta D_g - \Delta D_{gp}] + e.\Delta FOREX \qquad (1.4)$$

Rearranging Equation (1.4), the resulting expression yields:

$$\Delta D_g = \Delta M_b + \Delta D_{gp} - e.\Delta FOREX \qquad (1.5)$$

Equation (1.5) is the fundamental equation, which captures the changing financing modes of fiscal deficit and its consequent impact on macroeconomy. This shows that there are three ways to finance deficit, which is equal to the change in the government's debt (ΔD_g): (i) by an increase in the monetary base, ΔM_b; (ii) by an increase in bond financing, ΔD_{gp} or (iii) by a loss of foreign reserves at the central bank, $e.\Delta FOREX$. In short, to finance the fiscal deficit the government will have to print money, borrow from the public or run down foreign exchange reserves. As mentioned above, each of these sources of deficit financing can cause a particular kind of macroeconomic problem.

2
Fiscal Deficit and Macroeconomic Activity of Central and Subnational Governments

This chapter explores macroeconomic data. First, the trends in deficit and its financing pattern over the years and second, the movement of fiscal deficit in relation to the selected macroeconomic variables, namely, private capital formation, rate of interest, seigniorage, money supply and rate of inflation. Although the simple trend analysis will not provide a definite answer to the exact nature of relationship between fiscal deficit and macroeconomic variables, such analysis would provide indications regarding their movement of macrovariables in relation to fiscal deficit.

2.1 Trends in Central Government Deficits in India

As mentioned, the focus of policymakers has been to control the levels of fiscal deficits, revenue deficits and primary deficits as per the numeric fiscal rules. The gross fiscal deficit, which is the net borrowing requirement of the government, as percentage of GDP increased to the peak of 8.13 per cent in 1986–87 and then declined to 2.54 per cent in 2006–07 (Table 2.1). The fiscal deficit after reaching to a peak of seven per cent of GDP in 2007–08, has remained at around five per cent of GDP in the recent years. Despite the fiscal rules, the central government has not been able to contain the growth of fiscal

Table 2.1

Trends in Different Concepts of Deficit in India (as Percentage of GDP)

Year	Gross Fiscal Deficit	Gross Primary Deficit	Revenue Deficit	Budget Deficit	Monetised Deficit
1980–81	5.55	3.81	1.36	1.66	2.37
1990–91	7.61	3.95	3.17	1.94	2.52
2000–01	5.46	0.9	3.91	−0.05	0.31
2001–02	5.98	1.42	4.25	−0.06	−0.22
2002–03	5.72	1.08	4.25	0.07	−1.12
2003–04	4.34	−0.03	3.46	−0.14	−2.68
2004–05	3.88	−0.04	2.42	−0.05	−1.86
2005–06	3.96	0.37	2.5	−0.57	0.77
2006–07	3.32	−0.18	1.87	0.11	−0.07
2007–08	2.54	−0.88	1.05	−0.54	−2.34
2008–09	5.99	2.57	4.5	0.78	3.13
2009–10	6.46	3.17	5.23	−0.02	2.31
2010–11	4.79	1.79	3.24	0.08	2.37
2011–12	5.84	2.75	4.46	−0.18	1.58
2012–13	4.91	1.77	3.65	−0.51	0.55
2013–14	4.43	1.13	3.15	−0.17	0.95
2014–15	4.09	0.81	2.89	−0.12	−2.59
2015–16	3.94	0.71	2.80	0.09	–

Source: Handbook of Statistics on Indian Economy, RBI (2015).

deficit at the national level, now stand at around four per cent of GDP in 2015–16. At the same time, primary deficit, which is fiscal deficit excluding interest payments, has peaked in 1973–74 to 5.28 per cent in 1986–87 and then onwards declined to 0.51 per cent of GDP in 1996–97. After a period of primary surplus between 2003–04 to 2007–08 (except in 2005–06), the primary deficit has been less than one per cent by 2015–16. This is the reflection of high interest payment burden of central government since 2000–01.

Budget deficit, which is the conventional budgetary deficit of the central government, reflects deficit financing through the issue of ad hoc treasury bills by RBI. A high ratio of budget deficit may have implications in the conduct of monetary policy, as deficit would induce money supply and thereby may hamper the monetary policy objective of price stability. As noted from Table 2.1, budget deficit has shown wide fluctuations. During the mid-1980s, budget deficit sharply rose and reached a peak of 2.55 per cent in 1986–87. During the 1990s, budget deficit sharply declined and following the decision to phase out 91-day ad hoc treasury bills with effect from 1 April 1997, the conventional budget deficit is eliminated. The figures noted since 1996–97 in Table 2.1 is the Ways and Means Advances resorted by central government to correct the temporary mismatch of the government exchequer, which is around 0.09 per cent of GDP in 2015–16.

Apart from the conventional budget deficit, the monetary implication of the central government's budgetary operations is reflected in the level of the monetised deficit. Monetised deficit, which is the net RBI credit to central government, has been brought down in recent years through active open market operations (OMO). The decline in monetised deficit during the 1990s was due to the flexible use of interest rate through OMO. The use of OMO to signal the RBI's stance regarding monetary conditions and management of liquidity has emerged as an important feature of monetary management during the late 1990s (RBI, 1999a). However, the rise in monetised deficit since 2008–09 is a matter of concern, though it plummeted to 0.95 per cent of GDP in 2013–14, and further to −2.59 per cent of GDP in 2014–15.

Unlike other measures of deficit, no secular tendency to decline has been noted in revenue deficit. In 2009–10, the ratio of revenue deficit to GDP was all time high at 5.23 per cent of GDP, though it reduced to 2.80 by 2015–16. As can be seen in Figure 2.1, the share of revenue deficit in total fiscal deficit has increased steadily, reaching a peak of 81 per cent in 2009–10. As revenue expenditure by nature is current consumption expenditure and does not create tangible assets capable of generating financial returns, diversion of borrowed resources to finance the revenue deficit implies reduced availability of resources for capital expenditure meant for productive capital investment purposes. In other words, increasing share of revenue deficit in total fiscal deficit in the recent years implies crowding out the capital outlay by the government, which was intended to spend on the investment purposes.

Figure 2.1
Revenue Deficit/Fiscal Deficit (RD/FD) Ratio

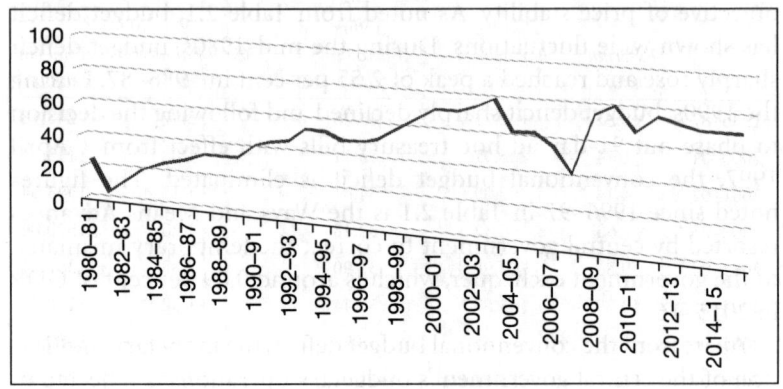

Source: Handbook of Statistics on Indian Economy, RBI (2015).

The financing pattern of fiscal deficit is shown in Table 2.2. The fiscal deficit is financed through issuance of bonds, seigniorage financing, financing through ad hoc treasury bills and external financing. It is evident from the table that over the years, government resorted more to internal financing than to external financing. Market borrowing has emerged as the most important source of financing of fiscal deficit since the early 1990s.

External financing of deficits is negligible in India. Increasing recourse to bond financing is reflected in the increase in the share of market borrowing during the 1990s and reached to 85.32 per cent of total financing by 2015–16 (Table 2.2). Has bond financing of fiscal deficit exerted upward pressure on rates of interest which needs an empirical validation?

While looking at the link between fiscal deficit and macroeconomic activity, it is imperative to analyse the composition of fiscal deficit. Fiscal deficit can be both structural and cyclical in nature. Cyclical deficit is linked to the changes in economic activity, which has got transitory effect on the budget balance; while structural deficit is linked to the structural changes in the economy due to discrete monetary and fiscal policies. For detailed discussion on structural and cyclical deficit, see Giorno et al. (1995), IMF (2001), Pattnaik et al. (1999), Tanzi and Blejer(1988) and Van den Noord (2000).

Table 2.2
Financing Pattern of Fiscal Deficit (as Percentage of Total)

	External (%)	Market Borrowings (%)	Other Borrowings (%)	Draw Down of Cash Balances (%)	Total (in ₹ billion)
1986–87	8.32	22.75	43.28	33.97	243.18
2000–01	6.74	65.97	35.11	−1.08	1113.11
2001–02	4.14	67.09	34.01	−1.11	1353.54
2002–03	−7.60	66.32	32.48	1.20	1570.06
2003–04	−9.86	64.98	37.90	−2.88	1367.61
2004–05	13.29	45.87	55.44	−1.32	1110.41
2005–06	5.38	76.45	38.58	−15.03	1389.63
2006–07	6.32	85.61	11.02	3.37	1341.01
2007–08	7.92	111.06	12.05	−23.11	1175.97
2008–09	3.38	75.76	10.79	13.45	3259.77
2009–10	2.71	96.79	3.55	−0.34	4074.44
2010–11	6.73	93.25	4.92	1.84	3500.35
2011–12	2.47	96.14	7.03	−3.18	5035.42
2012–13	1.49	105.06	5.50	−10.56	4829.89
2013–14	1.47	95.98	7.89	−3.87	4955.66
2014–15	1.93	92.56	10.56	−3.12	5029.23
2015–16	2.05	85.32	12.47	2.21	5444.76

Source: Handbook of Statistics on Indian Economy, RBI (2015).

This result is obtained by the RBI, adopting Organisation for Economic Co-operation and Development (OECD) methodology for decomposing fiscal deficit into structural and cyclical components. The OECD methodology distinguishes between discretionary budget changes and built-in-stabiliser as a prelude to define the structural budget balance. The first step to calculate the cyclical and structural fiscal deficit is to estimate the structural revenues and structural expenditures; that is revenues and expenditures that would have prevailed, had the actual output been at its potential level.

The cyclical and structural fiscal deficit is derived as follows:

Cyclical Deficit = [Built-in-Budget Balance] * [Actual Output − Trend Output]

$= [(g_0.E_g Y) - (r_0.E_r.Y)] * [(Y_t - Y_t^*)]$

Structural Deficit = [Base Year Budget balance] + [Balance arising out of discretionary policy induced revenue and expenditure] + [Fiscal Drag]

$= [G_0 - R_0] + [Gdt - Rdt] + \{[(g_0.E_g Y) - (r_0.E_r.Y)] * [Y_0(e^{rt} - 1)]\}$

Where,

$g_0 = G_0/Y$ = base year expenditure/actual output;
$E_g Y$ = expenditure elasticity;
$r_0 = R_0/Y$ = base year receipts/actual output;
$E_r Y$ = revenue elasticity; Y_t = actual output;
Y_t^* = trend output;
$Gdt = G_t - G_{at}$ = actual expenditure − expenditure responsive to change in output;
$Rdt = R_t - R_{at}$ = actual receipts − receipts responsive to change in output;
base year Y_0 = real potential GDP − real actual GDP;
e^{rt} = exponential rate of growth of trend output.

In the context of India, estimates have shown that structural deficit is predominant; and the cyclical component of fiscal deficit though present, is not significant. The RBI estimates of structural and cyclical fiscal deficit given in Table 2.3 confirms the predominance of structural fiscal deficit in India. The estimates of structural and cyclical deficit have not been constructed by the RBI for recent years. It can be seen that over the period 1980–81 to 1999–2000, the cyclical fiscal deficit has ranged between a deficit of 0.01 per cent of GDP and a surplus of 0.15 per cent of GDP as against the actual deficit of the central government, which ranged around 6–8 per cent of GDP. Given the small size of the automatic stabiliser, countercyclical measures would have to depend upon discretionary fiscal actions (RBI, 2002). The major discretionary fiscal policy actions could be the expenditure and tax reforms and policies relating to rising cost of borrowing, which can result in the compositional shift of expenditure pattern from developmental to non-developmental (and vice versa), shift in expenditure towards current revenue expenditure (or vice versa), growing revenue deficit and rising rate of interest in relation to the rate of growth of economy. After analysing the trends, composition and magnitude of fiscal deficit in relation to GDP, now we turn to examine the trends in fiscal deficit vis-à-vis selected macro-variables discussed in the first chapter, namely, public and private capital formation, rates of interest, seigniorage, money supply and rate of inflation. It is mentioned that high fiscal deficit pushes up rate of interest, crowds out private capital formation, creates seigniorage and in turn generate inflationary pressures in the economy. The following sections delve deep into the intertemporal trends in each of these macrovariables vis-à-vis fiscal deficit.

2.2 Fiscal Deficit and Private Capital Formation

Fiscal deficit arises due to the higher growth of expenditure in relation to the growth of non-debt-creating receipts of the government. The decline in capital expenditure—from around 40 per cent of total spending in the 1980s to around 10 per cent by 2015–16 has adversely affected the public investment in India[1] (Table 2.4).

---

[1] In the context of India, for the estimation of capital formation, the economy is divided into three broad institutional sectors, namely, public sector, private corporate sector and household sector. The household sector is conceived as the 'residual' sector embracing all economic entities other than the units of public and private corporate sector. In other words, the capital formation in household sector is derived by deducting the share of capital formation in organised public sector and private corporate sector from the global estimates of capital formation. The sources of data used in the estimation of household share are varied and divergent, and as a result, the estimates contain indeterminate sources of errors. In the light of these data problems, it should be noted that the disaggregation of private investment data is not entirely reliable for the same reason that investment in household sector is derived as a residual, so any estimation errors, both upward and downward bias in estimation of private corporate sector, gets correspondingly reflected in the estimation of investment by the household sector.

Table 2.3
Composition of Fiscal Deficit: Structural and Cyclical (as Percentage of GDP)

Year	Structural Deficit	Cyclical Deficit	Actual Deficit
1970–71	2.38	0.88	3.26
1975–76	3.41	0.43	3.84
1980–81	5.83	−0.05	5.78
1981–82	5.08	0.06	5.14
1982–83	5.64	0.01	5.65
1983–84	5.85	0.09	5.94
1984–85	7.07	0.02	7.09
1985–86	7.88	−0.02	7.86
1986–87	8.61	−0.15	8.46
1987–88	7.79	−0.15	7.64
1988–89	7.35	−0.01	7.34
1989–90	7.34	−0.01	7.33
1990–91	7.8	0.04	7.84
1991–92	5.55	0.01	5.56
1992–93	5.37	0.00	5.37
1993–94	7.03	−0.02	7.01
1994–95	5.68	0.02	5.70
1995–96	5.05	0.02	5.07
1996–97	4.87	0.01	4.88
1997–98	5.83	0.01	5.84
1998–99	6.42	0.02	6.44
1999–2000	5.36	−0.01	5.35

Source: RBI (1999) and RBI (2002).
Note: The series on cyclical and structural deficit is discontinued.

If we look at the movement of gross fixed capital formation to GDP ratio, it can be seen that the ratio increased steadily from 18 per cent in 1980–81 to a peak of around 36 per cent in 2011 (Table 2.4). However, in public sector, a decline in gross fixed capital formation-GDP ratio is noted from a peak of 13 per cent in the mid-1980s to around seven per cent in recent years. As a percentage of GDP, the private corporate investment gained momentum in the 1990s and reached the peak of 10 per cent of GDP in 1994–95, while the public

Table 2.4
Trends in Central Government Expenditure (as Percentage of GDP)

Year	Revenue Expenditure	Of Which			Capital Expenditure	Of Which			Total Expenditure
		Defence Expenditure	Interest Payments	Subsidies	(7+8)	Loans and Advances	Capital Outlay	Defence Expenditure	(2+6)
1	2	3	4	5	6	7	8	9	100
1980–81	63.29	14.40	11.44	8.91	36.71	23.21	13.50	1.43	100
1990–91	69.82	10.33	20.42	11.55	30.18	18.66	11.52	4.32	100
2000–01	85.33	11.44	30.50	8.24	14.67	7.07	7.60	3.80	100
2001–02	83.21	10.50	29.66	8.61	16.79	9.46	7.33	4.47	100
2002–03	81.96	9.85	28.51	10.53	18.04	7.66	7.04	3.62	100
2003–04	76.84	9.17	26.33	9.41	23.16	6.11	7.25	3.58	100
2004–05	77.14	8.80	25.48	9.22	22.75	5.80	10.50	6.42	100
2005–06	86.88	9.53	26.23	9.40	13.12	2.24	10.88	6.39	100
2006–07	88.21	8.86	25.76	9.79	11.79	1.46	10.33	5.80	100
2007–08	83.41	7.61	24.00	9.95	16.59	1.59	15.01	5.26	100

(*Continued*)

(Continued)

Year	Revenue Expenditure	Of Which Defence Expenditure	Of Which Interest Payments	Subsidies	Capital Expenditure (7+8)	Loans and Advances	Capital Outlay	Of Which Defence Expenditure	Total Expenditure (2+6)
1	2	3	4	5	6	7	8	9	100
2008–09	89.80	8.29	21.74	14.67	10.20	1.60	8.60	4.63	100
2009–10	89.00	8.85	20.80	13.80	11.00	1.53	9.47	4.99	100
2010–11	86.92	7.69	19.55	14.48	13.08	2.09	10.99	5.18	100
2011–12	87.84	7.90	20.94	16.71	12.16	1.59	10.57	5.21	100
2012–13	88.17	7.89	22.20	18.23	11.83	1.47	10.36	5.00	100
2013–14	87.97	7.98	24.00	16.33	12.03	1.23	10.80	5.07	100
2014–15	88.56	8.35	24.47	15.86	11.44	1.30	10.14	4.88	100
2015–16	86.42	8.56	25.66	13.72	13.58	1.36	12.23	5.32	100

Source: Handbook of Statistics on Indian Economy, RBI (2015).

Table 2.5
Gross Fixed Capital Formation in India and Its Major Components (as Percentage of GDP)

Year	gcfgdp	gcfhhgdp	gcfpvtgdp	gcfpubgdp
1980	18.05	6.35	2.52	9.17
1990	24.91	10.06	4.27	10.58
2000	24.21	11.46	4.91	7.16
2001	25.65	12.68	5.16	7.21
2002	25.02	12.29	5.73	6.46
2003	26.17	12.13	6.56	6.62
2004	32.45	13.44	10.33	7.42
2005	34.28	11.66	13.56	7.94
2006	35.87	11.88	14.53	8.3
2007	38.03	10.79	17.31	8.86
2008	35.53	13.50	11.30	9.44
2009	36.3	13.22	12.14	9.15
2010	36.98	13.14	13.35	8.39
2011	35.45	14.31	10.57	7.86

Source: National Account Statistics, new series, CSO, Government of India (various years).

Note: gcfgdp = gross capital formation/GDP, gcfhhgdp = gross capital formation in household sector/GDP, gcfpvtgdp = gross capital formation in private corporate sector/GDP and gcfpubgdp = gross capital formation in public sector/GDP.

investment to GDP ratio declined as mentioned earlier. The decline in the public sector investment during the 1990s can be attributed to the burgeoning fiscal crisis of 1990s. The growth of private corporate investment crossed over the public investment in relation to GDP in recent years. The gross capital formation as a percentage of GDP tended to increase over the years past three decades, irrespective of tiny fluctuations in trend.

It is evident from Table 2.5 that gross fixed capital formation in public sector and gross fiscal deficit are correlated having correlation coefficient of 0.54. At the same time, the correlation coefficient between GFCF in private sector and gross fiscal deficit is 0.874. However, within the private capital formation, the correlation of household investment with gross fiscal deficit is as low as 0.692 and private corporate investment is −0.68. From the correlation coefficients, prima facie, there appears to be a possibility of obtaining a negative

Table 2.6
Correlation Matrix of Fiscal Deficit and Capital Formation

Macrovariables	Gross Fiscal Deficit GDP	GFCF in Public Sector
Gross fixed capital formation	−0.49	−
GFCF in public sector	0.54	1
GFCF in private sector	−0.68	−0.39
GFCF in HH sector	−0.30	−0.66

Source: NAS (Basic Data), New Series, CSO (various years).

relationship between both private corporate investment and public investment (−0.39) and household investment (−0.66), however none of the correlation coefficients are statistically significant (Table 2.6).

2.3 Fiscal Deficit and Rate of Interest

Having analysed the movement of fiscal deficit and gross capital formation by public and private sectors, in this section we analyse the movement of fiscal deficit and rates of interest. This analysis assumes importance because theoretically, high fiscal deficit financed through domestic borrowing would induce rise in real rate of interest because increasing demand for funds by the government would create a shortage of funds in the financial market and to get the market equilibrium restored, the cost of funds, that is, the rate of interest has to increase. The relationship between fiscal deficit and rate of interest assumes added importance because rates of interest also determine investment demand. So, if increase in fiscal deficit pushes up the rate of interest that may adversely affect the private capital formation. In India, the major rates of interest are call money market rate, bank rate, prime lending rate (PLR) and gross redemption yield of Government of India Securities. The selected nominal and real rates of interests are shown in Figure 2.2. The real rates of interest are calculated by using Fisher equation, which defines nominal interest rate as a combination of real rate of interest and inflationary expectations. The point to be noted here is that though the nominal rate of interest of all the rates of interest except government securities showed a non-varying trend over the years in India, it has not been so in case of the real rate of interest series adjusted for the inflation (Figure 2.2).

Figure 2.2

Movement of Selected Real and Nominal Rates of Interest in India

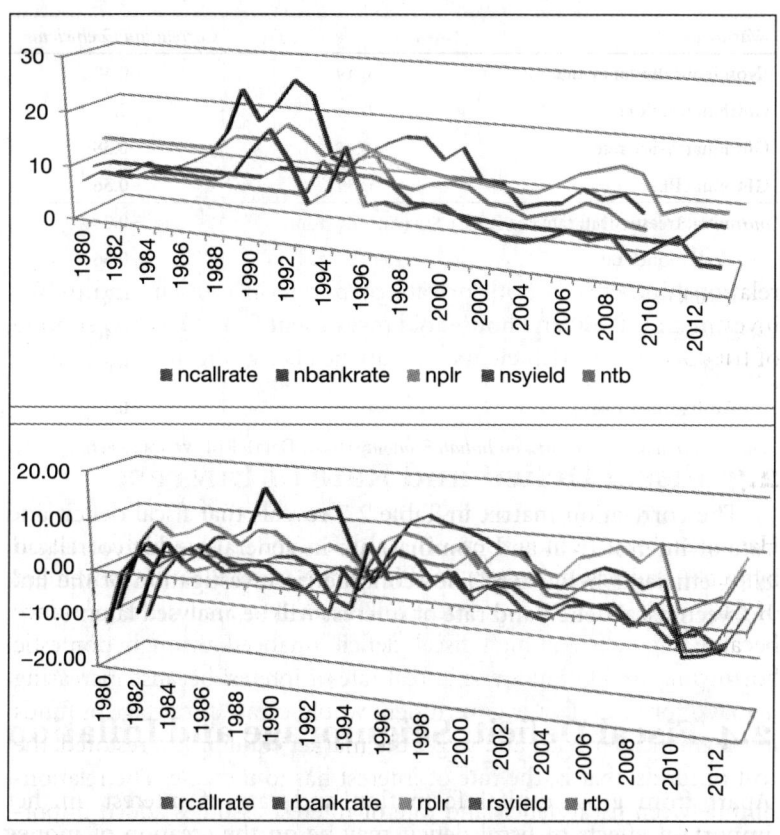

Source: Handbook of Statistics on Indian Economy (Basic Data), RBI (various years).

Figure 2.2 suggests that nominal bank rate has shown a stepwise increase till the mid-1990s and each increase in the rate is sustained over a period of time before further rise. The real bank rate showed considerable variations over the period. The nominal and real call money market rate of interest showed considerable variations. PLR has showed a distinct two-phased variation. In the administered interest rate regime, nominal PLR has shown a stepwise increasing trend. But in the financially deregulated regime since 1992, nominal PLR has shown fluctuating pattern. A similar trend is noted for short-term government security rate also.

Table 2.7
Correlation Coefficient of Fiscal Deficit and Rates of Interest

Variables	Correlation Coefficient
Nominal call money rate	−0.48
Nominal bank rate	−0.47
Nominal G-Sec rate	−0.38
Nominal PLR	−0.38
Nominal treasury bill rate	−0.01
Real call money rate	−0.36
Real bank rate	−0.27
Real G-Sec rate	−0.46
Real PLR	−0.01
Real call money rate	−0.23

Source: Handbook of Statistics on Indian Economy (Basic Data), RBI (various years).

The correlation matrix in Table 2.7 reveals that fiscal deficit and rate of interest (real and nominal) are in general weakly correlated; all coefficients below 0.5. The econometric investigation of the link between fiscal deficit and rate of interest will be analysed later.

2.4 Fiscal Deficit, Seigniorage and Inflation

Apart from gross capital formation and rate of interest, further important effects of fiscal deficit may be on the creation of money supply and inflation. The relationship between fiscal deficit, money supply and inflation depends largely on the mode of financing the deficit, in particular, whether seigniorage (through generating/print money in nontechnical sense) is preferred to other available modes of financing fiscal deficit. Technically, seigniorage is the change in reserve money to GDP ratio, which reached a peak of 4.40 in 2007–08 and declined to less than 1 in recent years (Figure 2.3). Despite efforts to control monetisation of deficits in the late 1990s, the seigniorage has not declined due to the increase in the net foreign exchange inflows. However, it is also argued that the conduct of monetary policy via monetisation of deficit does not cause inflationary pressures, when the economy is demand-constrained (Patnaik, 2001 and Rakshit, 2010).

Figure 2.3
Trends in Seigniorage

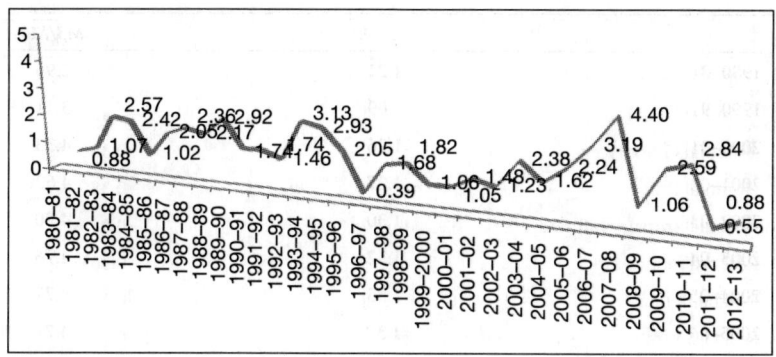

Source: Handbook of Statistics on Indian Economy (Basic Data), RBI (various years).

Table 2.8
Correlation Matrix of Fiscal Deficit, Seigniorage, M3 and Inflation

	Fiscal Deficit	Seigniorage	Money Supply	Inflation (WPI)
Fiscal deficit	1.	−0.15	0.96	−0.12
Seigniorage	−0.15	1	−0.012	−0.002
Money supply	0.96	−0.019	1	0.007
Inflation (CPI)	−0.12	0.074	−0.19	0.56
Inflation (WPI)	0.05	−0.002	0.007	1

Source: Handbook of Statistics on Indian Economy (Basic Data), RBI (various years).

The simple correlation exercise between seigniorage and fiscal deficit as per cent of GDP showed that both are correlated with coefficient at −0.15. The seigniorage itself cannot spillover into the money supply (correlation coefficient is −0.012). The correlation coefficient of fiscal deficit and money growth is weak at 0.96, while the fiscal deficit and inflation are weakly correlated and negative at −0.12 (Table 2.8). The transmission mechanism in which fiscal deficit (via seigniorage) affects money supply also depends on the stability of money multipliers. The money multipliers are defined as M1/M0 or M3/M0; which are the ratios of narrow money and broad money to monetary base respectively. The value of money multipliers is given in Table 2.9.

It is revealed in Table 2.9 that M3/M0 figures are higher than M1/M0. The extent of variability is more for M3/M0 than M1/M0. It is

Table 2.9

Money Multipliers of Indian Economy

	M1/M0	M3/M0
1980–81	1.21	2.95
1990–91	1.09	3.11
2000–01	1.26	4.33
2001–02	1.27	4.52
2002–03	1.30	4.80
2003–04	1.32	4.76
2004–05	1.35	4.77
2005–06	1.39	4.77
2006–07	1.39	4.78
2007–08	1.26	4.58
2008–09	1.25	4.75
2009–10	1.32	5.20
2010–11	1.27	4.97
2011–12	1.18	5.05
2012–13	1.22	5.40
2013–14	1.23	5.64
2014–15	1.23	5.73

Source: *Handbook of Statistics on Indian Economy*, RBI (2015).

deciphered from the Figure 2.4 that M1/M0 is relatively constant than M3/M0 over the period. The movement of money supply and fiscal deficit has shown no concomitant trend (Figure 2.4), but it is difficult to decipher at this point the exact money supply reaction to fiscal deficit, which would be empirically verified later.

2.5 The Story of Fiscal Consolidation at Subnational Level in India

The subnational governments in India have undertaken fiscal consolidation against the policy legislation of FRBM Acts (for details, see Chakraborty, 2015). This rule-based fiscal framework has been given emphasis by the Twelfth Finance Commission by providing

Figure 2.4
Trends in M1/M0 and M3/M0

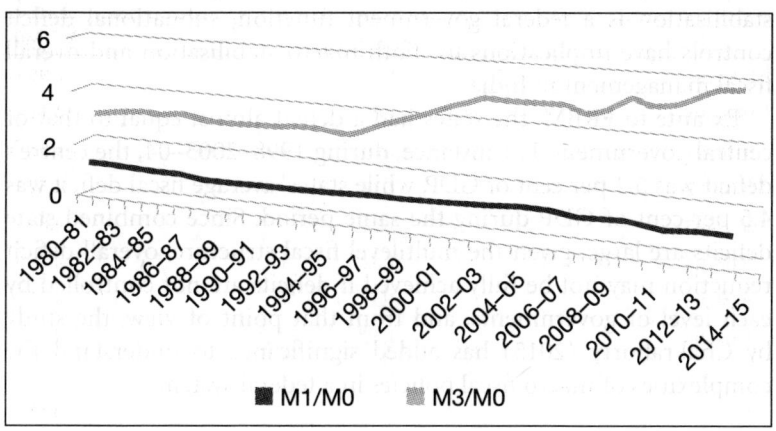

Source: Handbook of Statistics on Indian Economy, RBI (2015).

incentives to the states in terms of debt and interest rate relief. The Thirteenth Finance Commission has also continued incentivising the states for fiscal correction to maintain the deficits within the limits of FRBM Acts. The Thirteenth Finance Commission has proposed the fiscal consolidation path to be growth promoting in the sense the elimination of revenue deficit would ensure that net public borrowing would exclusively be used for growth enhancing public investment. The empirical analysis showed that this has not happened, as states have overadjusted to the fiscal rules by cutting down their capital spending to curtail deficits. This has long-term adverse implications on economic growth.

The refreshing perspective of the Fourteenth Finance Commission in its award decision to devolve 42 per cent of centres' tax pool to the states has become the gamechanger. Against the FFC recommendations, the medium-term fiscal consolidation of the states would be determined by the efficient utilisation of the enhanced resources through tax devolution under the Fourteenth Finance Commission award (RBI, 2015). There are only a few empirical analyses on fiscal consolidation at the subnational level. Chakraborty and Dash (2013) have found that fiscal rules have helped the states to control their deficits; however, the deficit targets have been met largely by reducing development expenditure. Chakraborty (Forthcoming) examined whether the application of fiscal rule has increased fiscal space for public investment spending in Indian states. A significant contribution of this study by Chakraborty (2015) is that although macroeconomic stabilisation is a federal government function, subnational deficit controls have implications for both macro-stabilisation and overall fiscal management in India.

Ex ante to FRBM, the states had a deficit almost equal to that of central government. For instance, during 1998–2003–04, the centre's deficit was 5.2 per cent of GDP, while states' average fiscal deficit was 4.5 per cent of GDP during the same period. Since combined state deficits are large, given the multilevel fiscal structure, overall deficit reduction may not be fully achieved if deficits are not controlled by each level of governments, and from that point of view, the study by Chakraborty (2015) has added significance to understand the complexities of macro fiscal policies in a federal system.

2.5.1 Trends in Subnational Fiscal Deficit and Revenue Deficit

Over the years, the revenue deficit as per cent of GDP has come down, especially in the post-FRBM era, and now the states are having revenue surplus (Figure 2.5). The state-specific analysis of revenue deficit

Figure 2.5

Trends in Revenue Deficit of Subnational Government (as Percentage of GDP)

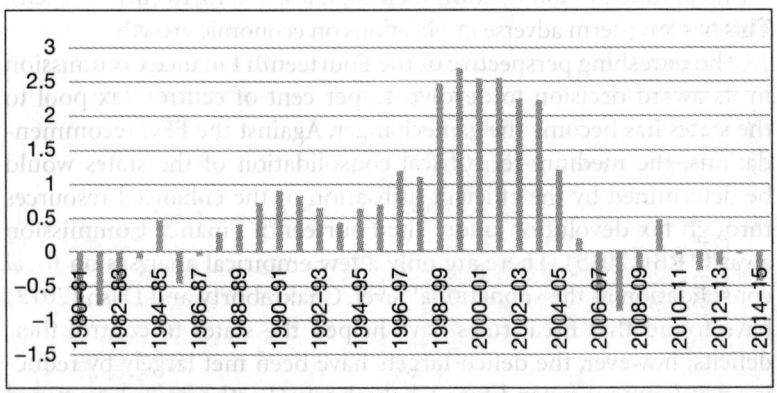

Source: Handbook of Statistics on Indian Economy, RBI (2015).

Fiscal Deficit and Macroeconomic Activity 31

would be carried out later. The states have reduced their fiscal deficit over the years, and the gross fiscal deficit to GDP ratio is around 2 per cent since 2005–06 (Figure 2.6). The striking outcome of fiscal consolidation at the state level has been its impact on capital formation. We will revisit this point later.

2.5.2 Trends in Subnational Deficits: Ex Ante and Ex Post FRBM

The ex ante and ex post FRBM analysis in terms of subnational deficits is carried out as a summary assessment of states' fiscal consolidation efforts in terms of key deficit indicators (as ratios of gross state domestic product (GSDP)) expressed as period averages. This grouping of states and the FRBM periods have been drawn from RBI (2015). The ex post and ex ante demarcation for each state is decided by the year in which FRBM legislation is undertaken in a particular state during 1992–93 and 2012–13. The point to be noted here is that ex ante and ex post FRBM periods differ across states. We follow the categorisation by RBI (2015) of states into non-special category (NSC) and special category (SC) states, and NSC states further classified into three groups high-income states (HIS), middle-income states (MIS) and low-income states (LIS)) on the basis of their per capita incomes. Ex ante to FRBM Acts, the revenue deficit of all HIS were around

Figure 2.6
Trends in Fiscal Deficit of Subnational Government (as Percentage of GDP)

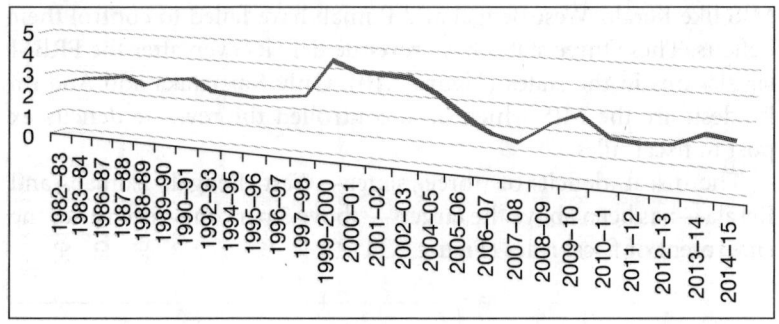

Source: Handbook of Statistics on Indian Economy, RBI (2015).

Figure 2.7
Revenue Deficit of High-Income States: Ex Ante and Ex Post FRBM

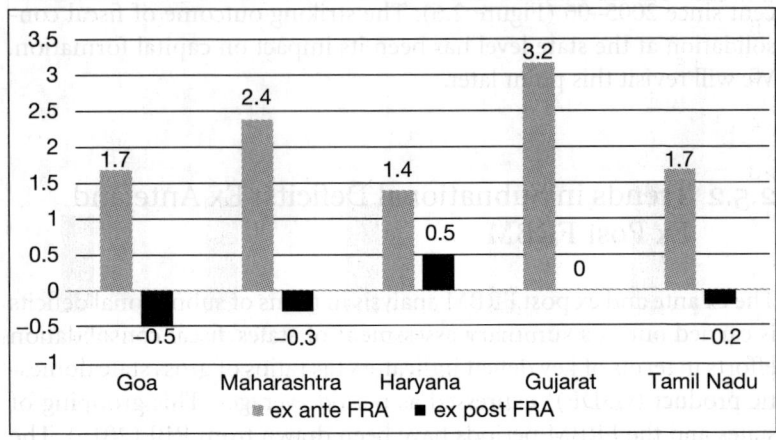

Source: RBI Study on State Finances 2014–15 (Basic Data).

2 per cent of GDP with exception of Gujarat at 3.2 per cent (Figure 2.7). However, ex post to the FRBM enactment, the HIS have shown revenue surplus, except for Haryana.

All HIS also maintained a deficit below the FRBM target of 3 per cent of GDP, ex post to the fiscal rules legislations (Figure 2.8).

The HIS experienced a period of low primary deficits after the FRBM legislation, with Maharashtra as exception with a primary surplus (Figure 2.9).

The ex ante and ex post behaviour of MIS have been much different from that of HIS and LIS. While HIS and LIS have adjusted to fiscal rules and maintained their deficits well below the FRBM targets, the MIS like Kerala, West Bengal and Punjab have failed to control their deficits. These three states have revenue deficits even after the FRBM legislations in the states (Figure 2.10). Only Karnataka and Andhra Pradesh are the MIS which have controlled the revenue deficits ex post to fiscal rules.

The fiscal deficit of three states—West Bengal, Punjab and Kerala—has been above the targets—above 3 per cent—even after the enactment of fiscal rules (Figure 2.11).

Fiscal Deficit and Macroeconomic Activity 33

Figure 2.8
Fiscal Deficit of High-Income States: Ex Ante and Ex Post FRBM

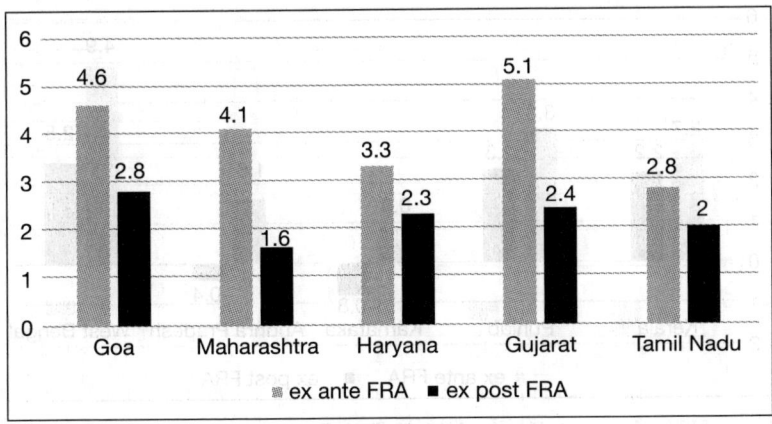

Source: RBI Study on State Finances 2014–15 (Basic Data).

Figure 2.9
Primary Deficit of High-Income States: Ex Ante and Ex Post FRBM

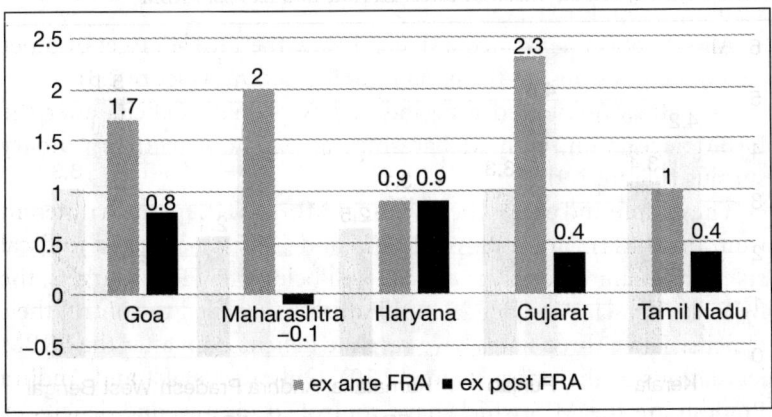

Source: RBI Study on State Finances 2014–15 (Basic Data).

Figure 2.10

Revenue Deficit of Middle-Income States: Ex Ante and Ex Post FRBM

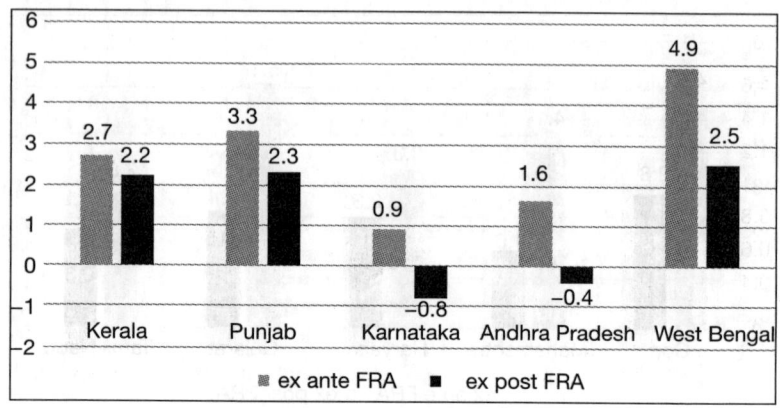

Source: RBI Study on State Finances 2014–15 (Basic Data).

Figure 2.11

Fiscal Deficit of Middle-Income States: Ex Ante and Ex Post FRBM

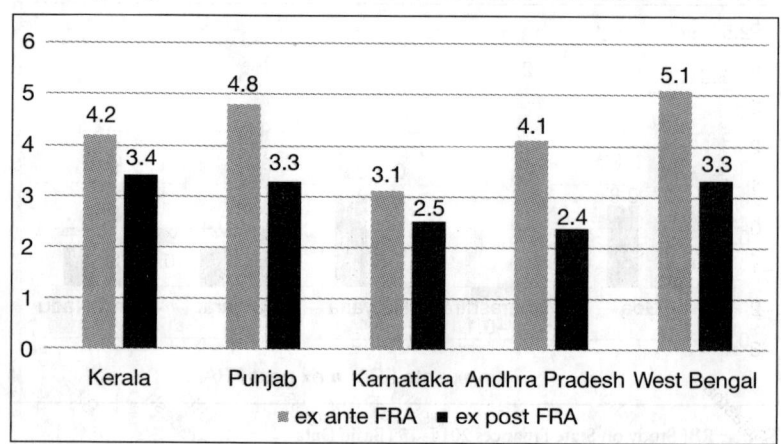

Source: RBI Study on State Finances 2014–15 (Basic Data).

Fiscal Deficit and Macroeconomic Activity **35**

Figure 2.12

Primary Deficit of Middle-Income States: Ex Ante and Ex Post FRBM

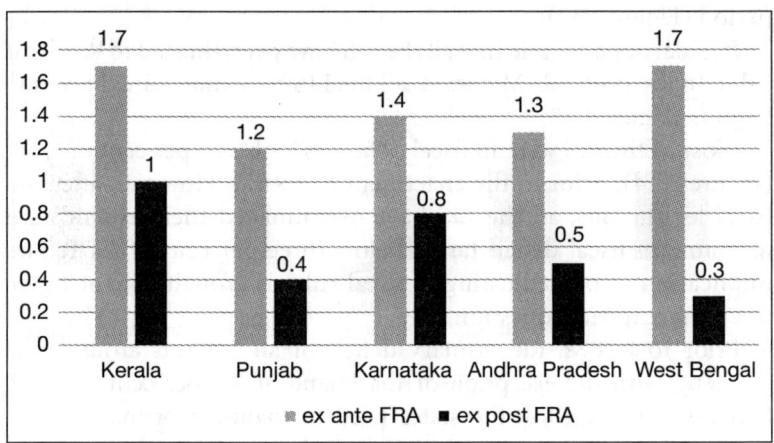

Source: RBI Study on State Finances 2014–15 (Basic Data).

Figure 2.13

Revenue Deficit of Low-Income States: Ex Ante and Ex Post FRBM

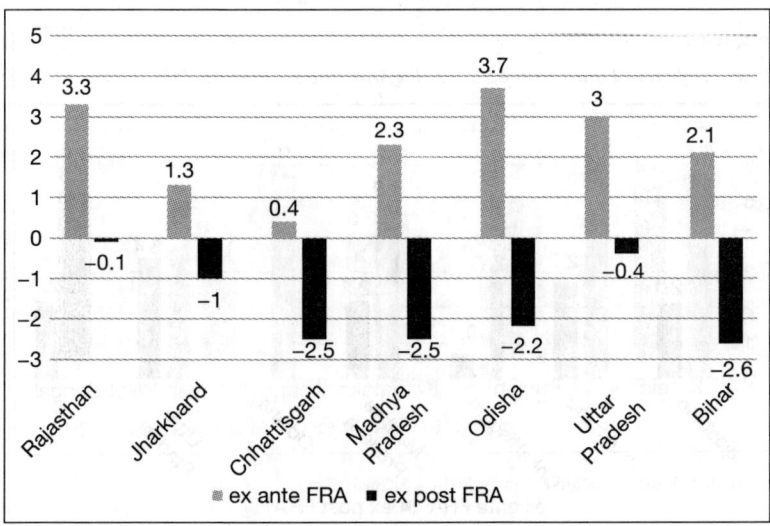

Source: RBI Study on State Finances 2014–15 (Basic Data).

Except Kerala, efforts have been made by the states to reduce the primary deficit to below one per cent of GDP in the post-FRBM period (Figure 2.12).

It is alarming to note that all the LIS have overadjusted to the fiscal rules. In the post-FRBM period, all the LIS have maintained revenue surplus (Figure 2.13).

Most of the LIS were in fiscal deficit as high as 5 per cent of GDP (Figure 2.14), prior to the enactment of FRBM. However, after the fiscal legislations, all the LIS have overadjusted their expenditure to maintain fiscal deficit target below three per cent of GDP. The implication of overadjusting to fiscal rules is growth enhancing or not is an empirical question.

Prior to FRBM, the primary deficit of all LIS was around two per cent, with the exception of Jharkhand at 4.5 per cent of GDP. However, after FRBM, the states tried to maintain primary deficit target to below 1 per cent of GDP, with three states in this category, namely Chhattisgarh, Jharkhand and Odisha, with prudent primary surplus (Figure 2.15).

Figure 2.14

Fiscal Deficit of Low-Income States: Ex Ante and Ex Post FRBM

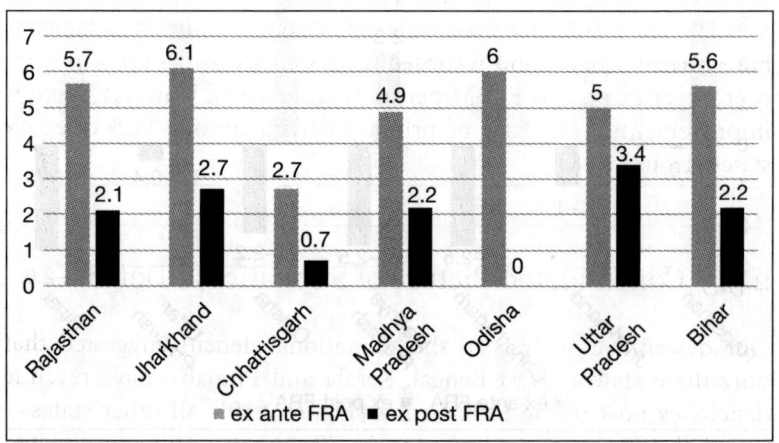

Source: RBI Study on State Finances 2014–15 (Basic Data).

Figure 2.15
Primary Deficit of Low-Income States: Ex Ante and Ex Post FRA

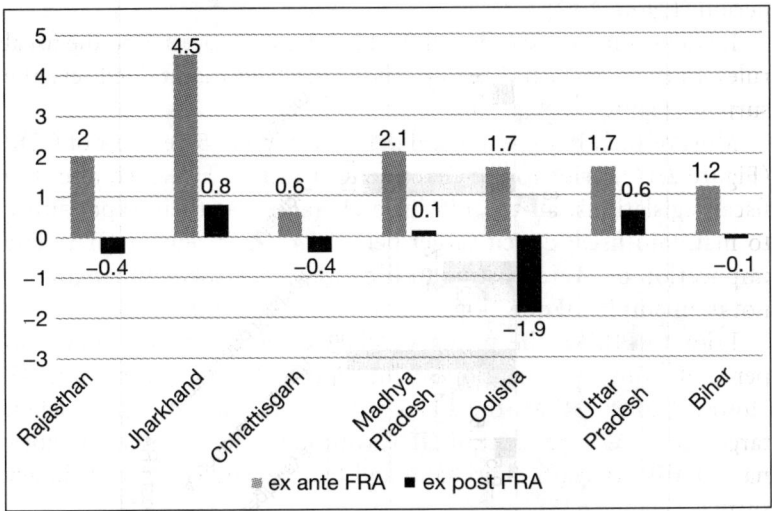

Source: RBI Study on State Finances 2014–15 (Basic Data).

All special category states (SCS) have eliminated revenue deficit. Prior to FRBM, only five states—Uttarakhand, Himachal Pradesh, Mizoram, Manipur and Assam were in revenue deficits among the SCS (Figure 2.16). However, only a few states of the SCS category have turned around and recorded fiscal deficits below the three per cent target ex post to FRBM period (Figure 2.17). However, there is improvement in the case of primary deficits among SCS category states (Figure 2.18).

2.5.3 Consolidated Picture of Subnational Deficits

Our descriptive analysis of the subnational deficits suggested that only three states—West Bengal, Kerala and Punjab—have revenue deficits ex post to the FRBM rules (Figure 2.19). All other states—especially LIS have overadjusted to the FRBM rules. This consolidated picture of revenue deficits given in Figure 2.19 has shown that the overall state-level fiscal balance had improved with the introduction of fiscal rule.

Figure 2.16
Revenue Deficit of Special Category States: Ex Ante and Ex Post FRA

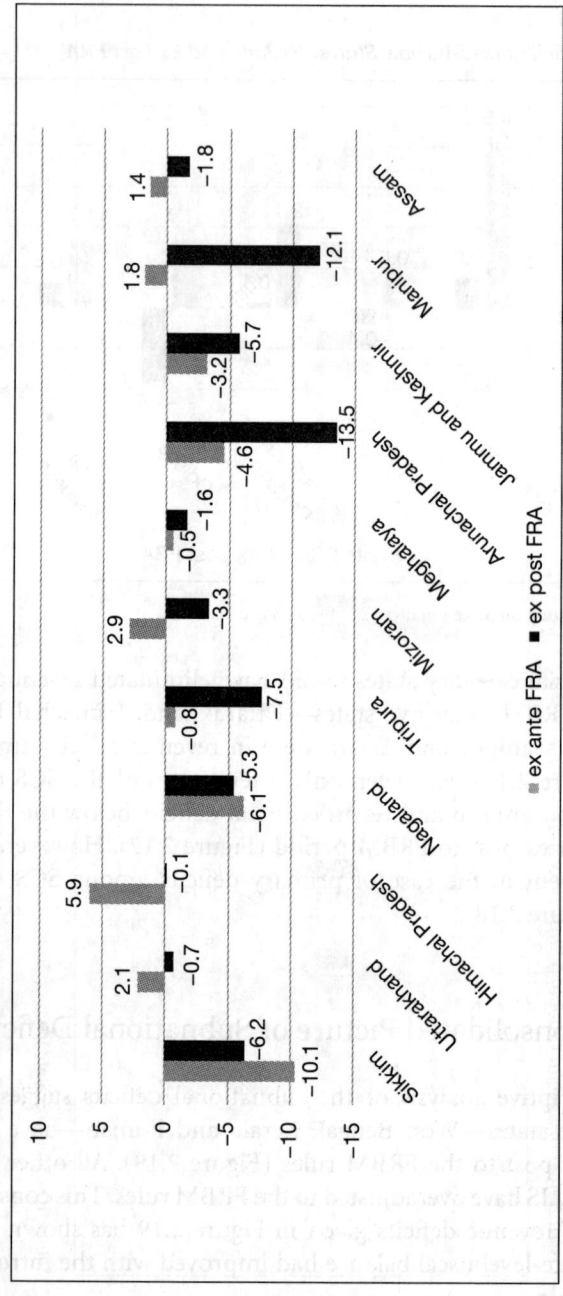

Source: RBI Study on State Finances 2014–15 (Basic Data).

Figure 2.17
Fiscal Deficit of Special Category States: Ex Ante and Ex Post FRA

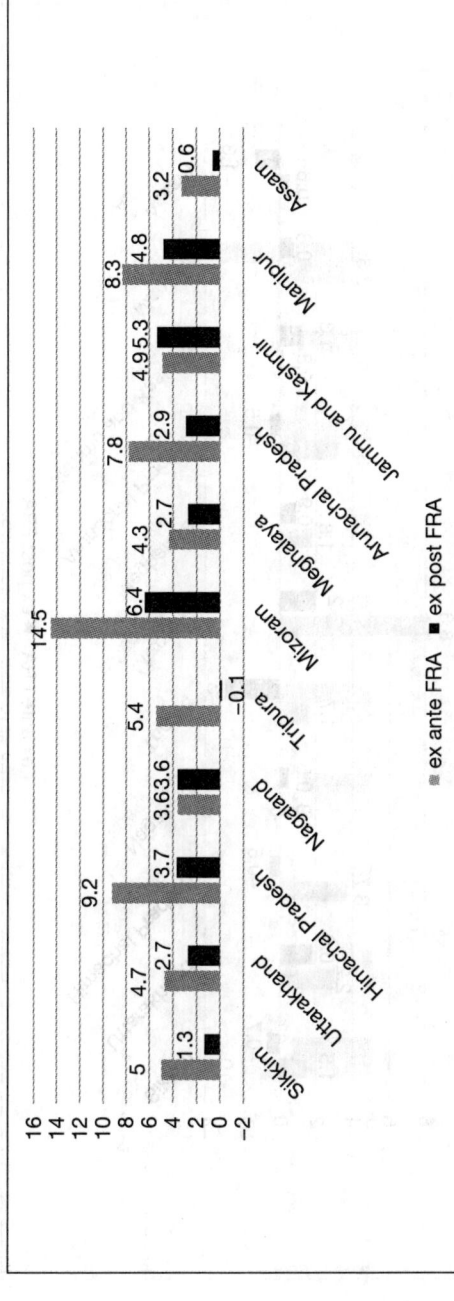

Source: RBI Study on State Finances 2014–15 (Basic Data).

Figure 2.18
Primary Deficit of Special Category States: Ex Ante and Ex Post FRA

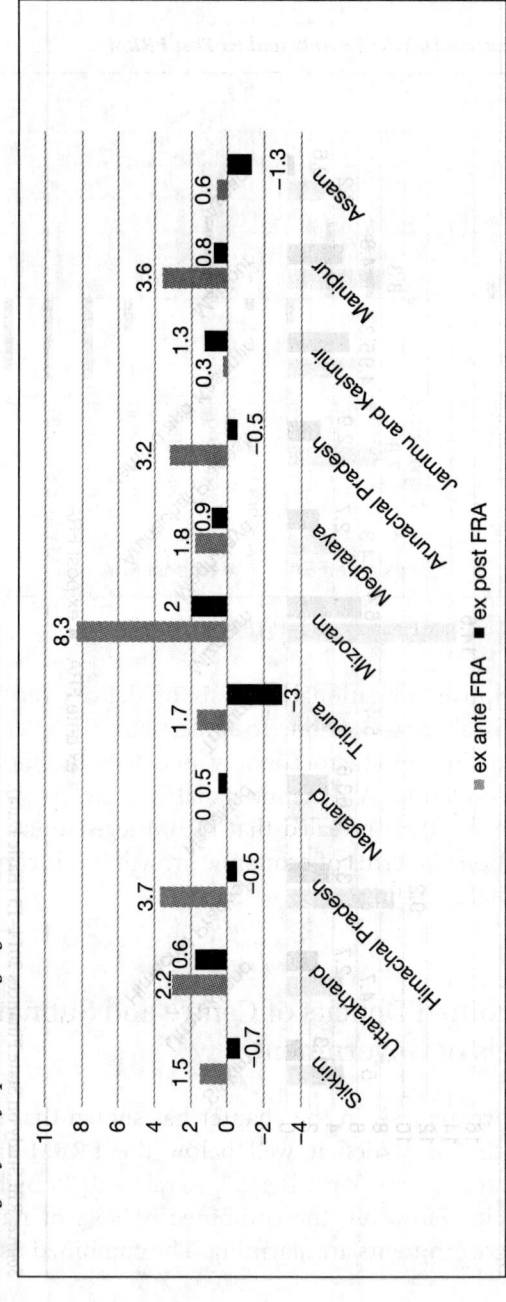

Source: RBI Study on State Finances 2014–15 (Basic Data).

Fiscal Deficit and Macroeconomic Activity 41

Figure 2.19
Subnational Revenue Deficit: Ex Ante and Ex Post FRBM

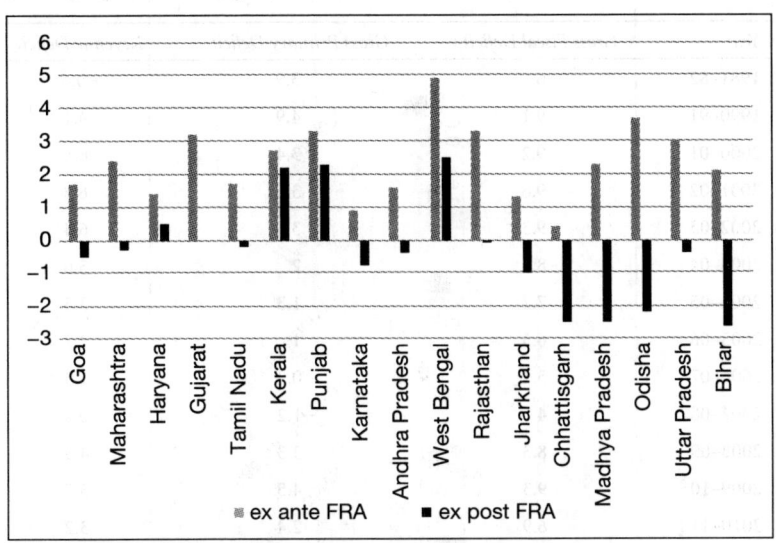

Source: RBI Study on State Finances 2014–15 (Basic Data).

The descriptive subnational analysis of deficits did not reveal the path of fiscal consolidation. To understand the effectiveness of fiscal consolidation on macroeconomy, one needs to know the path of fiscal consolidation. A dynamic panel data analysis carried out by Chakraborty (2015) revealed that FRBM legislations have long-term implications in terms of economic growth if it is carried out by reducing capital spending.

2.5.4 Combined Deficits of Centre and Subnational Levels of Government

The descriptive analysis in the chapter has shown that states have maintained the fiscal deficit well below the FRBM targets and almost all states (except West Bengal, Kerala and Punjab) have no revenue deficits. However, the combined deficits of national and subnational governments are alarming. The combined fiscal deficits

Table 2.10

Combined Deficits of the Central and State Governments (as Percentage of GDP)

Year	Gross Fiscal Deficit	Gross Primary Deficit	Revenue Deficit
1981–82	6	3.9	−0.6
1990–91	9.1	4.9	4.1
2000–01	9.2	3.4	6.4
2001–02	9.6	3.6	6.8
2002–03	9.3	3	6.4
2003–04	8.3	2	5.6
2004–05	7.2	1.3	3.5
2005–06	6.5	1	2.7
2006–07	5.1	−0.3	1.3
2007–08	4	−1.2	0.2
2008–09	8.3	3.3	4.3
2009–10	9.3	4.5	5.7
2010–11	6.9	2.4	3.2
2011–12	7.8	3.2	4.1
2012–13	6.9	2.3	3.4
2013–14	7.1	2.3	3.2
2014–15	6.6	1.7	2.6

Source: RBI (Basic Data, 2015).

of centre and states have been as high as 9 per cent of GDP in 2009–10, though it has marginally reduced to 7 per cent in recent years (Table 2.10). On the basis of these preliminary data analysis and tentative conclusions drawn, subsequent chapters will investigate the exact nature of relationships between these variables and fiscal deficit econometrically.

3
Fiscal Deficit, Capital Formation and Crowding Out

In recent years, in the context of macroeconomic management in India, it has often been argued that continuous pressure on market borrowing, arising out of high fiscal deficit, has led to an increase in the real rate of interest, which in turn crowded out private investment.[1] Also, the persistence of high fiscal deficits and increasing debt service payments is considered as one of the major constraints for the government at any level to undertake the necessary expenditures for productive capital formation. In other words, high fiscal deficit is affecting capital formation in the economy, both by reducing private investment through an increase in interest rate and also through reduction in public sector's own investment arising out of ever-increasing share of debt servicing obligation in total government expenditure.

The investment vacuum, if any, created by fiscal deficit would also depend on the nature of relationship between public and private investment. If the relationship between the two is complementary, then decline in public investment would lead to a decline in private investment even if the change in interest rate effect is controlled.[2] In this chapter, we will examine the nature of relationship between public and private investment.

---

[1] It has also been argued that the financing of public investment—whether through taxes, issuance of debt or seigniorage—will lower the resources available to the private sector and in turn would depress the private capital formation in the economy (Khan and Reinhart, 1990 and Modigliani 1961).

[2] Fiscal policy thus can affect capital formation through three channels; via public investment, via fiscal deficit and via rate of interest. In this chapter we examine the first two channels and following chapter looks into the third channel via rate of interest.

3.1 Unpacking the Effect of Deficits on Capital Formation

Theoretical literature identifies two variants of crowding out in an economy—real and financial. Blinder and Solow (1973) in their seminal paper 'Does Fiscal Policy Matter?' discuss three levels of crowding out at theoretical level. The first level of crowding out occurs when public investment displaces private investment broadly on a *dollar-for-dollar* basis. This level of crowding out occurs irrespective of the mode of financing the deficit. The second level of crowding out, as Blinder and Solow (1973) put, is an integral part of Keynesian tradition. It is based on the notion that deficit spending *not accompanied by new issuances of money* carries with it the need for government to float debt issues which compete with the private debt instruments in financial markets. The resulting upward pressure on interest rates will reduce any private expenditure, which is interest rate sensitive. In other words, this financial side effect of crowding out occurs via rate of interest (that is, bond financing of deficit causes market rate of interest to rise and in turn crowds out private investment). As discussed by Blinder and Solow (1973), there is no theoretical controversy over this second level of crowding out; the only contested issues are empirical. The rationale for third level of crowding out is that any government deficit requires the issuance of some sort of debt instrument—outside money or interest bearing bonds—and this increase in private wealth will have further reverberations in the economy. In other words, debt financing of deficit simultaneously results in the creation of bonds, which is considered as net wealth in the private sector. It is a matter of debate whether bonds are considered as net wealth in the context of India. However, this third level of crowding out is beyond the scope of this book.

The *real* crowding out occurs when the increase in public investment displaces private capital formation, which is also termed as *direct* crowding out. Real crowding out is important to be analysed in the context of developing countries, such as India, because of the large share of public investment in gross capital formation, and moreover, the nature of public investment (whether infrastructure or non-infrastructure) itself can affect private investment differently.

The phenomenon of partial loss of private capital formation in the economy due to increase in the interest rates emanating from the pre-emption of real and financial resources by the government through bond-financing of fiscal deficit is termed as *financial crowding out*. Financial crowding out occurs due to the upward pressures on rate of interest induced by the debt financing of fiscal deficit (interest rate effect). The phenomenon of financial crowding out is separately examined in Chapter 4.

The taxonomy of crowding out was discussed in detail by Buiter (1990). According to Buiter, *direct* crowding out (or crowding in) refers to substitution or complementary relationships between public and private spending that occur not through changes in prices, interest rates or required rate of return by changes in public sector activity, but through public sector consumption/investment being an argument in private utility functions and through the public sector capital stock being in argument in private sector production functions (Buiter, 1990: 34). Buiter defined *indirect* crowding out as the consequence of public actions that affect private behaviour either by altering budget constraints or by influencing the prices faced by private agents, namely, rate of interest. As mentioned, crowding out that occurs via interest rate changes are referred to as *financial crowding out* in this chapter.

Kotlikoff (1984) also pointed out that 'financial crowding out' is advanced in literature through the testing of causal link between fiscal deficit and rate of interest. He further pointed out that much of the concern with 'financial crowding out' revolves round the transaction of selling bonds to finance fiscal deficit. As the argument goes, a government's sale of bonds, regardless of its use of the proceeds, raises the total supply of bonds in the market. The greater supply of bonds, according to this view, means a lower bond price, that is a higher interest rate, which reduces (crowds out) the private investment.

The existing studies on *crowding out* are completely dichotomised. One set of studies looked into the link between public investment and private investment directly without incorporating the macroeconomic channel of crowding out phenomenon via the deficit-induced interest rate mechanism (Aschauer, 1989; Erenburg, 1993; Erenburg and Wohar, 1995; Khan and Kumar, 1990 and Sundararajan and Thakur, 1980). Another set of studies looked into the link between budget deficit and rate of interest and concluded the evidence of crowding out if rate of interest is deficit linked, without further analysing whether private investment is interest rate sensitive (Ahamad, 1994;

Cebula, 1990; Correia and Stemitsiotis, 1995; Dalamagas, 1987; Evans, 1985; Kulkarni and Erickson, 1996; Ostrosky, 1979 and Tanzi, 1985).

This analysis is different from the existing studies on crowding out in India for three reasons. First, the study bridged the lacuna of *partial analysis status* of financial crowding out in India by analysing not only whether private investment is interest rate sensitive but also whether the rise in interest rate is deficit-induced. This two-fold analysis is significant because even if private investment is interest rate sensitive, this aspect by itself does not mean occurrence of financial crowding out if rate of interest is not deficit induced. This is because the ad hoc configurations of demand and supply of loanable funds in the market is affected by myriad factors and these factors may have their respective roles in the determination of rate of interest. However, from the perspective of crowding out hypothesis, what is relevant is the extent to which the rate of interest is induced by the fiscal deficit operations of the government, and, in turn, the extent to which such increase in the rate of interest adversely affect the level of private capital formation.

Second, while analysing the real (direct) crowding out, it is important to analyse whether the infrastructure and non-infrastructure mix of public capital formation has differential impacts on private capital formation. Third, the study has taken care of certain acute methodological deficiencies of existing studies on *crowding out* debate. Most of the studies assumed the respective time series as stationary and proceeded with the analysis by applying ordinary least squares. Earlier studies have failed to address that time series may contain unit root and be non-stationary at levels, which can lead to spurious regression results, which would yield inconsistent estimates. The problems of simultaneity and ad hoc specification of lag structure are eliminated by applying Hsiao's asymmetric vector autoregressive (VAR) framework.

3.2 Theory and Empirics: A Synoptic View

Any analysis of investment can be done at different levels of aggregation, namely, firm, industry and the macroeconomy. Given the focus of the study, which intends to examine whether public investment crowds out private investment, the analysis is confined to aggregate macroeconomy level analysis of the determinants of private investment. At the aggregate level, theories on investment can be broadly categorised into three: Neoclassical accelerator models, financial theories on investment and the theories of uncertainty.

In the early accelerator theory, investment is related linearly to past changes in output (Clark, 1917). According to the accelerator principle, the size of capital stock desired by entrepreneurs depends on the aggregate demand, which in turn is represented mostly by the level of output. Later, flexible accelerator models were introduced, where adjustment to capital stock to the desired level is not instantaneous, but involves delivery lags due to the delayed response to the changes in aggregate demand. The Neoclassical theory of investment, which followed, viewed that investment spending depends on the user cost of capital and is geared to maintaining the optimal capital stock and an associated level of output. Jorgenson's Neoclassical theory (1963) on investment relies on the theory of profit maximising firm subject to a production function. The production function links the capital stock to the relative prices between capital and output. Once these relative prices are kept constant or if technology requires that capital and labour used in fixed proportions (in which case the elasticity of substitution is zero) then with constant returns to scale, the desired capital stock is proportional to the demand for output, which implies Jorgenson's model (1963) boils down to Clark's simple accelerator model, and rate of interest is not a determinant of investment. However, accelerator and relative price of capital models have together formed the foundation of numerous empirical models, which incorporate the demand-side (aggregated demand proxied by output) and the supply-side factors (cost of capital) in a single expression. In the late 1950s, financial theories were developed based on the premise that investment decisions are determined by the availability of internal funds and access to external funds (Meyer and Kuch, 1957 and Modigliani and Miller, 1958). These financial theories of investment looked into the implications of corporate financing through alternate routes namely debt versus equity and internal versus external funds on the capital formation and in turn established a strong relationship between real and financial variables in the economy. Tobin's q theory also falls in this stream, where investment is considered to be positively related to the value of 'q', which is the ratio of market value of capital to its replacement cost (Brainard and Tobin, 1968). All 'q' models are based on static expectations. A recent study by Alesina et al. (2002) estimated the effects of fiscal policy on business investment in q theory framework. Using a panel of OECD countries, the study found a sizable negative effect of fiscal spending—and in particular wage component—on investment. The results showed that an increase of one percentage point in the ratio of primary spending to GDP leads to a decrease in investment as a share of GDP of 0.15 percentage points on impact and a cumulative fall of 0.74 percentage points after five years. This effect was found particularly strong when fiscal expenditure increases occur in the government wage bill: in this case, the decrease in the investment to GDP ratio is 0.48 on impact and 2.56 cumulatively after five years. Also the study found that increases in taxes reduce profits and investment, but the magnitude of the effects on the revenue side is smaller than those on the expenditure side.

The recent theories on investment, emanating from the poor empirical performance of Neoclassical and Tobin's 'q' models in the context of developing countries, focussed on *irreversibility and uncertainty* as determinants of investment (Dixit and Pindyck, 1994; Pindyck and Solimano, 1994). These theories are based on the dual assumptions that *investment decisions are inherently irreversible* and *investment returns are uncertain*. The existence of sunk costs (that is, irreversible investment) implies that investment today carries an additional cost in the loss of option to invest tomorrow. This 'real options' view of investment gives a significant role to *uncertainty*; corporate investment tends to postpone or reduce the level of investment when greater is the level of uncertainty. These recent theories on investment suggest that macroeconomic environment arising from change in policy regarding interest rates; exchange rates and the inflationary pressures in the economy affect investment decision.

Based on the micro-foundations of these investment theories, the empirical studies on investment found that private corporate investment is associated with public (infrastructure) investment, aggregate demand and availability of financing, price and exchange rate stability and cost of investment. The empirical studies on link between private investment and public investment are summarised in Table 3.1. Many authors have tested the relationship between public investment and

Table 3.1

Selected Empirical Evidences on Crowding Out

Study	Period and Country	Model	Variables Selected	Results
Cebula (1978)	1949–76 US and Canada	ISLM	Capacity utilisation, lagged domestic investment, budget deficit	Budget deficit crowd out private investment in Canada and the US
Blejer and Khan (1984)	1971–79 24 developing countries	Flexible Accelerator Model	Output, real bank credit, real public investment	It is not the level, but the change in public investment that crowd out private investment
Ramirez (1994)	1950–90 Mexico	Flexible Accelerator Model	Public investment, flow of credit, exchange rate	Public investment crowds in private investment
Krishnamurty (1985)	1975–90 India	Sectoral Model	Public infrastructure investment, etc.	Infrastructure investment crowds in private investment in almost all sectors
Nemat Shafik (1992)	1970–88 Egypt	Neoclassical Model	Rate of interest, markup (WPI/Wage), private credit, public infrastructure, GDP	Public investment crowds out Private investment. Rate of interest determines private investment
Greene and Villanueva (1991)	1975–87 23 developing countries	Neoclassical Model	GDP, Public gross capital formation, debt ratio, etc.	Gross public capital formation crowds in private investment
Sundararajan and Thakur (1990)	1960–78 India and Korea	Neoclassical (Jorgenson)	Public investment, capital stock, rate of interest, capital stock	Evidence of crowding out in India Complementary relationship between public and private investment in Korea
Pradhan, Ratha, and Sarma (1988)	1960–90 India	Computable General Equilibrium (CGE) Model	Interest rate, modes of financing public investment, money creation, market borrowing, taxation and mark up	The extent of crowding out varies with the different modes of financing the public investment

(*Continued*)

(Continued)

Study	Period and Country	Model	Variables Selected	Results
Mohanty (1995)	1960–1990 India	RET (Ricardian Equivalence Theorem)	Real Disposable Income, Capital stock, public debt, government expenditure, interest payments.	Direct crowding out impact of government expenditure on private consumption. Government consumption and transfer payments have positive while public investment and interest payments have negative impact on private consumption.
Karen Parker (1995)	1974–1994 India	Accelerator Model	Interest rate, public investment, credit rate, real effective exchange rate, WPI inflation, index of industrial production, GDP	Public investment crowds out private investment. Public Infrastructure crowds in private investment.
K L Gupta (1990)	1960–1985 10 Asian countries	RET	Transitory and permanent income, taxes, transitory and permanent government expenditure.	RET is rejected for Sri Lanka, India, Indonesia and Philippines among 10 Asian countries. Evidence of Crowding out in all Asian countries except India
Sankar (1997)	1960–94 India	Accelerator model	Private corporate investment = f[public infrastructure investment, public non-infrastructure investment, ratio of public infrastructure to noninfrastructure investment, bank rate]	Infrastructure investment crowds in private corporate investment

Study	Period/Country	Model	Variables	Findings
Ostrosky (1979)	1950–75 US	ISLM	Capacity utilisation rate, average profit rate, net change in the government debt, etc.	Investment is affected by the net change in the debt, and hence crowding out
Feldstein (1984)	1950–82 Australia	Intertemporal CGE Model	Government deficit, government expenditure, etc.	Increase in debt financed proportion of government deficit crowds out private investment
Tun and Chong (1982)	1965–75 five countries of same development pattern	Flexible Accelerator Model	Public investment, quantity of credit, private sector output	Public investment crowds out private investment. Quantity of credit is also a significant factor
Chakraborty (2007)	1980–81 to 2002–03 India	Asymmetric VAR	Public investment (infrastructure and non infrastructure), bank credit, rate of interest, REER, output gap	Public investment (especially infrastructure investment) crowds in private corporate investment

Source: Author's compilations.

private investment and found contradictory results. Ramirez (1994), Greene and Villanueva (1990), Buiter (1977), Aschauer (1989) and Erenburg (1993) found that public investment and private investment have a complementary relationship. These studies showed that increase in public capital formation stimulate aggregate demand and in turn increases private investment. Another link for the existence of this complementary relationship is that a higher stock of public capital, in particular infrastructure may increase the return of private investment projects. Contrary to the complementary relationship, another set of studies showed that public investment might also act as a substitute for private investment. This substitutability can arise when private sector utilises the public capital for its required purposes rather than expand private capacity. Alternately, higher private investment can result in lower public capital formation; for instance, firms might construct physical infrastructure such as roads and bridges themselves, thereby allowing the public sector to withhold from this investment. In other words, there exists a forward and backward linkage between private and public investment (Aschauer, 1989; Blejer and Khan, 1984; Cebula, 1978; Kulkarni and Balders, 1998; Ostrosky, 1979; Parker, 1995; Shafik, 1992 and Tun and Chong, 1982).

In the context of developing countries including India, there are only few studies that looked into the link between public investment and private investment. Sundararajan and Thakur (1980) conducted the study on crowding out for two countries, namely, India and Korea in a Neoclassical framework. The study found that public investment exerts a short-term crowding out effect on private investment and hampers the growth of national income; this effect is found to be larger in the case of India than in Korea. Krishnamurty (1985) found that a rise in public investment resulted in crowding out of private investment, but led to higher growth. Pradhan et al. (1990) examined the question of complementarity between public and private investment in India under different modes of allocation and financing of public investment in an 18 sector computable general equilibrium framework. The study noted that though public investment crowds out private investment, in terms of its effect on total investment and economic growth, the economy is better off with increased public investment. Kulkarni and Balders (1998) analysed the phenomenon of crowding out in Mexican economy for the period 1970–96 in

Fiscal Deficit, Capital Formation and Crowding Out 53

terms of interest rate effect, price level effect and exchange rate effect. The study gave evidence of link between budget deficit and interest rate, but did not examine the link between interest rate and private investment.

To establish the evidence of financial crowding out, one ought to examine if increase in fiscal deficit increases rates of interest; even if the private investment is found interest rate sensitive. If fiscal deficit does not induce increase in the rates of interest, mere interest sensitivity of private investment does not mean financial crowding out. The present study does a two-fold analysis of crowding out debate in India by examining the relationship between fiscal deficit and interest rates after analysing the linkage between interest rates and private investment.

3.3 Modelling Private Investment in India

Though the Neoclassical-flexible accelerator model has been the most widely accepted general theory of investment behaviour, the application of these models in the context of developing countries posed certain challenges due to the key assumptions of the models such as perfect capital markets and little or no government investment (Greene and Villanueva, 1991). With the relatively significant role of government in capital formation and other certain structural and institutional factors peculiar to developing countries, the standard models of investment could not be directly adapted to developing countries. However, certain studies, for instance, Sundararajan and Thakur (1980), Tun and Wong (1982), Shafik (1992), Blejer and Khan (1984) attempted to incorporate features of standard accelerator and Neoclassical models of investment through relaxation of basic assumptions underlying these models. Furthermore, even if standard models could be directly adapted to developing countries, severe data constraints arise when attempts are made to implement them empirically (Blejer and Khan, 1984).

This chapter attempts to develop a model for private investment focusing on fiscal policy and tries to derive an explicit relationship between the principal policy instrument—variations in public expenditure (in particular, public investment in infrastructure and non infrastructure), the level of fiscal deficit and variations in bank credit to commercial sector along with real rates of interest—and private capital formation. In the process, model allows an assessment of possibility of *crowding out* phenomenon, financial and real, that may occur. This chapter attempts to derive the model in line with the existing attempts on modelling private investment in the context of developing countries using Neoclassical-flexible accelerator models, for instance, Blejer and Khan (1984) and Tun and Wong (1982).

Theoretically, gross investment in private sector is defined equal to net investment in private sector plus depreciation of the previous capital stock. While net investment in private sector is defined as the difference between the desired stock of capital in period t and the actual stock in the previous period $t - 1$,

$$I_{pvt} = \Delta KP_t + \delta KP_{t-1} \tag{3.1}$$

where I_{pvt} = Gross Private Investment
$\Delta KP_t = N_{pvt}$ = Net Private Investment
δ = rate of depreciation

$$N_{pvt} = \Delta KP_t = \beta\left(KP_t^* - KP_{t-1}\right) \tag{3.2}$$

where KP_t^* = desired stock of capital in private sector
KP_{t-1} = actual stock of capital in private sector in the previous period
β = coefficient of adjustment, $0 \leq \beta \leq 1$

Substituting Equation (3.2) in (3.1), we get:

$$I_{pvt} = \beta(KP_t^* - KP_{t-1}) + \delta KP_{t-1}. \tag{3.3}$$

In the standard lag-operator notation, Equation (3.3) can be rewritten as:

$$I_{pvt} = [1-(1-\delta)L]KP_t, \tag{3.4}$$

where L is the lag operator, $LKP_t = KP_{t-1}$. Now, we specify a partial adjustment function for gross investment as follows:

$$\Delta I_{pvt(t)} = \beta\left(I_{pvt(t)}^* - I_{pvt(t-1)}\right), \tag{3.5}$$

where $I^*_{pvt(t)}$ is the desired level of private investment. In the steady state, desired private investment is given by:[3]

$$I^*_{pvt} = [1-(1-\delta)L]KP^*_t. \qquad (3.6)$$

Combining the Equations (3.5) and (3.6), and solving for $I_{pvt(t)}$ yields the equation as follows:

$$I_{pvt(t)} = \beta\left[1-(1-\delta)L\right]KP^*_t + (1-\beta)I_{pvt(t-1)} \qquad (3.7)$$

We know that in the accelerator models, desired stock of capital can be assumed to be proportional to the output expectations in the economy.

$$KP^*_t = \alpha Y^*_t \qquad (3.8)$$

where Y^*_t is the expected output in the economy.[4]

Substituting Equation (3.8) in Equation (3.7), we get:

$$I_{pvt(t)} = \beta\alpha\left[1-(1-\delta)L\right]Y^*_t + (1-\beta)I_{pvt(t-1)} \qquad (3.9)$$

The beta coefficient in the equation, which captures the response of private investment to the gap between desired and actual investment, which in turn is assumed to vary systematically with the economic factors that influence the ability of private investors to achieve the desired level of investment. We hypothesise that the response of private investment depends on the availability of financing (cost and quantity of credit), uncertainties in an open macroeconomy and the level of public sector investment. Blejer and Khan (1984) hypothesised that beta coefficient depends on (i) the stage of economic cycle, (ii) the availability of financing and (iii) the level of public sector investment. While Tun and Wong (1982) hypothesised that beta coefficient depends positively on the change in the bank credit to the private sector and net capital inflow to the private sector.

---

[3] This equation requires that $KP^*_{t-1} = KP_{t-1}$. This equality would generally hold in the steady state.

[4] We follow the assumption of Blejer and Khan (1984) that private sector investment depends on output expectations of the economy, not in the private sector alone. Blejer and Khan (1984) also noted that private sector output is proportional to total output.

With regard to availability of financing, a hypothesis emerged in recent years that in contrast to developed countries, one of the principal constraints on investment in developing countries is the quantity, rather than cost of the financial resources. This view is associated with McKinnon (1973) in his controversial work on Money and Capital in Economic Development. McKinnon (1973) was the first to challenge the conventional wisdom intrinsic in the Keynesian and Neoclassical models that investment is interest rate sensitive and low interest rate would promote investment spending and economic growth in developed and developing countries[5] (Molho, 1986). Similarly, the movements in exchange rate can also cause changes in private investment, which reflects the uncertainties in the open macroeconomy, with surge of capital flows.

The phenomenon of real crowding out is incorporated in the model through the link between level of public investment and private investment. In the context of developing countries, it is a matter of debate whether public investment crowds out or crowds in private investment. In broad terms, crowding out phenomenon is expected if the public sector investment utilises scarce physical and financial resources that would be otherwise available to the private sector, or if it produces marketable output that competes with private output (Blejer and Khan, 1984). The non-homogeneous nature of public investment receives attention in this context; that the public investment, which is infrastructure in nature, can attract private investment while public investment in non-infrastructure may or may not crowd in private investment. Theoretically, this relationship remains ambiguous. On the basis of the arguments above, we can assume the reaction coefficient beta depends on monetary and fiscal policies; in particular, availability of credit to private sector (ΔC_{pvt}), rate of interest (i_r), real exchange rate (e_r), and public investment (I_{pub}).

$$\beta = f\left(\Delta C_{pvt}, i_r, e_r, I_{pub}\right) \quad (3.10)$$

A linear regression model for private investment can thus be constructed assuming Equations (3.9) and (3.10) are linear.

---

[5] Shaw (1973) also challenged the conventional wisdom that low interest rates are adopted in the countries as a way of promoting economic growth. A detailed discussion of various rationale for a policy of low interest rates is given in Shaw (1973, 92–112).

$$I_{pvt} = a + b_1 I_{pvt(-1)} + b_2 I_{pub} + b_3 i_r + b_4 \Delta C_{pvt} + b_6 e_r + b_7 Y^* + v_t. \quad (3.11)$$

Now we turn to discuss the nature of link between each of these explanatory variables with private investment.

3.3.1 Private Investment and Output Expectations

The output expectations as a determinant of private investment emanates from the accelerator theories of investment. In consistent with the flexible accelerator models of investment behaviour, a priori we expect that lagged private corporate investment is determined by the output expectations in the economy, which in turn is represented most closely by the level of output gap. The concept of output gap is synonym to the concept of capacity utilisation of an industry or firm. Like 'capacity utilisation', it is also a measure of the intensity with which national economy makes use of its resources. The economy-wide measure of 'capacity utilisation' or the *output gap* index can be defined as

$$OG = [(\text{Actual GDP} - \text{Potential GDP})/\text{Potential GDP}] * 100 \quad (3.12)$$

This is also known as the 'economic activity index' (Congdon, 1998; and Tanzi, 1985). It can be seen from the Equation (3.12) that 'output gap' or the index of economic activity is defined as the difference between the actual and trend/potential level of national output as a percentage of trend/potential output.

Definitionally speaking, potential level of output would be higher than the actual as the resource utilisation is maximum at potential level. However, it is argued that cyclical factor such as recession or boom could cause the actual to be below or above the potential output respectively (Tanzi, 1985). The major problem of estimation of 'output gap' lies on the estimation of potential level of output.

Theoretically, the 'production function method' estimates the trend/potential output by determining the quantity and productivity of inputs, namely, labour and capital.[6] The relative importance of the two inputs are determined by assuming that their return is determined by their marginal products and their share in the national

---

[6] It is called 'production function method,' as production is represented as the functions of inputs.

output is equal to their quantity multiplied the return (Adams and Coe, 1990 and Congdon, 1998). Trend output estimation through 'production function method' requires data on labour force and capital stock. If data on one of these series or both are not available, one has to search for other methods of estimation of trend output.

One of the most commonly used methods of estimation of trend output is the moving average method. Another method is known as 'trend through peaks' (hereafter, TTP) developed by Klein with Wharton Econometric Forecasting Associates. The steps involved in estimation are delineated below. First step is to plot the data on GDP adjusted for price fluctuations and identify the peaks. Second, it is assumed that identified peaks in the series are the points where resources in the economy are used at 100 per cent of their capacity. Third step is to intrapolate between the major peaks including the first and last observation. The strong assumptions beneath the TTP method itself deterred us from using it as a tool for estimating potential output.

The Hodrick-Prescott filter (HP filter) is yet another method for the derivation of the potential output. The idea of this filter is to decompose a non-stationary time series such as actual output into a stationary cyclical component and a smooth trend component (Y_t and Y_t^* denote the logarithms of actual and trend/potential output respectively) by minimising the variance of cyclical component subject to a penalty for the variation in the second difference of the trend component. This results in the following constrained least square problem

$$Min \sum_{t=1}^{T} (Y_t - Y_t^*)^2 + \lambda \sum_{t=2}^{T-1} \left[\left(Y_{t+1}^* - Y_t^* \right) - \left(Y_t^* - Y_{t-1}^* \right) \right]^2 \qquad (3.13)$$

The first term in the equation is a measure of fit. The second term is a measure of smoothness. The *Langrange* multiplier λ is associated with the smoothness constraint and must be set a priori. As a weighting factor, it determines how smooth the resulting output series is. The lower the λ, the closer potential output follows actual output. We have used the HP filter method for the calculation of potential level of output. Figure 3.1 traces the path of actual and potential output in India. The series showed a smooth increasing trend over the period 1950–51 to 1999–2000.

Figure 3.1
Movement of Trend and Cyclical GDP in India: 1980–81 to 2013–14

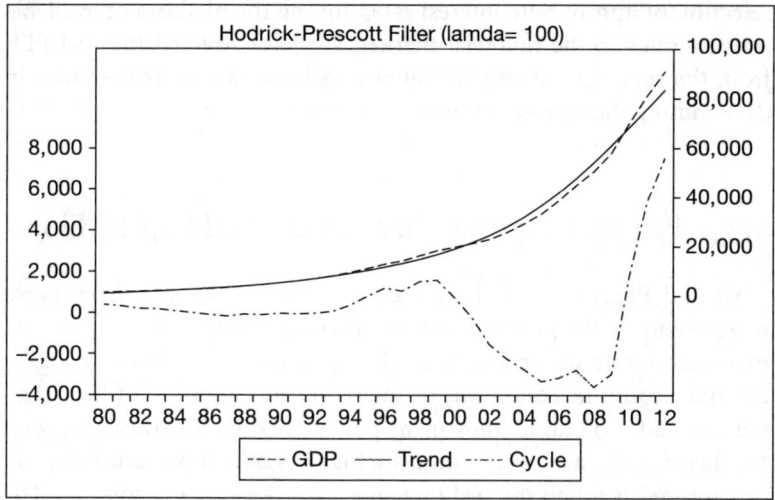

Source: Handbook of Statistics on Indian Economy (Basic Data), RBI (2015).

3.3.2 Private Corporate Investment and Price versus Quantity of Credit

Theoretical literature argued that both price and quantity of credit have a bearing on investment. It is important in this context to examine whether principal constraint on investment in developing countries is the quantity or the cost of financial resources (McKinnon, 1973). It is noted that one of the principal constraints on investment in developing countries is the quantity, rather than the cost, of financial resources and it would be legitimate to hypothesise that private investor in a developing country is restricted by the level of bank financing (Blejer and Khan, 1984). The variable 'availability of credit' is the first difference of outstanding credit from the banking sector to the commercial sector. This variable is included in our study to understand whether it is the credit that gets rationed in the investment decisions in India. It is to be noted that moral hazards and adverse selection problems can lead to credit rationing since the riskiness of investments cannot be identified a priori (Stigliz and Weiss, 1981). In order to analyse whether there is any impact of the cost of funds, that is the impact of rate of interest on private corporate investment, the study encountered the problem of selection of appropriate interest rates among the plethora of available interest rates in the financial market. We have selected the real PLR from the spectrum of rates of interest in India due to its relevance in determining the investment process in the economy.[7]

3.3.3 Private Corporate Investment and Capital Flows

Dixit and Pindyk (1994) have shown in their study that irreversible investments in the private sector would be postponed when there are macroeconomic uncertainties in the open economy about changing external economic conditions or the scope and duration of key stabilisation and structural adjustment policy reforms. In consistent with the theories, the macroeconomic fluctuations of an open economy can be captured through the real exchange variations in an economy. The macroeconomic uncertainties arising from the external financing constraints which reflect in foreign exchange reserves or debt-service ratio do not appear to have impact on private capital formation in India, unlike some other developing countries mainly because of the fact that Indian economy has not been open to foreign capital and trade flows until the late 1990s. Moreover, the financing pattern of fiscal deficit in India showed that it comprises mostly the internal liabilities. External debt financing of fiscal deficit has been highly negligible in India over the years of the period under concern. The overall external debt GDP ratio is also maintaining a moderate level. Thus, private investment disincentives in India cannot be associated with an external debt overhang as it happens in heavily indebted developing countries. Therefore, external debt overhang theories[8] of disincentive effect on investment efficiency can be insignificant in the context of India.[9] Krugman's hypothesis argued that when a country is unable to fully service its debt,

---

[7] The process of transforming nominal rate of interest into ex-ante real rate of interest using HP filter method is discussed in detail in Chapter 4.
[8] For details on external debt overhang theories, please see Krugman (1988), Sachs (1988), Husain (1992).
[9] Dixit and Pindyk (1994) analysed the detrimental effects of price uncertainties on private capital formation.

actual payments tend to depend on the country's economic performance. He further argued that the existence of a heavy debt burden then depresses the return on investment and weakens the incentive to invest, since the part of the profits will need to be diverted towards debt servicing and amortisation. When such disincentives becomes important, debt reduction is the appropriate policy action than private investment decisions. Yet another competing explanation for the fall in investment has also been offered by Krugman (1988), with very different policy implications. It argues that the debt crisis is a liquidity issue as opposed to a solvency issue. According to this view, lucrative private investment opportunities are available in debtor countries, but some sort of market failure associated with debt crisis has prevented creditors from lending any further (Krugman, 1988). Thus external debt overhang theories literature captures two types of investment inefficiency—a disincentive effect caused by the existence of future debt burden and a liquidity effect arising from a shortage of current resources available for investment. However, with the surge of capital flows in the recent decade, to capture the macroeconomic uncertainties, we have used real effective exchange rate and capital flows as a determinant of investment.

3.4 Econometric Estimation

The methodology used for the analysis is Hsiao's asymmetric VAR framework. We have used VAR methodology because it avoids the imposition of potentially spurious a priori constraints. Furthermore, as noted by Fischer (1981), Genberg, Salemi, and Swaboda (1987) and McMillin and Koray (1989), VARs are well suited to examine the channels through which a variable operates since few restrictions are imposed on the way the system's variables interact. In particular, the Hsiao's asymmetric VAR model we have used in the book has got an advantage of judicious parametrisation using Akaike's Final Prediction Error (FPE), in addition to causality detection and solving simultaneity bias. That is, the asymmetric VAR methodology does not permit every variable to enter every equation with equal lag length. The practical disadvantage of symmetric models with large number of parameters to be estimated is that it quickly eats up the degrees of freedom in the estimation procedure. And often a substantial number of parameters hardly differ from zero. Moreover, Ahking and Miller (1985) have shown that imposing equal lag lengths to all variables does not have any basis in theory and can distort the estimates and lead to misleading inferences concerning causality, if lag structure differ across variables (Sturm, 1998). To overcome this problem, Hsiao (1981) suggests an asymmetric VAR approach that starts from univariate autoregression and sequentially adds lags and variables using Akaike's FPE criterion, which is often referred as VAR-FPE model. The order in which variables enter the equation in the VAR-FPE model is guided by *specific gravity criterion* of Caines, Keng and Sethi (1981).

A series X_t is said to be integrated of order d, denoted by

$$Xt \sim It(d) \quad (3.13)$$

If it becomes stationary after differentiating d times and thus X_t contains d unit roots. Using the augmented Dickey Fuller (ADF) methodology,[10] the fundamental regression equation to test unit roots is,

$$\Delta y_t = \alpha_0 + \alpha_{1t} + \gamma y_{t-1} + \sum_{i=1}^{k} \beta_i \Delta y_{t-1} + \varepsilon_t \quad (3.14)$$

The null hypothesis of unit root is accepted if $\gamma = 0$. If the null hypothesis $\alpha_1 = \gamma = 0$ is rejected, the series is trend stationary.

The unit root test results of private corporate investment and its apriori determinants are presented in the Table 3.2. All the variables are integrated of order 1.

Having established that macrovariables are non-stationary and have same order of integration at $I \sim (1)$, we proceed to test whether the linear combination of these macroseries is stationary, that is, they are cointegrated. Cointegration is a test for equilibrium between

---

[10] One of the major problems of the ADF test is that the selection of appropriate lag length. Including too many lags reduces the power of the test to reject the null hypothesis since the increased number of lags requires the estimation of additional parameters and loss of degrees of freedom. On the other hand, very few lags will not capture the actual error process, which would fail to give a proper estimate of Δ and its standard error (Enders, 1995). The approach suggested for the selection of appropriate lag length is to start with a relatively long lag length and pare down to the model by the usual t-test and/or F-test. Thus, one can estimate the equation using a lag length of n^*. If the t-statistics is insignificant in the lag n^*, repeat the procedure until the lag is significantly different from zero.

Table 3.2
Unit Root Test Results for Private Corporate Investment and Its Apriori Determinants

Macro Variables	Lags	t-statistics	Mc Kinnon Critical Value	Order of Integration
Private corporate investment	0	−5.960311	−4.296729	$I \sim (1)\ c,t^*$ at 1%
Public investment	0	−5.026341	−4.296729	$I \sim (1)\ c,t^*$ at 1%
Real rate of interest	0	−7.296329	−4.284580	$I \sim (1)\ c,t$ at 1%
Output gap	0	−3.729007	−3.661661	$I \sim (1)\ c$ at 1%
Real effective exchange rate	0	−5.342808	−4.284580	$I \sim (1)\ c,t$ at 1%
Public infrastructure investment	0	−5.684418	−4.309824	$I \sim (1)\ c,t$ at 10%
Public non-infra investment	0	−7.355331	−4.296729	$I \sim (1)\ c,t$ at 1%
Gross fiscal deficit	0	−5.731913	−4.284580	$I \sim (1)\ c,t^*$ at 1%

Source: National Account Statistics (Basic Data), New Series, CSO (various issues), and *Handbook of Statistics on Indian Economy*, RBI (various issues).

non-stationary variables integrated of same order. We employ cointegration test to determine whether the simple Granger causality test is appropriate. In case of multivariate models, Johansen's cointegration test, based on trace and the eigenvalue tests, is superior to Engle–Granger methodology, for three reasons. First, the Johansen and Juselius method tests for all the number of cointegrating vectors between the variables. These tests are based on the trace statistic test and the maximum eigenvalue test. Second, it treats all variables as endogenous, thus avoiding an arbitrary choice of dependent variable. Third, it provides a unified framework for estimating and testing cointegrating relations within the framework of a vector error correction model. Before endeavouring Johansen's FIML approach to cointegration, we need to ascertain the nature of intercept and trend in the underlying VAR model and choose the order of VAR. The order of VAR is detected using the model selection criteria of Akaike Information Criteria (AIC), Schwarz Bayesian Criteria (SBC) and Log Likelihood method, setting the sample to maximum order of 3. The SBC suggests a VAR of order 1, while AIC and Log Likelihood of order 2. Since we have a short time series data, we cannot afford the risk of over-parametrisation and therefore chose 1 as the order of VAR as per the SBC criteria. According to Ho and Sorensen (1996), when Johansen's cointegration procedure is applied to small samples, the precision of the estimator is much better when the lag length is short. The next important step is to ascertain the nature of intercept and trend. It is proved that most of the series under consideration are trended, but it seems unlikely that there will be a trend in cointegrating relation between the variables. Using deterministic or non-deterministic trends in data, the maximum eigenvalue test and λ-trace test suggested that the rank (number of cointegrating vectors) is two. Hence, we concluded that there are two cointegrating relationships among the variables such as private investment, public investment, output gap, real rate of interest, real effective exchange rate and availability of credit to private sector.[11] The next step is to conduct asymmetric VAR model to find the causality between the variables. The appropriate parametrisation of the model manifests the critical part of Granger-causality test, as the results depend on the lag length chosen. Arbitrary or ad hoc parametrisation can lead to econometric problems. Under parametrisation may lead to estimation bias and over parametrisation results in the loss of degrees of freedom and thus the power of the test.[12] Hsiao's (1981) method is one of the alternatives to unconstrained Sims type symmetric VAR.[13] Hsiao's procedure starts from univariate autoregression

---

[11] Here lies an important econometric question, is it better to have one or many cointegrating vectors among the group of the system variables? The existence of many cointegrating vectors may indicate that the system under examination is stationary in more than one direction and hence it is stable. As discussed by Dickey, Jansen and Thorton (1994), 'the more cointegrating vectors there are, the more stable the system... it is desirable for an economic system to be stationary in as many directions as possible'. From the angle of policymaking, the existence of more than one long-run cointegrated relationship between a set of variables has significant policy implications. In the framework of cointegrated series, policymakers could determine their targets on one variable seeking to stabilise effectively the long run- level of some other variables.

[12] On the basis of parametrisation, VAR modelling can be of two types. The first type of VAR model is standard Sims-type VAR model in which every variable enters every equation with the same lag length. This is symmetric VAR model since it employs symmetrical lag specifications. The second type is asymmetric VAR model. Asymmetric VAR model is defined as VAR where each variable may have a unique number of lags. The advantage of asymmetric VAR over symmetric VAR is that the latter employs the same lag length for each variable, exhausts considerable degrees of freedom and consequently often estimates many statistically insignificant coefficients.

[13] Litterman (1986) used Bayesian VAR model, which another alternative to symmetric VAR. Hsiaos' (1981) asymmetric VAR has an advantage against Littermans' Bayesian VAR. Litterman imposes Bayesian prior restrictions on VAR coefficients. Since these prior

and sequentially adds lags and variables using Akaike's (1969) FPE criterion. This asymmetric VAR model using FPE criterion to select the appropriate lag specification takes care of *parametrically prolific symmetric VAR models*. An advantage of Hsiao (1981) asymmetric VAR is that along with the appropriate parametrisation, we can detect the causality of the variables also in the autoregressive framework. Asymmetric VAR models permit more flexibility in modelling dynamic system. In asymmetric VAR, each equation has the same explanatory variables, but each variable may have different number of lags. Hsiao noted that FPE criterion is appealing since it balances the risk due to the bias when a lower order is selected and the risk due to the increase of variance when a higher order is selected. And by combining FPE criterion and Grangers' (1969) definition of causality, a practical method for identification of the system of equations was suggested.

VAR models can be written in general form as

$$y_t = \alpha + \psi(L) y_t + \mu_t \qquad (3.15)$$

where y_t is vector of model variables

that is, first difference of (I_{pub}), (O_g), (i_r), (ΔC_{pvt}), (e_r)

α is vector of constants

μ_t is vector of white noise error terms

$\psi(L)$ is vector of polynomials in the lag operator, L

where $\varphi_{ij} = \sum_{t=1}^{k} \varphi_{iji} L^i$ where L is the lag operator.

μ_t and v_t are white noise error terms.

To choose the order of lags in $\psi_{ii}(L)$ and $\psi_{ij}(L)$ by the minimum FPE is equivalent to applying an approximate F test with varying significance levels (for details, see Hsiao ([1981]).

Akaikes' definition of FPE criteria is expressed as

$$FPE_y(m,n) = \frac{T+m+n+1}{T-m-n-1} * \frac{\sigma^2 y(m,n)}{T}$$

---

restrictions are almost always based on forecasting performance instead of economic theory, parameter estimates from Bayesian VARs are likely to be biased. Bias may be acceptable in forecasting, but biased structural parameters estimates are undesirable if the goal is to answer questions about macroeconomic structure and the channels of operation of a macrovariable (Keating, 2000).

where T is the number of observations, m and n are the order of lags of the variables under the concern, private corporate investment [y] and determinants [x_s] respectively and $\sigma^2 y(m,n) = \sum_{t=1}^{T}(y_t - \psi_{ii}^m)(L)y_t - \psi_{ii}^n (L)x_{s_t} - \hat{a})^2$ where superscripts m and n denote the order of lags in $\psi_{11}(L)$ and $\psi_{12}(L)$. And $\psi_{11}^m(L)$, $\psi_{12}^n(L)x_{(s)t}$ and $\hat{a}$ are the least square estimates. The causality can be detected as follows: If $FPE\, y(m, n) < FPE\, y\,(m, 0)$ then $x_{(s)t}$ Granger causes y_t, denoted by $x_{(s)t} \Rightarrow y_t$.

The FPE of fitting one-dimensional autoregressive process for private corporate investment is computed with upper bound of lag length (L^*) assumed equal to 5 in all the models discussed in the chapter. First, we have considered private corporate investment as controlled variable, holding the order of its autoregressive operator to 1, we sequentially added the lags of the manipulated variables such as public investment, real rate of interest, output gap, availability of credit to private sector and exchange rate upto the L^* of 5 and found respective order which gives the smallest FPE.

The order in which variable enter into the equation is as per the *specific gravity criteria*. Caines et al. (1981) suggested the following procedure for multivariate autoregressive modeling for stationary processes: For a pair of stationary processes (X, Y) construct bivariate AR models of different orders, then compare the multivariate FPEs of these models, and choose the model of order k possessing minimum FPE to be the optimal model for the pair of processes (X, Y).

(i) Construct bivariate AR (k) models (both causal models and non-causal (independent) models) for (X, Y) and apply the stage wise causality detection procedure to determine the endogeneity, exogeneity or independent relations between X and Y.
(ii) If a process, say X, has n multiple causal variables, $y^1, y^2, \ldots, y^n$, we rank these multiple causal variables according to the decreasing order of their specific gravities.
(iii) For each caused (endogenous) process, X, we first construct the optimal univariate AR model using FPE criterion, then we include X's multiple causal variables, one at a time, according to their causal ranks and use FPE criterion to determine the optimal orders of the model at each step.

Table 3.3
Public Investment Model

Controlled Variable	Manipulated Variables				Optimum Lags of Manipulated Variable	Final Prediction Error	Causality Inference
I_{pvt} (1)	–				–	0.079103	–
I_{pvt} (1)	I_{pub}	–			1	0.0087050	$I_{pub} \Rightarrow I_{pvt}$
I_{pvt} (1)	I_{pub}	C_{pvt}	–		1	0.0080240	$\Delta C \Rightarrow I_{pvt}$
I_{pvt} (1)	I_{pub}	C_{pvt}	O_g		1	0.0658400	$O_g \Rightarrow I_{pvt}$
I_{pvt} (1)	I_{pub}	C_{pvt}	O_g	$(i_r - \pi_t)$	1	0.0751980	$(i_r - \pi_t) \Rightarrow I_{pvt}$
I_{pvt} (1)	I_{pub}	C_{pvt}	O_g	$(i_r - \pi_t)$ $(e_r)_t$	1	0.0503591	$(e_{rt})_t \Rightarrow I_{pvt}$

Source: National Account Statistics (Basic Data), New Series, CSO (various issues), and Handbook of Statistics on Indian Economy, RBI (various issues).

Note: Figures in the parentheses denotes the lag length of controlled variable.

(iv) Pool all the optimal univariate AR models constructed in (iv) and estimate the system.

As per the specific gravity criteria, the explanatory variables sequenced as follows: public investment, credit availability to private sector, output gap, real interest rate and finally real effective exchange rate. The results showed that private corporate investment is sensitive to real rate of interest and public investment (Table 3.3). The macroeconomic instability in the open economy arising from fluctuations in exchange rate adjusted for inflationary expectations, output gap and the availability of credit to private sector are also found significant in determining the private corporate investment.

The econometric results are provided in Table 3.3, showed the interest rate sensitivity of private corporate investment and also the link between public investment and private corporate investment.

In addition to detection of causality, the sign of the causal relationship between private corporate investment and other macrovariables is also of great significance in understanding the mechanism of crowding out phenomenon. The evidence of cointegration implies the error correction modeling of private corporate investment, which combines both the long-run information and short-run dynamics in the equation.

$$I_{pvt} = -2.346 + 0.370 \Delta I_{pvt(t-1)} + 1.224 \Delta I_{pub} - 0.363 \Delta I_{pub(t-1)}$$
$$(-1.334) \quad (1.189)^* \quad (1.757)^* \quad (-0.554)$$
$$+ 2.166 \Delta C_{pvt} - 2.131 \Delta C_{pvt(-1)}$$
$$(2.371) \quad (0.0393)$$
$$0.029 \Delta i_r - 0.006 \Delta i_{r(t-1)} + 0.003 \Delta(e_r) - 0.005 \Delta(e_r)_{(t-1)}$$
$$(-1.775)^* \quad (-0.387) \quad (0.609) \quad (-1.180)$$
$$+ 0.018 \Delta(O_g) + 0.001 \Delta(O_g)_{(t-1)} - 0.402 \text{ecm}_{(-1)}$$
$$(1.146) \quad (-0.706) \quad (1.005)$$
$$R^2 = 0.99$$
$$DW = 1.81$$

The figures in parentheses denote t-statistics and * denote one per cent level of significance.

The equation showed that public investment and real rate of interest affect private capital formation in India. There is no evidence of direct crowding out of private corporate investment by public investment; instead it is observed that one per cent increase in public capital formation increased private capital formation in the corporate sector by 1.224 per cent. The estimated equation reinforced that quantity and cost of the credit (proxied by real interest rate) also matter for the capital formation in the private corporate sector in the context of developing countries. The confirmation of no financial crowding out can be detected only after checking whether real interest rate rise is induced by fiscal deficit operations of the government, which would be dealt in the next chapter. Before going into discussion on these issues, it is imperative to analyse the link between private corporate investment and public investment based on the non-homogeneity of public capital formation in India.

3.4.1 Non-Homogeneity of Public Investment

The public capital formation in India is of non-homogeneous in nature and can broadly divided into infrastructure and non-infrastructure investment. The public infrastructure investment is defined as the aggregate of capital formation in agriculture, electricity, water supply, oil and

Figure 3.2
Trends in Infrastructure and Non-Infrastructure Investment in India

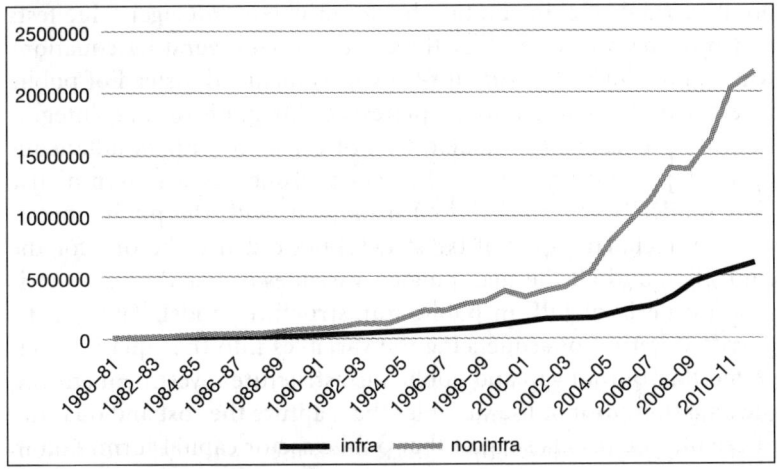

Source: National Account Statistics (Basic Data), New Series, CSO (various issues).

transport and communication. While the public non-infrastructure is defined as capital formation in manufacturing, mining and quarrying, trade, hotels and restaurant, finance and insurance etc. Karen Parker (1995) categorised infrastructure and non-infrastructure investment in similar manner. Based on the nature of investment, it is deciphered from Figure 3.2 that gap between both series widened over the years. The decline in public capital formation in case of infrastructure is a matter of concern. It is important in this context to analyse the heterogeneity of public investment—whether it implies that different types of public investment likely to have conflictive or mutually reinforcing effects on private capital formation; public investment in infrastructure prima facie tend to attract private investment while public investment in non-infrastructural activities where public enterprises do what private firms too can do might have substitution effects.

Now we turn to econometrically investigate the link between private corporate investment with the infrastructure and non-infrastructure public capital formation. The model specified is same as above in case of public investment model, but with separate inclusion of infrastructure and non-infrastructure investment instead of aggregate public investment. The unit root tests revealed that both infrastructure and non-infrastructure investment are integrated of order one. Johansen's full information maximum likelihood method of cointegration based on maximum eigenvalue tests and trace tests revealed that there are two cointegrating equations when public infrastructure investment is included instead of public investment. Subsequent to the pretests of integration and cointegration, we proceeded to the detection of causality with simultaneous optimal parametrisation of the model using Hsiao's asymmetric VAR model. The results moved in tandem with the public investment model. The optimal lag structure is tested to be one for the controlled and all the manipulated variables as per the parametrisation criteria of FPE in public infrastructure-model. The specific gravity criterion of sequencing the variables into the equation suggested that output gap and public infrastructure investment entered the equation prior to the variables that capture the cost and quantity of credit. The results suggest that public sector capital formation in infrastructure, quantity of non-food credit to the economy and real rate of interest proved to be the effective causal factors of private corporate investment while the macroeconomic instabilities front were found not the causal variables of the private capital formation in the corporate sector (Table 3.4).

The evidence from the equation inclusive of error correction term revealed that public infrastructure investment crowds in public

Table 3.4

Public Infrastructure Investment Model

Controlled Variable	Manipulated Variables (MV)					Optimum Lags of MV	FPE	Causality Inference
I_{pvt} (1)	–	–	–	–	–	–	0.079103	–
I_{pvt} (1)	O_g	–	–	–	–	1	0.0949530	$O_g \neq I_{pvt}$
I_{pvt} (1)	O_g	$I_{pubinfra}$	–	–	–	1	0.0081339	$I_{pubinfra} \Rightarrow I_{pvt}$
I_{pvt} (1)	O_g	$I_{pubinfra}$	C_{pvt}	–	–	1	0.069296	$C_{pvt} \Rightarrow I_{pvt}$
I_{pvt} (1)	O_g	$I_{pubinfra}$	C_{pvt}	$(i_r - \pi_t)$	–	1	0.059268	$(i_r - \pi_t) \Rightarrow I_{pvt}$
I_{pvt} (1)	O_g	$I_{pubinfra}$	C_{pvt}	$(i_r - \pi_t)$	$(e_{r-})_t$	1	0.063313	$(e_{r-})_t \Rightarrow I_{pvt}$

Source: National Account Statistics (Basic Data), New Series, CSO (various issues), and *Handbook of Statistics on Indian Economy*, RBI (various issues).

Note: Figures in the parentheses denotes the lag length of controlled variable.

investment. The lagged rate of interest is also found to be negative and significant in determining the private investment. The estimated coefficient value of error correction term of 0.249 is found insignificant. The macroeconomic activity captured through output gap has also been significant in the public infrastructure equation.

$$I_{pvt} = 2.61 + 0.47 I_{pvt(t-1)} + 0.077 \, \Delta I_{pubinfra} - 0.442 \, \Delta I_{pubinfra(t-1)}$$
$$(0.98) \quad (1.65)^* \quad (2.924)^* \quad (-1.33)$$
$$+ 1.490 \, \Delta C_{pvt} - 0.609 \, \Delta C_{pvt} + 0.12 \, \Delta i_r - 0.055 \, \Delta i_{r(t-1)}$$
$$(1.621)^* \quad (-0.648) \quad (0.703) \quad (-2.67)^*$$
$$- 0.019 \, \Delta(e_r) - 0.361 \, \Delta(e_r)_{(t-1)} + 0.033 \, \Delta(O_g)_{t-1}$$
$$(-0.053) \quad (-0.918) \quad (2.214)^*$$
$$- 0.018 \, \Delta(O_g) - 0.249 \, \text{ecm}$$
$$(-1.697)^* \quad (-0.570)$$
$$R^2 = 0.99$$
$$DW = 1.96$$

The figures in parentheses below the coefficients denote t-statistic. Now we turn to analyse the link between public non-infrastructure investment and private investment in India. Theoretically, considerable ambiguity remains in the direction of magnitude of public non-infrastructure investment and private capital formation, especially in the context of developing countries. If government invests in the sectors, which are of competing in nature with private firms, it may lead to crowding out of private investment. At the same time, private firms operate in a *level playing field* provided by the government in the investible sectors and government continue investing in non-infrastructure projects like manufacturing, finance and insurance, business services etc. a healthy co-existence of private and public sector investment can be a priori expected. It is therefore important to econometrically investigate whether public non-infrastructure investment have mutually reinforcing effects on private corporate investment or substitution effects.

The pretest of Johansen's Full Information Maximum Likelihood estimates based on maximum eigenvalue test and trace test for public non-infrastructure and private corporate investment model showed that there are at the most two cointegrating vectors as the rank is detected two. Then we proceeded to optimal parametrisation and causality detection whose results are shown in Table 3.5. The analysis showed that public non-infrastructure investment is found significant in determining private investment in India. The cost of credit rather than quantity of credit is found significant when we included public non-infrastructure investment instead of public investment (Table 3.5). The output gap is also a significant causal variable in non-infrastructure model.

The evidence from equation with error correction term revealed that cost rather than quantity of credit is a significant determinant of private investment. The coefficient of non-infrastructure investment in public sector was found to be instantaneously crowding in private corporate investment, however in the period with lag 1, the results have shown crowding out effect.

$$I_{pvt} = 0.319 + 1.003\,\Delta I_{pvt(t-1)} + 1.675\,\Delta I_{pubnoninfra} - 1.491\,\Delta I_{pubnoninfra}$$
$$(0.07) \quad (2.263)^* \quad\quad (3.339)^* \quad\quad (-1.719)^*$$
$$- 0.179\,\Delta C_{pvt} + 0.03\,\Delta C_{pvt} + 0.005\,\Delta i_{r(t-1)} - 0.017\,\Delta i_{r(t-1)}$$
$$(-0.163) \quad\quad (0.025) \quad\quad (0.325) \quad\quad (-1.167)^*$$
$$- 0.183\,\Delta(e_{r\_}\pi_t) - 0.117\,\Delta(e_{r\_}\pi_t)_{(t-1)} - 0.008\,\Delta(O_g)$$
$$(-0.471) \quad\quad -0.357 \quad\quad (-0.437)$$
$$+ 0.012\,\Delta(O_g)_{t-1} - 0.458\,ecm$$
$$(0.148) \quad\quad (-0.797)$$

$R^2 = 0.99$

$DW = 1.93$

As discussed in the beginning of the chapter, fiscal policies can affect private investment through three channels: via public investment, fiscal deficit and rate of interest. The above models of public (infrastructure and non-infrastructure) investment showed that there is no evidence of *direct crowding out* of private corporate investment by public investment. But the confirmation of no *financial* crowding out can be detected only after checking whether real interest rate rise is induced by fiscal deficit operations of the government, which would be dealt in the next chapter. If the real rate of interest is not induced by fiscal deficit, then no evidence for the occurrence of financial crowding out though private corporate investment is interest rate

Table 3-5
Public Non-Infrastructure Model

Controlled Variable	Manipulated Variables		Optimum Lags of Manipulated Variable	Final Prediction Error	Causality Inference
I_{pvt} (1)	—	—	—	0.079103	—
I_{pvt} (1)	$I_{pubnoninfra}$	—	1	0.070988	$I_{pubnoninfra} \Rightarrow I_{pvt}$
I_{pvt} (1)	$I_{pubnoninfra}$	O_g	1	0.073634	$O_g \Rightarrow I_{pvt}$
I_{pvt} (1)	$I_{pubnoninfra}$	O_g, C_{pvt}	1	0.098767	$C_{pvt} \neq I_{pvt}$
I_{pvt} (1)	$I_{pubnoninfra}$	O_g, C_{pvt}, $(i_r - \pi_t)$	1	0.059051	$(i_r - \pi_t) \Rightarrow I_{pvt}$
I_{pvt} (1)	$I_{pubnoninfra}$	O_g, C_{pvt}, $(i_r - \pi_t)$, $(e_{r-})_t$	1	0.093118	$(e_{r-}) \neq I_{pvt}$

Source: National Account Statistics (Basic Data), New Series, CSO (various years), and *Handbook of Statistics on Indian Economy* (various years).

Note: Figures in the parentheses denotes the lag length of controlled variable.

sensitive. Now we turn to look into the possibility of fiscal deficit directly (not via investment expenditure we discussed in the earlier models) crowding out private investment. We know that the variables under consideration are integrated of order 1. As the next step, we have applied cointegration analysis which is based on trace test statistics and maximum eigenvalue statistics in identifying the number of cointegrating vectors. After detecting the number of cointegrating relations to be three, we turn to sequential causality tests based on Hsiao's autoregressive framework of VAR-FPE method.

The results of VAR-FPE causality showed that gross fiscal deficit per se does not have any causal links with the private capital formation in India. Fiscal deficit affects private capital formation via the leverage of public investment activities through capital expenditure. It is noted that to the extent public expenditure is in investment activities, in particular, infrastructure investment, such as power, transport and communication, it could be complementary to private investment rather than crowding out. Also these investments by government can enhance the profitability and productivity of private investment, which could provide a demand and supply-side stimulus to private investment. The rate of interest is the only variable found significant in determining private investment in fiscal deficit model (Table 3.6).

Table 3.6

Fiscal Deficit and Private Corporate Investment Links

Controlled Variable	Manipulated Variables					Optimum Lags of Manipulated Variable	Final Prediction Error	Causality Inference
$I_{pvt}(1)$	–	–	–	–	–	–	0.079103	
$I_{pvt}(1)$	f_d	–	–	–	–	1	0.09933	$f_d \neq I_{pvt}$
$I_{pvt}(1)$	f_d	O_g	–	–	–	2	0.098405	$O_g \neq I_{pvt}$
$I_{pvt}(1)$	f_d	O_g	C_{pvt}	–	–	1	0.091955	$C_{pvt} \neq I_{pvt}$
$I_{pvt}(1)$	f_d	O_g	C_{pvt}	$(e_{r-})_t$	–	1	1.608984	$(e_r)_t \neq I_{pvt}$
$I_{pvt}(1)$	f_d	O_g	C_{pvt}	$(e_{r-})_t$	$(i_r - \pi_t)$	1	0.061916	$(i_r - \pi_t) \Rightarrow I_{pvt}$

Source: (Basic Data): National Account Statistics, New Series, CSO, 2001 and 2002, and *Handbook of Statistics on Indian Economy*, RBI (2001).

Note: Figures in the parentheses denotes the lag length of controlled variable.

$$I_{pvt} = 0.184 + 0.900\, \Delta I_{pvt(t-1)} + 0.156\, \Delta DEF_{(t-1)} - 0.048\, \Delta C_{pvt(t-1)} -$$
$$(0.302) \quad (3.518)^* \quad\quad (0.935) \quad\quad (-0.171)$$
$$-0.031\, \Delta i_{r(t-1)} + 0.002\, \Delta(e_r)_{(t-1)} - 0.014\, \Delta(O_g)_{t-1} - 0.0144\, ecm_{(-1)}$$
$$(-1.805)^* \quad\quad (0.557) \quad\quad (-1.722)^* \quad\quad (-0.038)$$
$$R^2 = 0.984$$
$$DW = 2.02$$

The figures in parentheses denote t-statistic and * denote 1 per cent level of significance. The error correction model also revealed that fiscal deficit does not have any direct effect on private corporate investment. In this model, the rate of interest adjusted for inflationary expectations and the output gap matter for investment.

3.5 Conclusion

The results suggest that there is no evidence of direct crowding out of private capital formation by public investment in India. The analysis found that the public investment has a complementary relationship with private corporate investment and evidence is for crowding in phenomenon in India. The reasons for no crowding out may be twofold. One of the plausible reasons for no crowding out in the context of India could be that the increase in financial resources raised through capital flows against the backdrop of integration of financial markets gives an indication that the private corporate sector, on the aggregate, did not face a shortage of investible resources. The second reason could be the overall liquidity in the system might not have pushed up the interest rate and, in turn, crowded out the private corporate investment.

Though there is no evidence of direct crowding out of private corporate investment by public investment, the confirmation of no financial crowding out can be detected only after analysing whether the real interest rate rise is induced by fiscal deficit operations of the government. If the real rate of interest is not induced by fiscal deficit, then no evidence for the occurrence of financial crowding out though private corporate investment is interest rate sensitive. This would be taken up in Chapter 4.

Appendix

Johansen–Juselius Full Information Maximum Likelihood Procedure of Cointegration

Johansen–Juselius tried to develop a methodology as follows to study the long-run relationship among non-stationary variables. Let us define z_t as 'n' potentially endogenous variables and model z_t as an unrestricted VAR of k lags,

$$z_t = A_1 z_{t-1} + \ldots + A_k z_{t-k} + u_t \quad \text{where} \quad u_t \sim IN(0\,\Sigma) \tag{i}$$

where z_t is $(n \times 1)$ and each of the Ai is an $(n \times n)$ matrix of parameters.[14]

Equation (i) can be reformulated into a vector error correction (VECM) form:

$$\Delta z_t = \Gamma_1 \Delta z_{t-1} + \ldots + \Pi z_{t-k} + \mu_t \tag{ii}$$

where $\Gamma_i = -(I - A_1 - \ldots - A_i)$, $(I - A_1 - \ldots - A_k)$
and

$$\Pi_i = -(I - A_1 - \ldots - A_k)$$

Equation (ii) contains information on both the short-run and long-run adjustment to changes in z_t, via the estimates of $\hat{\Gamma}_i$ and $\hat{\Pi}$ respectively. As shown in Johansen (1988), $\Pi = \alpha\beta$, where α represents the speed of adjustment to disequilibrium, while β is a matrix of long-run coefficients such that the term $\beta` z_{t-k}$ represents up to $n-1$ cointegrating relationships in the multivariate model which ensure that the z_t converge to their long-run steady state solution.

Assuming that z_t is a vector of non-stationary $I(1)$ variables, then all the terms in (ii) which involve Δz_{t-i} are $I(0)$. We need to have u_t as $I \sim (0)$ for existence of long-run relationship. This can happen only when Πz_{t-k} is stationary, which can be met in three instances: when all variables in z_t

---

[14] This type of VAR-model is to estimate dynamic relationships among jointly endogenous variables without imposing strong a priori restrictions (such as particular structural relationships and/or exogeneity of some of the variables). The system is in reduced form with each variable in zt is regressed on only lagged values of both itself and all other variables in the system. Thus OLS is an efficient way to estimate each equation comprising (i) since right hand side of each equation in the system comprises a common set of (lagged and thus predetermined) regressors (Harris, 1995).

Fiscal Deficit, Capital Formation and Crowding Out

are in fact stationary. The second instance when there is no cointegration, that is Π is an $(n \times n)$ matrix of zeros. The third way for Πz_{t-k} to be $I \sim (0)$ is when there exists upto $(n-1)$ cointegration relationship: $\beta`z_{t-k} \sim I(0)$. In this instance, $r \le (n-1)$ cointegration vectors exist in β (that is r columns of β form r linearly dependent combinations of variables, each of which is stationary, together with $(n-r)$ nonstationary vectors (that is $n-r$ columns of β form $I \sim (1)$ common trends). Only the cointegrating vectors enter Equation (ii), otherwise Πz_{t-k} would not be $I \sim (0)$, which implies that $(n-r)$ columns of α are effectively zero. The problem of estimating the number of cointegrating vector in a multivariate system boils down to estimating the rank of Π matrix.

Rewriting Equation (ii) as:

$$\Delta z + \alpha \beta' z_{t-k} = \Gamma_1 \Delta z_{t-1} + \ldots + \Gamma_{k-1} \Delta z_{t-k+1} + u_t \qquad \text{(iii)}$$

It is possible to correct for short-run dynamics by regressing Δz_t and z_{t-k} separately on the right hand side of Equation (iii). That is, the vectors R_{0t} and R_{kt} are obtained from:

$$\Delta z_t = P_1 \Delta z_{t-1} + \ldots + P_{k-1} \Delta z_{t-k-1} + R_{0t} \qquad \text{(iv)}$$

$$z_{t-k} = T_1 \Delta z_{t-1} + \ldots + T_{k-1} \Delta z_{t-k-1} + R_{kt} \qquad \text{(v)}$$

which can then be used to form residual (product moment) matrices.

$$S_{ij} = T \sum_{i=1}^{T} R_{ij} R'_{jt} i, j = 0, k \qquad \text{(vi)}$$

The maximum likelihood estimate of β is obtained as the eigenvectors corresponding to the r largest eigenvalues from solving the equation:

$$\left| \lambda_{skk} - S_{k0} S_{00}^{-1} S_{0k} \right| = 0 \qquad \text{(vii)}$$

which gives the n eigenvalues $\hat{\lambda}_1 > \hat{\lambda}_2 > \ldots > \hat{\lambda}_n$

and the corresponding eigenvectors $\hat{V} = (\hat{v}_1, \ldots, \hat{v}_n)$.

Those r elements in $\hat{V}$ which determines the linear combinations of stationary relationships can be denoted by $\hat{\beta} = (\hat{v}_1 \ldots \hat{v}_r)$, that is these are cointegration vectors. This is because the eigenvalues are the largest squared canonical correlations between the 'level' residuals R_{kt}

and the difference residuals R_{0t}, that is we obtain estimates of all the distinct $\hat{v}'_i z_t (i=1,2,...,r)$ combinations of the $I(1)$ levels of z_t which produce high correlations with the stationary $\Delta z_t \sim I(0)$ elements in Equation (iii), such combinations being the cointegration vectors by virtue of the fact that they must themselves be $I(0)$ to achieve a high correlation. Thus the magnitude of $\hat{\lambda}_i$ is a measure of how strongly the cointegration relations $\hat{v}'_i z_t$ (which we can denote as $\hat{\beta}'_i z_t$) are correlated with the stationary part of the model. The last $(n-r)$ combinations obtained from solving (vii), that is $\hat{v}'_i z_t$ $(I=r+1,...,n)$, indicate the non-stationary combinations, and theoretically these are uncorrelated with the stationary elements in (ii). Consequently, for the eigenvectors corresponding to the non-stationary part of the model, $\hat{\lambda}_i = 0$ for $i=r+1,..., n$. So, for example, Johansen and Juselius (1992) points out that the test that $r=1$ is really a test that $\hat{\lambda}_2 = \hat{\lambda}_3 = ... = \hat{\lambda}_n = 0$, where as $\hat{\lambda}_i > 0$.

The values of Likelihood Ratio (LR) test statistic is used for the hypothesis that number of cointegrating vectors is not greater than r. One can use two LR tests. These are LR test based on maximum eigenvalue (λ_{max}) and LR test based on trace (λ_{trace}) of the stochastic matrix. These are defined as follows:

$$\lambda_{max}(r,r+1) = -T\ln(1-\hat{\lambda}_{r+1})$$

$$\lambda_{trace}(r) = -T\sum_{i=r+1}^{n}\ln(1-\hat{\lambda}_i)$$

where λ_i = estimated values of the characteristic roots (also called eigenvalues) obtained from the estimated π matrix.

T = the number of usable observations.

4
Deficit—Interest Rate Link and Financial Markets

In Chapter 3, no evidence of *direct* crowding out of private investment in India was established. The absence of direct crowding out does not necessarily imply the absence of *financial* crowding out. It has also been mentioned that *financial* crowding out may occur due to the upward pressures on the rate of interest induced by the debt financing of fiscal deficit. In other words, even if public sector investment does not crowd out private investment, private capital formation in the economy may suffer due to the increase in interest rates arising due to the pre-emption of real and financial resources by the government to finance the increasing fiscal deficits. In this chapter, we will examine whether fiscal deficit affects interest rate. It is all the more important to examine such a link in the present context, as it has already been noted in Chapter 3 that the rate of interest is a significant determinant of private investment. If increase in fiscal deficit increases the rate of interest, it would imply financial crowding out.

Theoretically, an analysis of the link between fiscal deficit and interest rate assumes importance mainly for three reasons. First, in the context of the growing global integration of financial markets, the macroeconomic effects of an increase in the domestic interest rate due to the rise in the fiscal deficit can spread globally. Second, if the increase in the fiscal deficit leads to an increase in the interest rate, it may lead to a crowding out of the interest-sensitive components of private spending, especially private corporate investment. And third, if such a relationship is verified, the fiscal and monetary policy linkage in the macro management of a country is established. For instance, a reduction of budget balances could moderate upward pressure on interest rates and could therefore provide monetary policy with additional degrees of freedom in interest rate management.[1]

In the recent credit policy announcements, the Central Bank of India (Reserve Bank of India—RBI) kept the interest rates (repo rates) unchanged and advised the government of India's Ministry of Finance to cut the fiscal deficit prior to cutting the interest rates. Keeping interest rates high has detrimental effects on the economic growth of the country. Globally, when central banks have proceeded with the cutting of interest rates, RBI has kept the interest rates unchanged in all recent policy announcements. This invites a compulsory revisiting of the question of whether fiscal deficit affects the interest rate in India. This chapter presents a rare examination of the link between the two. Chakraborty (2002) made an attempt to address this empirical link and concludes that a deficit does not induce a rise in the interest rate in India; it is rather the other way around. Two years later, incorporating the monetary variables, the model by Chakraborty (2002) was re-examined by a study of RBI, which found the results consistent with the former (Goyal, 2004). These are the two empirical studies on the fiscal deficit and the interest rate exclusively concerning India. Though Chakraborty (2007) revisited the question of crowding out in India, the aspects of the 'financial' crowding out channel via the interest rate mechanism was not analysed in the context of capital flows; rather, the focus of the paper was on 'direct' crowding out. However, the study found that fiscal deficit is not a determinant of interest rate in India.

This chapter takes the literature forward by incorporating the capital flows in the macro model of interest rate determination. Chapter 3 established no evidence of direct crowding out of private corporate investment in India; the absence of direct crowding out does not necessarily imply the absence of financial crowding out. The financial crowding out may occur due to the upward pressures on the interest rate induced by the debt financing of fiscal deficit. In other words, even if public sector investment does not crowd out

---

[1] In a large number of industrial countries, actual fiscal imbalances prevent monetary policy from properly managing interest rates. Thus, in order to stimulate economic activity, the setting of both monetary and fiscal policies needs to be reassessed within a comprehensive framework of sound and stable fiscal balances over the medium term (CorreiaNunes and Stemitsiotis 1995).

private corporate investment, the private capital formation in the economy may suffer due to the increase in interest rates occurring due to the pre-emption of real and financial resources by the government to finance the increasing fiscal deficits. In this chapter, we will examine the plausibility of whether fiscal deficit affects interest rate. It is all the more important to examine such a link in the present context, as the analysis in Chapter 4 found that interest rate is a significant determinant of private corporate investment. If increase in fiscal deficit increases the interest rate, it would imply financial crowding out.

It is well known that the Indian financial system was characterised by administered interest rate structure until the 1990s. The process of financial deregulation since 1991 has been aimed at making the financial sector market-oriented to improve allocative efficiency.[2] The debatable question is, as the interest rate was administered until the financial deregulation, how could a functional relationship be justified between fiscal deficit and the administered interest rate? Even if it is assumed that the administered interest rate truly reflects the market signals, there is a need to establish such a relationship empirically. The task of establishing such a relationship is ambiguous and might be the reason that thwarts the analysis of this link prior to the deregulation of interest rates. However, contrary to the popular belief that an administered interest rate in developing countries is insensitive to market perceptions, the literature revealed that an administered interest rate does accommodate market signals and in order to analyse that, the literature has suggested examining the intertemporal movement of the interest rate and its variability (Gupta, 1984). The analysis of intertemporal movements in the selected interest rates adjusted for inflationary expectations also

---

[2] The major highlights of financial liberalisation are interest rate deregulation, a phased reduction of cash reserve requirements and statutory liquidity ratios, simplifying directed credit programs, and development of money markets, etc. The administered interest rates were simplified beginning in 1992–93. A small number of fixed rates for priority sector loans were retained, while large commercial borrowers faced a floor-lending rate. From 1993–94, the markets for commercial paper and certificates of deposit were deregulated, allowing companies to access credit at market terms that were considerably below the minimum lending rate. In October 1994, the minimum lending rate was eliminated. The deregulation of interest rates has been accompanied by the introduction of new instruments like 14-day and 182-day auction treasury bills in addition to the 91-day and 364-day auction treasury bills. It is to be noted that the 182-day treasury bill was reintroduced in mid-1999.

showed that the interest rates in India, though administered, have shown variations over the years, and real interest rates remained positive in a substantial number of years. Chakraborty (2007), using the annual data, established no evidence of fiscal deficit causes in interest rate determination. However, the model was not controlled for the capital flows. This chapter takes the debate forward in the context of capital flows, focusing on the financially deregulated regime, using the recent high-frequency data of fiscal deficit and the interest rate for the period 1980–81 to 2013–14.

4.1 Theoretical Paradigms and Empirics

At the theoretical level, an extensive debate has developed to explain the link between deficit and interest rate. There are three different theoretical paradigms under which this relationship can be viewed and empirically tested: Neoclassical, Keynesian, and Ricardian. According to the Neoclassical view, a rise in the deficit leads to an increase in the interest rate and, in turn, crowds out private investment. The Keynesians visualise that though an increase in the deficit leads to an increase in the interest rate, such an increase stimulates savings and capital formation. In between the Neoclassical and Keynesian view, there exists the observation of the RET, which argued that deficits merely postpone taxes and, therefore, tax financing and debt financing of deficit have equal impacts on the economy; thus, deficit does not have any impact on the interest rate (Barro, 1974).

It is to be noted that the empirical literature on the fiscal deficit and interest rate link is largely confined to developed countries (Table 4.1). To start with, in the context of the US, Tanzi (1985) examined the relationship between fiscal deficit and the interest rate. He observed that for the period 1960–84, the sensitivity of the interest rate to fiscal deficit decreased over the years. Tanzi pointed out that the plausible explanation of this phenomenon was the growing global integration of financial markets in recent years and correspondingly increasing flow of global capital to finance the domestic deficit. On the basis of the multivariate loanable funds model (which incorporates the effect of term structure on interest rate), Cebula (1990) and Correia and Stemitsiotis (1995) showed that deficit, inflation, short-run interest

Table 4.1
Selected Empirical Evidences on Link between Fiscal Deficit and Rate of Interest

Author Period Country	Model	Macrovariables	Results
Evans (1985) 1858–1950 US	ISLM Model in 2SLS	Real rate of interest = f{pubexp/GDP, deficit/GDP, money stock/GDP, expected inflation}	Deficit does not have impact on rate of interest.
Ahamad (1994) 1970–91 Pakistan	ISLM in OLS	Real interest rate = f{gov.exp., gov. deficit, change in money stock, expected inflation}	No variable except inflation is significant. Monetary and fiscal policy variables do not have any impact.
Tanzi (1985) 1960–84 US	Neoclassical	Nominal interest rate = f{GAP, expected inflation, money supply, government deficit, gov. exp, trade balance}	Sensitivity of rate of interest to fiscal deficit has come down in the recent years of study, in 1980–84 time span.
Balkan and Balkan (1995) 1960–84 UK	ISLM in 2SLS	Real rate of inflation = f{gov. deficit, gov. exp., trade balance, expected inflation, money supply}	Significant and positive impact of government deficit on real rate of interest.
Cebula (1990) 1973–93 US	Loanable Funds Model In cointegration	Nominal long-run rate of interest = f{budget deficit-GDP ratio, capital flow/gdp, expected inflation, short-run rate of interest, percentage change in real GDP}	Deficit Granger causes rate of interest.
Correia and Stemitsiotis (1995) 1970–93 10 OECD countries	Loanable Funds Model in 2SLS	Long-run rate of interest = f{short-run rate of interest, expected inflation, deficit/GDP}	Deficit affects long-run rate of interest.

(*Continued*)

(Continued)

Author / Period / Country	Model	Macrovariables	Results
Gupta (1990) 1960–85 10 Asian countries	RET in OLS	Private real percapita consumption = f{transitory and permanent income, taxes, transitory and permanent gov. exp}	RET is rejected for Sri Lanka, India, Indonesia, Philippines among 10 countries.
Kulkarni and Erickson (1996) 1960–88 India	Accelerator Model in OLS	Short-run rate of interest = f{lagged short-run rate of interest, inflation based on CPI, exchange rate, budget deficit}	Deficit does not affect rate of interest.
Chakraborty (2002) India	Asymmetric bivariate VAR Model	Short-run interest rate = f{fiscal deficit}	Deficit does not cause interest rate. Interest rate causes deficits.
Goyal (2004) India	VAR Model	Short-run interest rate = f{fiscal deficit, money supply}	Deficit does not cause rate of interest.
Chakraborty (2012) India	VAR Model	Short-run rate of interest = f{fiscal deficit, inflationary expectations, capital flows, output gap}	Deficit does not cause interest rate. Inflationary expectations cause deficits.
Vinod, Chakraborty and Karun (2014) India	MEBOOT Model	Short-run rate of interest = f{fiscal deficit, capital flows, reserve money, inflationary expectations, output gap}	Deficit does not cause interest rates.

Source: Author's compilations.

rate, percentage change in GDP and capital flows Granger-cause the nominal long-term interest rates, and hence crowding out of private investment occurs. The advantage of the loanable funds model is that in addition to capturing the monetary and fiscal variables like real deficit, real money stock, government spending, expected inflation rate and so on, it also captures the term structure of interest rates. In other words, the loanable funds model's framework allows for the combination of the characteristics of the term-structure with the fiscal and monetary policy variables, influencing the interest rate. In Correia and Stemitsiotis's (1995) study, which was based on cross-country data of 10 OECD countries, there was evidence of crowding out as the interest rate was positively linked to the deficit. Further, Cebula (1997b) examined the direction of causality between long-term interest rates and structural budget deficits in the US for the period 1973–91, and found that there is bidirectional causality between the interest rate and the deficit. Gale and Orszag (2002) argued that interest rates do not increase as a result of fiscal expansions due to foreign capital savings replacing domestic savings. However, economic performance may still be negatively affected by persistent fiscal imbalances as capital stock accumulation declines either because of a decline in domestic or foreign net investment.

In the context of developing countries, studies are few on the link between budget deficit and the interest rate (Table 4.6). In the context of Pakistan, Ahamad (1994) found that there is no link between interest rates and deficit. In India, paucity of data on market interest rates might be the reason for no specific studies on the causal relationship between the deficit and interest rates. Sundararajan and Thakur (1980), Pradhan, Ratha and Sarma (1980) and Parker (1995) addressed the issue of 'direct' crowding out between public and private investment in India, but these studies did not analyse the macroeconomic link of fiscal deficit and interest rates through which the crowding out phenomena should theoretically be operating.

4.2 Analytical Framework

The analytical framework for the study is derived from an extended version of Sargent's (1969) paper 'Commodity Price Expectations and the Interest Rate'. The extended version of Sargent's model is flexible enough to incorporate the macroeconomic link that may operate in the determination of interest rates. Sargent (1969) expressed the nominal interest rate as a combination of three components: the equilibrating interest rate, the spread between market interest rate and the equilibrating real interest rate and the spread between nominal interest rate and market interest rate. It can be expressed as follows:

$$r_{n(t)} = r_{e(t)} + \left[r_{m(t)} - r_{e(t)} \right] + \left[r_{n(t)} - r_{m(t)} \right] \qquad (4.1)$$

In Equation (4.1), $r_{n(t)}$ is the nominal interest rate, $r_{e(t)}$ is the real interest rate that equilibrates desired savings and desired investment, and $r_{m(t)}$ is the nominal interest rate adjusted for the expected rate of inflation. Each of the three specific components is determined in turn by specific macroeconomic variables. The logical step that follows is to identify the determinants of each of the three terms in Equation (4.1).[3] One of the significant determinants of the first term, $r_{e(t)}$, which is the real interest rate that equilibrates desired savings and desired investment, is the deficit of the government.[4]

$$r_{e(t)} = \alpha + \beta_1 (def_t) + \mu_t \qquad (4.2)$$

The determinant of the second term, $[r_{m(t)} - r_{e(t)}]$ is determined by the growth rate of high-powered money.[5] In the open economy

---

[3] The derivations of determinants of each term in the model are drawn from Gupta and Moazzami (1996). But as the objective of their study was to test the validity of alternative paradigms of the link between deficit and interest rate—neoclassical, Keynesian, and Ricardian Equivalence Theorem—across countries and to distinguish between the short-term and long-term impact of deficits on interest rate, we have not drawn heavily on the derivations of the determinants of the model; rather we improvise the specification according to our purpose to undertake the impact of fiscal deficit on the interest rate in the context of India, irrespective of the paradigm-specific details and the dichotomy of transitory and permanent effects of deficits on the interest rate .

[4] The other determinants of term (1) in the Gupta-Moazzami model constituted government consumption expenditure, national income, private consumption expenditure, private savings, etc., which we omit in our specification due to multicollinearity problems, and moreover, these explanatory variables are not required for our analysis as we have not gone into the testing of validity of each of the alternative paradigms of fiscal deficit and interest rate in the context of India; rather, our prime concern was to assess the role of fiscal deficit in the interest rate to understand the transmission channel of the crowding out phenomenon

[5] For details, see Sargent (1969).

model, capital flows also determine the spread between the market rate and the equilibrium real interest rate. The real exchange rate can also be inserted into the Equation (4.3) to capture the effect on the interest rate in an open economy macro model.

Assuming linearity, we thus have:

$$\left[r_{m(t)} - r_{e(t)}\right] = \lambda + \beta_2 (\Delta M_3)_t + \beta_3 (k_r)_t + \delta_t \qquad (4.3)$$

where $(\Delta M_3)_t$ = changes in high-powered money and $(k_r)_t$ = net capital flows.

The last term of Equation (4.1) is assumed to depend linearly and positively on the inflationary expectations.

$$r_{n(t)} - r_{m(t)} = \theta + \beta_4 (\pi_t^e) + v_t \qquad (4.4)$$

where, π_t^e = expected rate of inflation.

Now, by substituting Equations (4.2), (4.3) and (4.4) in Equation (4.1), we get Equation (4.5):

$$r_{n(t)} = \phi + \beta_1 (def_t) + \beta_2 (\Delta M_3)_t + \beta_3 (e_r)_t + \beta_4 (\pi_t^e) + \omega_t \qquad (4.5)$$

According to Equation (4.5), interest rate is a function of fiscal deficits, change in high-powered money, capital flows and expected inflation. Capital flows are an important variable for the model, especially when the period under study experiences volatility in capital flows; therefore, controlling for this fluctuation in liquidity, whether fiscal deficit affects interest rate or not is an interesting aspect to examine. The theoretical derivation mentioned earlier is econometrically estimated.

Each of these determinants is linked to the interest rate through various macroeconomic channels; a few are attempted as follows. The unsettled relationship between money supply and interest rate is reviewed extensively by Nachane et al. (1997). These are mainly unanticipated monetary announcement effect, Keynesian liquidity effect, financial effect, price expectations effect (Fisher effect) and income effect. Due to unanticipated monetary announcement effect, permanent higher money growth rate induces an increase in expected inflation and a resulting increase in interest rates to reflect an inflation premium (Girton and Nattress 1985). According to the Keynesian 'liquidity effect', income and prices are slow to react as the money supply increases, and thus the monetary system experiences excess liquidity at unchanging nominal income levels. Contemporaneous with the liquidity effect, there runs the financial effect. As per the financial effect, as the growth of money increases, banks find themselves saddled with excess reserves, and these excess reserves have to be temporarily parked in short-term market securities. This temporary spurt in the demand for short-term marketable securities lowers short-term interest rates. When the supply of money increases with the rise in income, the demand for money rises. As a result, the real balance of the economy decreases, finally pushing up the nominal interest rate.

Price expectation effect (Fisher effect) shows that when money supply increases, the expected inflation increases and thereby the nominal interest rate also increases. All five effects will be present in any given situation, though their duration, strength and timing are largely an empirical matter and will vary from situation to situation. The relationship between monetary expansion and interest rate has been obscure in the empirical literature. While Mishkin (1982) found that the interest rate and money growth surprises have a significant positive correlation, Makin (1983) found that it is negative and significant. Makin explained that these contradictory findings were a result of the different method used to measure interest rates. Makin implied that his period-average short-term interest rate is responding to the initial liquidity effect, while Mishkin's end-of-period short-term interest rate measure is sampled after the Fisher effect begins to dominate. Grier (1986) also showed that lagged money surprises have a significant positive impact on rates.

Robert Lucas (1980) finds no empirical support for the hypothesis, which he calls one of the central implications of the quantity theory of money. Beginning with Irving Fisher (1930), most of the empirical investigations have discovered that fully anticipated inflation has less than a unit effect on the nominal interest rate, and thus reduces the real interest rate even in the longest of runs. Fama (1975) concluded that 'one ... cannot reject the hypothesis that all variation through time in one-to-six nominal rates of interest mirrors variation in correctly assessed one-to-six month expected rates of purchasing power'. Fama's conclusion rests on two assumptions: (i) there is a constant expected real interest rate and (ii) all relevant information about future inflation is fully incorporated in the expected-inflation component of the market interest rate. Both assumptions are contradicted by evidence by Carlson (1977). Carlson pointed out that variations in short-term interest rates are not good predictors of variations in inflation rates. Furthermore, both of the key assumptions are of dubious validity. Evidence has been presented that expected short-term real interest rates do have notable variation.

In the scenario of large capital flows in a flexible exchange rate regime, the nominal exchange rate appreciation leads to the deterioration of international competitiveness. So to prevent the real appreciation of the exchange rate and to preserve external competitiveness, the central bank intervenes in the Forex market to sterilise the incremental liquidity thus generated, thereby keeping the monetary expansion under control. This process has, however, quasi-fiscal costs associated with it, as it imposes the danger of increasing the real interest rate, which can further induce the capital flows. Another explanation is that an increase in the exchange rate of the previous year would make the domestic currency less valued in the international market and therefore would attract the demand for domestic financial assets from abroad. This may lead to increase in the interest rate. Capital flows have been incorporated in the macro model; however, exchange rate is dropped in the econometric model for empirical reasons of non-stationary series as well as multicollinearity between capital flows and exchange rate.

4.3 Stylised Links of Rate of Interest with Macro Variables

Although the focus of the analysis is to examine the relationship between fiscal deficits and interest rates, an appropriate model specification is extremely important as other macroeconomic variables may also affect the movement of rate of interest.

4.3.1 Money Supply and Interest Rate

The unsettled relationship between money supply and rate of interest effect is reviewed extensively by Nachane et al. (1997). These are mainly unanticipated monetary announcement effect, Keynesian liquidity effect, financial effect, price expectations effect (Fisher effect) and income effect. Due to unanticipated monetary announcement effect, permanent higher money growth rate induces an increase in expected inflation and a resulting increase in interest rates to reflect an inflation premium (Girton and Nattress, 1985). According to the Keynesian 'liquidity effect', income and prices are slow to react as the money supply increases and thus the monetary system experiences excess liquidity at unchanging nominal income levels. Contemporaneous with the liquidity effect there runs the financial effect. As per the financial effect, as the growth of money increases, banks find themselves saddled with excess reserves and these excess reserves have to be temporarily parked in short-term market securities. This temporary spurt in the demand for short-term marketable securities lowers short-term interest rates. When money supply increases with the rise in income, the demand for money rises. As a result, the real balance of the economy decreases, finally pushing up the nominal rate of interest.

Price expectation effect (Fisher effect) manifests that when money supply increases, the expected inflation increases and thereby the nominal rate of interest also increases. All five effects will be present in any given situation though their duration, strength and timing are largely an empirical matter and will vary from situation to situation.

The relationship between monetary expansion and interest rate has been obscure in the empirical literature. While Mishkin (1982) found that the interest rate and money growth surprises have a significant positive correlation, Makin (1983) found that it is negative and significant. Makin explained these contradictory findings as a result of the different methods used to measure interest rates. Makin implied that his *period-average* short-term rate of interest is responding to the initial liquidity effect, while Mishkin's *end-of-period* short-term rate of interest measure is sampled after the Fisher effect begins to dominate. Grier (1986) also showed that lagged money surprises have a significant positive impact on rates.

4.3.2 Rate of Interest and Expected Inflation

Fisherian theory predicts that the nominal rate of interest will tend to change at the same rate as changes in expected inflation. Thus it manifests one-to-one relationship between the expected inflation and the nominal rate of interest. According to Fisher equation, a one per cent increase in the expected rate of inflation in turn causes a one per cent increase in the nominal rate of interest. Only a few studies in the context of the US by Feldstein (1976), Gibson (1970) have found coefficients close to unity. But Sargent (1976), Shiller (1979) and Wood (1981) have observed that these findings of 'coefficients close to unity' are limited to a particular period of the US history, till the early 1970s. Furthermore, even a unit coefficient would contradict superneutrality hypothesis; that an increase in inflation will not affect real interest rates in the long-run.

4.3.3 Rate of Interest and Nominal Exchange Rate

Under the scenario of large capital flows in a flexible exchange rate regime, the nominal exchange rate appreciation leads to the deterioration of international competitiveness. So to prevent the real appreciation of the exchange rate and to preserve external competitiveness, central bank intervenes in Forex market to sterilise the incremental liquidity thus generated, thereby keeping the monetary expansion under control. This process has however quasi-fiscal costs associated with it as it imposes the danger of raising the real interest rate, which can further induce the capital flows. Another explanation is that an increase in the exchange rate of the last year would make the domestic currency less valued in the international market, and therefore would attract the demand for domestic financial assets from abroad. This may lead to increase in interest rate.

4.4 Econometric Estimation: Asymmetric VAR

As a prelude to the estimation, unit root test is undertaken to avoid spurious results. The results of unit root shown in Table 4.2 revealed that all variables are integrated of order 1 except the bank rate, which is integrated of order 2. Another point to be noted here is that the unit root results showed that there is no significant trend and drift (c and t) for all variables except money supply.

Table 4.2
Unit Root Test Results for Rate of Interest and Its Apriori Determinants

Macrovariables	Lags	t-statistics	McKinnon Critical Value	Order of Integration
Call money market rate	0	−3.326854	−3.215267	$I\sim(0)$ c, t. at 10%
Bank rate	0	−3.317587	−2.641672	$I\sim(1)$ no c, t. at 1%
Prime lending rate	0	−7.296329	−4.284580	$I\sim(1)$ c, t. at 1%
Government security rate	0	−5.263349	−4.323979	$I\sim(1)$ c, t. at 1%
Ch reserve money	0	−4.419979	−4.284580	$I\sim(1)$ c^*, t^* at 1%
Inflationary expectations	0	−10.29430	−4.296729	$I\sim(1)$ c^*, t^* at 1%
Output gap	0	−3.729007	−3.661661	$I\sim(1)$ c at 1%
Real effective exchange rate	0	−5.342808	−4.284580	$I\sim(1)$ c, t at 1%
Fiscal deficit	0	−5.731913	−4.284580	$I\sim(1)$ c, t^* at 1%

Source: Handbook of Statistics on Indian Economy (Basic Data), RBI (various issues).

Having checked the unit roots, the next logical task is the selection of appropriate interest rate from the available spectrum of interest rates in India for an elaborate analysis of link between rate of interest and fiscal deficit. The major rates of interest are called money market rate, bank rate, prime lending rate (PLR) of term lending institutions and interest rate on dated securities of Government of India. Among these rates of interest, call money market rate has exhibited large volatility and the bank rate appeared to be non-varying in nature, which intuitively can be opted out in analysing the link between fiscal deficit and rate of interest. We have selected PLR and rate of interest on dated securities of Government of India to analyse whether there is any link between fiscal deficit and these rates of interest. PLR is all the more important as it is a significant determinant of private investment behaviour, and to establish whether there exists any financial crowding out in India, we need to analyse whether fiscal deficit has any role in exerting pressure on PLR. The redemption yield on dated securities of India is selected on the ground that shift from seigniorage financing to bond financing of deficit in India can have some pressure on rate of interest, especially the rate of interest on bonds or securities. Both these rates of interest are adjusted for inflationary expectations and the real rate of interest is used for analysis. As analysed in Chapter 2, real rates of interest shows much variability than the nominal rate of interest.

Figure 4.1

Plot of Hodrick–Prescott: Filtered Expected Inflation WPI Series in India

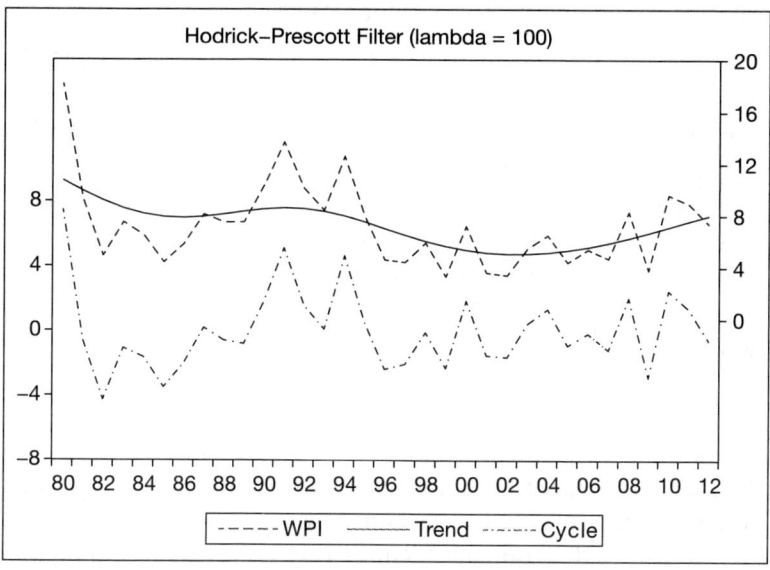

Source: Handbook of Statistics on Indian Economy (Basic Data), RBI (various issues).

Having selected the relevant rates of interest for the analysis, the next task is to transform these rates of interest into ex ante real rate of interest. According to Fisher hypothesis, nominal rate of interest (γ^n) is given by:

$$\gamma^n = \gamma^r + \pi^e \qquad (4.6)$$

where γ^r is the real rate of interest and π^e is the expected rate of inflation. The real rate of interest in any period, thus, is postulated to evolve as a deviation between nominal rate of interest and the expected inflation. Recently, Correia et al. (1995) used the low-frequency component of consumer price changes as generated by Hodrick–Prescott (HP) filter to model *expected* inflation. We use HP filter for computing expected inflation (Figure 4.1).[6]

---

[6] Apart from HP filter method, various other econometric methods have also been employed to construct appropriate proxies for the market's expectations of future inflation. Tanzi (1985) used surveys of inflationary expectations such as Livingston index to generate series on expected inflation in the context of the US. Autoregressive models have also been used to generate series of expected inflation.

Using HP filter, how to capture expected inflation from the observed series?[7] Let us assume that observed inflation π contain both expected π^e and unexpected components π^u.

$$\pi = \pi^e + \pi^u \qquad (4.7)$$

The HP filter decomposes observed inflation into a stationary cyclical component and a smooth trend component (π and π^e denote the logarithms of observed and expected inflation respectively) by minimising the variance of cyclical component subject to a penalty for the variation in the second difference of the trend component. This results in the following constrained least square problem.

$$\text{Min} \sum_{T=1}^{i} (\pi - \pi^e)^2 + 1 \sum_{t=2}^{T} [(\pi_{t+1}^e - \pi_t^e) - (\pi_t^e - \pi_{t-1}^e)]^2$$

Now we turn to analyse the link between fiscal deficit and rate of interest along with other relevant parameters. The real rate of interest $(R-\pi)_t$ model is specified for India in an open economy macro-framework where interest rate is determined by fiscal, monetary and external factors. The determinants identified are expected rate of inflation (π_t^e), seigniorage ($\Delta M0/GDP_t$), fiscal deficit $(def)_t$ and exchange rate $(e_r)_t$. The optimal parameterisation of variables through final prediction criteria suggested that the controlled and manipulated variables take the lag structure one in real interest rate model. Before analysing the causal relationship in Hsiao's autoregressive framework, we tested the series for cointegration. We used Johansen full information maximum likelihood test of cointegration for this purpose by identifying the order of VAR as one and including a linear deterministic trend. The results of cointegration in Johansen's maximum likelihood method confirm that there are three cointegrating vectors. After estimating the number of cointegrating vectors, we turn to analyse the causal relationship between fiscal deficit and PLR along with certain

---

[7] HP filter has good mathematical properties in order to extract the unobservable variable of expected inflation out of the observed series. The expected inflation series computed using HP filter contains both forward and backward looking information on inflation rates, which makes it relevant in rational expectations framework. Past information is necessary to adjust prices from a disequilibrium position, while information regarding future trends is also required because rational economic agents look forward in time to form expectations about the future inflation rate (Correia et al., 1995).

Table 4.3
Real Long-Run Rate of Interest Model

Controlled Variable	Manipulated Variables				Optimum Lags of Manipulated Variable	Final Prediction Error	Causality Inference
$(PLR-\pi)_t$	–	–	–	–	–	2.643016208	
$(PLR-\pi)_t$	$(e_r)_t$	–	–	–	1	2.589608998	$(e_r)_t \Rightarrow (PLR-\pi)_t$
$(PLR-\pi)_t$	$(e_r)_t$	π^e_t	–	–	1	2.570014063	$\pi^e_t \Rightarrow (PLR-\pi)_t$
$(PLR-\pi)_t$	$(e_r)_t$	π^e_t	$\Delta M0_t$	–	1	2.986422882	$\Delta M0_t \neq (PLR-\pi)_t$
$(PLR-\pi)_t$	$(e_r)_t$	π^e_t	$\Delta M0_t$	$(def)_t$	1	2.712582282	$(def)_t \neq (PLR-\pi)_t$

Source: Handbook of Statistics on Indian Economy (Basic Data), RBI (various issues).

Note: Figures in the parentheses denotes the lag length of controlled variable.

other relevant macrovariables in Hsiao's autoregressive framework. As per the specific gravity criteria for ordering the variables in model, the monetary variables entered the equation prior to the entry of fiscal variables in the PLR of interest model (Table 4.3). The results reinforced the absence of financial crowding out in India, as fiscal deficit is found insignificant in determining the real PLR of interest. Instead, the results showed that real PLR is affected by the the inflationary expectations and exchange rate in an open economy macromodel. Quite contrary to the crowding out debate, that is deficit-induced rise in the rate of interest displaces private investment, our analysis proved no significant relationship between interest rate and deficit though private corporate investment is found interest rate sensitive in India (reference to chapter three).

Now we turn to undertake an analysis using the redemption yield on dated securities of government instead of PLR to understand whether the results vary. We tested the variables for cointegration by identifying the optimal order of VAR is equal to one and including a linear deterministic trend. The results showed that there are three cointegrating vectors.

After testing for cointegration, we turn to analyse the causal relationships between the macrovariables in Hsiao's VAR framework. The results showed that long-term government security yield rate is determined by inflationary expectations and exchange rate fluctuations in

Table 4.4
Real Long-Run Rate of Interest Model: Hsiao (1981) Detection of Optimal Lags of the Manipulated Variables and FPE of the Controlled Variable (G-Sec Rate)

Controlled Variable	Manipulated Variables				Optimum Lags of Manipulated Variable	Final Prediction Error	Causality Inference
$R_{g\text{-sec}(t)}$	–	–	–	–	–	11.76643966	
$R_{g\text{-sec}(t)}$	π_t^e				1	11.49474994	$\pi_t^e \Rightarrow R_{g\text{-sec}(t)}$
$R_{g\text{-sec}(t)}$	π_t^e	$(e_r)_t$			1	11.12544934	$(e_r)_t \Rightarrow R_{g\text{-sec}(t)}$
$R_{g\text{-sec}(t)}$	π_t^e	$(e_r)_t$	$(def)_t$		1	12.72214193	$(def)_t \neq R_{g\text{-sec}(t)}$
$R_{g\text{-sec}(t)}$	π_t^e	$(e_r)_t$	$(def)_t$	$(\Delta M0)_t$	1	13.48035857	$\Delta M0_t \neq R_{g\text{-sec}(t)}$

Source: Handbook of Statistics on Indian Economy (Basic Data), RBI (various years).

Note: Figures in parentheses denote the lag length of controlled variable.

the open economy (Table 4.4). In this model also, fiscal deficit is not found to be a significant variable in determining the real rate of interest. However, changes in reserve money is found insignificant in the determination of government bond yield rate.

Now we turn to analyse whether the link between fiscal deficit and rate of interest holds good in the deregulated financial regime in India in the next section.

4.5 Analysis of Link between Fiscal Deficit and Rate of Interest in Deregulated Financial Regime

This section examines whether in the financially deregulated regime, shift in the financing pattern of fiscal deficit away from seigniorage and external debt financing to bond financing has the probability of creating an upward pressure on the rate of interest in India. As we are using high-frequency data, another problem encountered was the selection of appropriate interest rate from the available spectrum of interest rates in deregulated financial regime. As short-term rates are always considered as reference rate, the imperative is to select the appropriate short-term interest rates, which acts as the reference rate in the market.

Figure 4.2

Intertemporal Variations in 91-Day Treasury Bill: 2006:03–2015:07

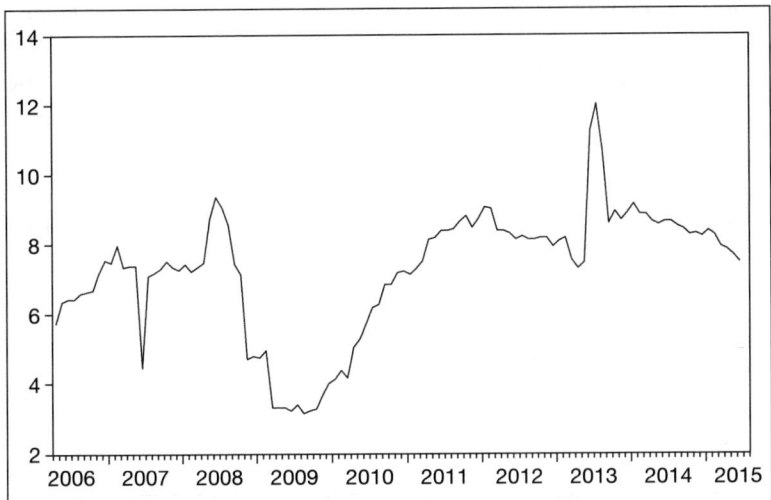

Source: Handbook of Statistics on Indian Economy (Basic Data), RBI (various years).

In the analysis of fiscal deficit and rate of interest link in India using annual data in the previous section, we did not use a 'reference rate of interest', instead we tried to analyse the link using all relevant rates of interest and found that there is no link between these rates of interest and fiscal deficit. Moreover, the concept of 'reference rate' is all the more relevant in the financially deregulated regime.

Theoretically, a reference rate is defined as the price of a short-term low-risk instrument in a free liquid market. It is revealed from the Table 4.7 that the call money market rate, one of the short-term rates of interest, has exhibited large volatility. Another short rate, namely the bank rate appeared to be non-varying in nature. Long-term rates of interest are opted out as a reference rate. A potential short-term low-risk rate of interest is the 91-day treasury bill rates which exhibited a non-volatile and non-sticky trend.

The implicit cut-off yield rate of 91 auction day treasury bills is plotted in Figure 4.2.

As we discussed in the earlier section, in order to analyse whether there is any impact of rising fiscal deficit on the real rate of interest, the

Figure 4.3

Plot of Actual Rate of Inflation and Hodrick–Prescott Filtered Expected Inflation Series in India: 2006:03–2015:07

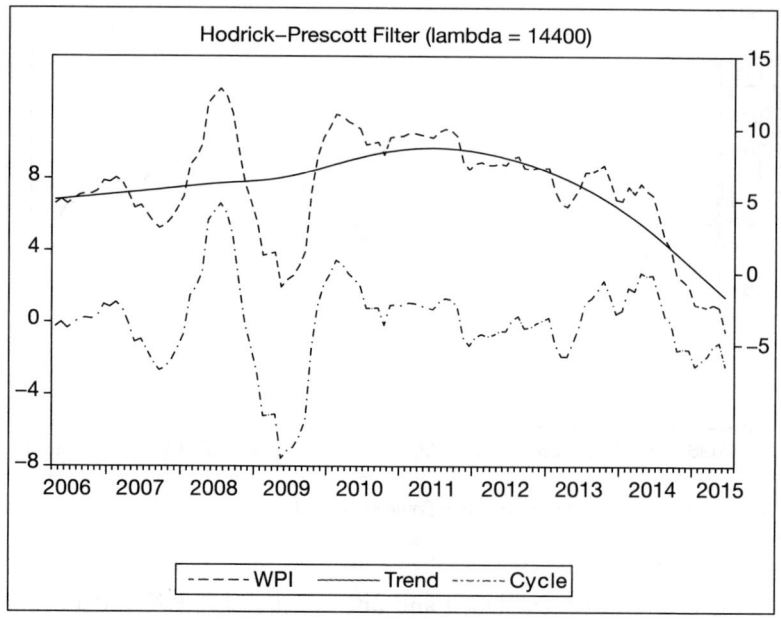

Source: Handbook of Statistics on Indian Economy (Basic Data), RBI (various years).

first step is to calculate the ex ante real rate of interest. As we have already selected the treasury bill rate[8] as the reference rate from the spectrum of short-term rate of interest in India, the next task is to transform the treasury bill rate into ex ante real rate of interest. Using Fisher equation the nominal rate of treasury bill is transformed into real rate of interest, the details of HP methodology involved in this procedure is discussed in the above section. The HP filtered expected rate of inflation along with the nominal rate of inflation using the high-frequency data in the deregulated financial regime is plotted in Figure 4.3.

The series of expected inflation generated through HP filter method depicted in Figure 4.3. The ex ante real rate of interest is

---

[8] Weighted rate of interest of 91- and 364-day treasury bills with corresponding amount of borrowing done via the auction of 364-day treasury bills and 91-day treasury bills as the weights.

Figure 4.4

Co-Movement of Rate of Interest and WPI Rate of Inflation

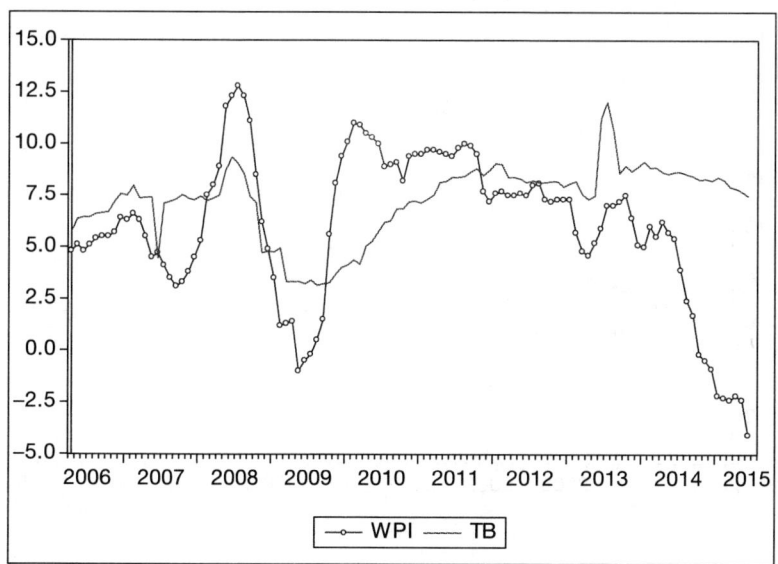

Source: Handbook of Statistics on Indian Economy (Basic Data), RBI (various issues).

derived by subtracting the expected rate of inflation from the nominal rate of interest. The plots of ex ante real rate of interest and nominal inflation—both WPI and CPI—in the financially deregulated period of India are given in Figures 4.4 and 4.5. The co-movement of WPI and CPI is given in Figure 4.6. As noted, the analysis of deregulated financial regime covers a period based on the availability of monthly data on fiscal deficit. The nominal and real rates of interest are given in Figure 4.7.

The high-frequency data based unit root test results of ex ante real rate of interest and fiscal deficit are presented in the Table 4.5. The series of fiscal deficit and ex ante real rate of interest are found stationary at levels with drift and trend. The macroseries of real effective exchange rate, change in money supply and expected inflation were also found to be stationary.

The FPE of fitting one-dimensional autoregressive process for fiscal deficit $(def)_t$ and rate of interest (TB) are computed with upper bound of lag length (L^*) assumed equal to 15. First, we have considered real

Figure 4.5

Co-Movement of Rate of Interest and CPI Rate of Inflation

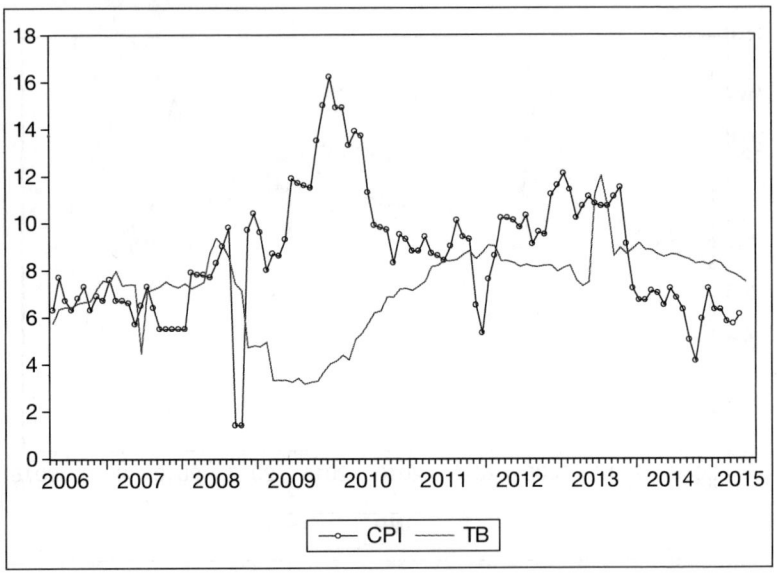

Source: Handbook of Statistics on Indian Economy (Basic Data), RBI (various issues).

rate of interest as controlled variable, holding the order of its autoregressive operator to 3, we sequentially added the lags of the manipulated variables upto the L^* of 15. In this treatment of real rate of interest as the manipulated variable we found that $FPE_{(def)t}\,(m^*,n^*) > FPE_{(def)t}\,(m^*,0)$ which implies fiscal deficit does not Granger-causes rate of interest (Table 4.6).

4.6 Analysing Deregulated Financial Regime

The econometric estimation in Chapter 3 revealed that private corporate investment is interest rate sensitive, but as the transmission channel of financial crowding out is via rate of interest, it became imperative to analyse whether rise in rate of interest is fiscal deficit induced. Thus, in this chapter we have examined whether there is any evidence of

Figure 4.6

Co-Movement of WPI and CPI Rates of Inflation

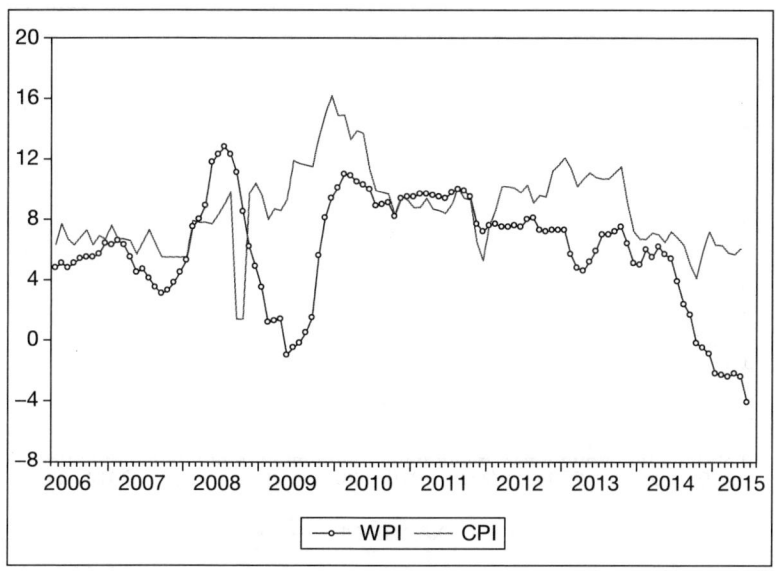

Source: Handbook of Statistics on Indian Economy (Basic Data), RBI (various issues).

financial crowding out for both administered and deregulated interest regime using high-frequency data. In both the regime, quite contrary to the popular belief that increase in fiscal deficit induces a rise in the rate of interest, no significant relationship between the two is established. The relationship between the two in the deregulated regime was based on monthly data of fiscal deficits and rates of interests. For the administered interest rate regime, the study examined the link between fiscal deficits and major short- and long-run rates of interests. However, in the case of deregulated regime, the relationship is examined between the monthly fiscal deficits and the treasury bill rate. The treasury bill rate is empirically found to be the reference rate for the market in the deregulated regime. Thus, an analysis of the link between the reference rate and fiscal deficits was considered sufficient to arrive at the conclusion regarding the relationship between other interest rates and fiscal deficits.

The overwhelming conclusion drawn from the multivariate VAR analysis for the period between 1980–81 and 2015–16 revealed that

Figure 4.7

Nominal and Ex Ante Real Rate of Interest in India: Deregulated Financial Regime

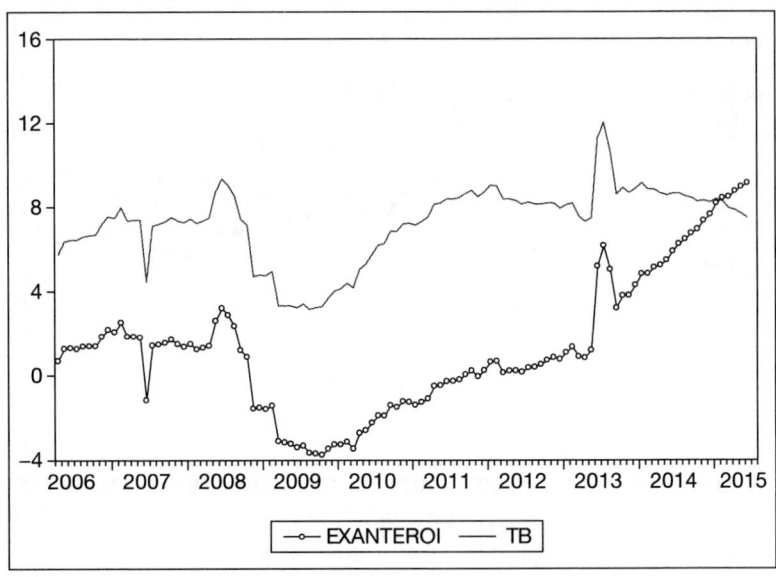

Source: Handbook of Statistics on Indian Economy (Basic Data), RBI (various issues).

Table 4.5

High-Frequency Regime: Unit Root Test Results for Ex Ante Real Rate of Interest and Fiscal Deficit

Macrovariables	Lags	t-statistics	McKinnon Critical Value	Order of integration
Ex ante rate of interest	0	−8.878902	−3.490772	$I\sim(0)$ with c^*, at 1%
Fiscal deficit	0	−9.656189	−4.043609	$I\sim(0)$ with c^*,t^* at 1%
Ch reserve money	0	−3.696334	−3.451184	$I\sim(0)$ with c^*,t^* at 5%
Ex ante real effective exchange rate	10	−3.153438	−2.889753	$I\sim(0)$ with c^*, at 10%
Ex ante rate of inflation	5	−1.614713	−1.040803	$I\sim(0)$, with c^*,t^* at 10%

Source: Handbook of Statistics on Indian Economy (Basic Data), RBI (various issues).

Table 4.6
High-Frequency Regime: Detection of Optimal Lags and FPE

Controlled Variable	Manipulated Variables				Optimum Lags of Manipulated Variable	Final Prediction Error	Causality Inference
$(i_r - \pi_t^e)$ [2]	–	–	–	–	–	1.199668111	
$(i_r - \pi_t^e)$ [2]	$(def)_t$	–	–	–	1	1.221850845	$(def)_t \neq (i_r - \pi_t^e)$
$(i_r - \pi_t^e)$ [2]	$(def)_t$	ΔM_{3t}	–	–	1	1.199721239	$\Delta M_{3t} \neq (i_r - \pi_t^e)$
$(i_r - \pi_t^e)$ [2]	$(def)_t$	ΔM_{3t}	$(er)_t$	–	1	1.212263408	$(er)_t \neq (i_r - \pi_t^e)$
$(i_r - \pi_t^e)$ [2]	$(def)_t$	ΔM_{3t}	$(er)_t$	π_t^e	1	1.10393091	$\pi_t^e \Rightarrow (i_r - \pi_t^e)$

Source: Handbook of Statistics on Indian Economy, RBI (various years).
Note: Figures in parentheses denote the lag length of controlled variable.

both short-term and long-term rates of interest are affected by the expected inflation and real exchange rate fluctuations. The change in reserve money is also found significant in some models of rate of interest. As the results from this chapter showed that there is no significant positive relationship between fiscal deficits and rates of interest, no evidence for financial crowding out is reinforced in Indian context. The asymmetric VAR modeling of Granger-causality test conducted between fiscal deficit and real rate of interest for the deregulated regime revealed that contrary to the Neoclassical paradigm, direction of causality does not run from real rate of interest to deficit. Also, it is empirically found that inflationary expectations determine rate of interest in the deregulated financial regime in India.

5
Monetary–Fiscal Policy Coordination: Fiscal Rules and Testing for Monetary Seigniorage

There is a growing concern about the tendency of considering the monetary and fiscal policies in isolation while assessing the impact of macroeconomic institutions on policy outcomes (Jean-Louis et al., 2014). This chapter attempts to revisit this dichotomy which prevails in the contemporary macro policy space and analyses the plausible linkages between fiscal and monetary policy coordination in the context of India.

The significance of institutional linkages between fiscal and monetary authorities can be traced back to 'Unpleasant Monetary Arithmetic' of Sargent and Wallace (1981), who showed that when the fiscal authority dominates and sticks to a given path of primary surpluses, sooner or later when bond financing of deficits becomes unsustainable, the monetary authority has to give in and generate the seigniorage revenues to eventually monetise the deficits. Under this fiscal dominance regime, attempts by the central bank to keep inflation low through tight money issuance cannot last and must ultimately give in to higher inflation in the longer run—that 'inflation today or inflation tomorrow' is the only plausible macro policy option—which is referred to as the 'unpleasant monetarist arithmetic'.

A recent treatment of the Sargent-Wallace argument of fiscal-monetary policy linkages is the 'fiscal theory of the price level' (FTPL), pioneered by Leeper (1991), Sims (1994), Woodford (1994) and Cochrane (1998a). The fiscalist literature argues that the price level is independent of monetary policy but dependent strictly on fiscal policy; price level indeterminacy problems can be solved by having the central bank peg the nominal interest rate at a level consistent with the central bank's desired inflation rate, rather than by controlling the growth rate of the (base) money supply (Sims, 1994 and Woodford, 1994).

These theoretical debates find relevance in contemporary macro policy transition in India from discretion to rules. The fiscal policy institutions have moved away from discretionary fiscal stance towards fiscal rules—the efficacy of fiscal authorities to keep the deficits within the numerical threshold level of deficits normalised to GDP (for details, see Schaechter et al., 2012). Recently, the monetary policy authorities have begun floating the policy rules to 'inflation targeting' and 'central bank independence' in India (for details, see RBI, 2014). This new dimension of rule-based monetary policy stance in India has spurred from Taylor's rule (for details, see Taylor and Williams, 2010).

The contemporary macroeconomic policy transition from discretion to rules gives rise to one pertinent question: does monetary rule require a fiscal rule? Such monetary–fiscal linkages are treated in the literature (for instance, Sargent and Wallace, 1981) through analysing the macroeconomic channels through which deficits affect monetary policy stance. Unfortunately, over the years, the debates have confined to just numeric values of deficits—just the 'levels' of deficit to three per cent of GDP—in attempting such linkages. There has been a widening acceptance that numeric fiscal rules are associated with greater fiscal discipline (Alesina and Perotti, 1995).

What is missing in the design of numeric fiscal rules is the macroeconomic channel through which the deficits affect the output gap. It is not only the levels of deficit but also the financing pattern of deficits that creates macroeconomic consequences. This aspect was surpassed in the debates related to fiscal rules and budget management policies. The fiscal rules have taken the deficit financing rules as granted and deal with only numerical targets of deficits. However, excessive use of any financing mode of deficits has macroeconomic repercussions and cannot be tackled by focusing on the fiscal rules alone.

If we take recourse to the original arguments for monetary–fiscal linkages, for instance, unpleasant monetary arithmetic is a telling case, how bond financing of deficits can be flawed even under a fiscal dominance regime. Does bond financing—the dominant source of financing the deficit in India—has an upper bound? If so, does it imply when the rate of interest on government bonds exceed the growth rate of the economy, we need to eventually monetise the deficits through generating seigniorage? The fiscal stance, however, would not be unsustainable soon, as the present structure of deficit financing has a negligible share of external financing of debt and the composition of debt is more of long-term maturities. Still the assumption that the monetary regime has no influence on the conduct of fiscal policy needs a revisit, especially when the economic growth rate (g) is plummeting and the rates of interest (r) have shown no signs for a downward trend in recent years in India? This concern is not because of any straightjacket unsustainability condition of $r>g$ impending for India, but the monetary policy stance contains relevance for the term structure of interest rates (the relationship between short- and long-term rates of interest) and has a catalytic role in promoting economic growth. As mentioned earlier, India is also moving towards a rule-based monetary policy stance—inflation targeting—to begin the pegging of policy rate to inflationary expectations and output gap. One can contest this recent move of RBI towards monetary rules; however, one question remains: does inflation targeting need a gen-Next fiscal rule? If gen-Next fiscal rules are formulated to attain a striking balance between fiscal sustainability and growth, one cannot surpass the deficit financing rules anymore.

As a prelude to all these questions, it is important to test the existence of a seigniorage Laffer curve—which is derived through deficit and seigniorage linkages—in the context of India. If such curve exists, one can explore two possible domains. One could be the monetary and fiscal policy linkages through generating seigniorage to finance deficits. Second could be a seigniorage-maximising inflation rate for India, which suggests a threshold level of seigniorage financing of deficits. If seigniorage Laffer curve does not exist, it could reflect the deficit financing rule which has prevailed in India (outside the purview of fiscal rules) to move away from seigniorage to bond financing of deficits. However, it is interesting to recall heterodox economists' emphasis to seigniorage finance of deficits for public investment, as they believe it is 'free lunch' if the economy has not attained the full employment levels (Rakshit, 2005 and 2010). Does the 'functional finance' encourage to 'taking the free lunch first' when facing a hard intertemporal budget constraint?

Do the gen-Next fiscal rules incorporate deficit financing rules along with golden rule (financing of current expenditure from current revenue, without any recourse to deficits)? While redesigning the fiscal rules for a long-term fiscal consolidation, three elements need to be considered; (i) the size of the government (G/GDP ratio), (ii) tax structure and reforms for increased tax realisation and (iii) a judicious mix of seigniorage and bond financing. While putting constraints on (i) can be detrimental to economic growth in long-term and (ii) depends itself on greater economic growth (higher levels of GDP than the rate of growth of GDP), a plausible mix of deficit financing rules becomes an impending one. The moment we incorporate the macroeconomic channel of fiscal deficit, the rules take the form of not mere fiscal rules, but Macro-Fiscal Rule. Therefore, 'macro-fiscal rule' should be the gen-Next rule-based fiscal policy.

This chapter attempts to examine the theoretical and empirical linkages between fiscal and monetary policy linkages. It presents an illustrative estimation of seigniorage and deficit linkages through arriving at a plausible seigniorage Laffer curve. The chapter is organised in four sections. Section 5.1 explores the fiscal rules and pattern of financing the deficits, while Section 5.2 deals with the estimation of seigniorage and inflation tax. Using maximum entropy ensembles of bootstrapping algorithms, an attempt to develop a threshold level of seigniorage maximising inflation and checking out for any occurrence of seigniorage Laffer curve would be attempted in Section 5.3; the estimation is preliminary and illustrative. Section 5.4 concludes and suggests policy options.

5.1 Fiscal Rules and Deficit Financing

A fiscal rule imposes a long-lasting constraint on fiscal policy through numerical limits on budgetary aggregates (Kopits and Symansky, 1998). This implies that a domain is set for fiscal policy which cannot be frequently changed and a roadmap is provided by specifying a numerical target that limits a particular budgetary aggregate. The fiscal rules aim at correcting distorted incentives and containing pressures to overspend, in particular in good times, so as to ensure fiscal responsibility and debt sustainability (Schaechter et al., 2012).

In India, the 'golden rule' is invoked for the reduction of revenue deficit to zero or negative levels. A limit on fiscal deficits to four–five per cent of GDP was imposed with an emphatic rationale to avoid 'crowding out' of private investment. However, many empirical evidences do not suggest 'direct' or 'financial' crowding out in the context of India (Chakraborty, 2002, 2006, 2007 and 2012; Chakraborty and Chakraborty, 2008; Goyal, 2004 and Vinod et al., 2014) that deficits crowd out private corporate investment and does not induce rise in interest rates or output gap either.

As the importance of analysing the impact of deficit on the real economy increased, attention has also been given to develop an appropriate concept of deficit, which can capture the exact impact of fiscal policy on the macroeconomy. It is argued that unless a correct indicator of government deficit is adopted, there is a possibility of miscalculation of pre-emption of resources by the government and thus the assessment of the fiscal policy and its impact on macroeconomy (Boskin, 1988). This evolution towards a series of *purpose-specific* deficit measures worldwide, as a prelude to fiscal rules, from the conventional approach of *single measure* of budget deficit resulted in construction of primary deficit, fiscal deficit, monetised deficit and revenue deficit (for details, see four pioneering surveys by IMF on the measurement of *purpose-specific* budgetary deficits by Blejer and Cheasty, 1993; Blejer and Chu, 1988; Blinder and Solow, 1974; Heller et al., 1986 and Pattnaik et al., 1999 for details on India-specific measurement issues of deficit).

The generation of purpose-specific deficits through pioneering IMF surveys has huge relevance of facilitating the analysis of the impacts of fiscal policy stance on macroeconomic activity. However, the formulation of numerical bound fiscal rules has shrunk the possibility of maturing such debates of macroeconomic impacts of fiscal stance, and the debates have confined to the numerical fiscal rules. The trends in different concepts of deficits in India as per cent of GDP are given in Figure 5.1.

The fiscal deficit is financed through issuance of bonds, seigniorage financing, financing through ad hoc treasury bills and external financing. The financing pattern of fiscal deficit is shown in

Figure 5.1

Trends in Deficits

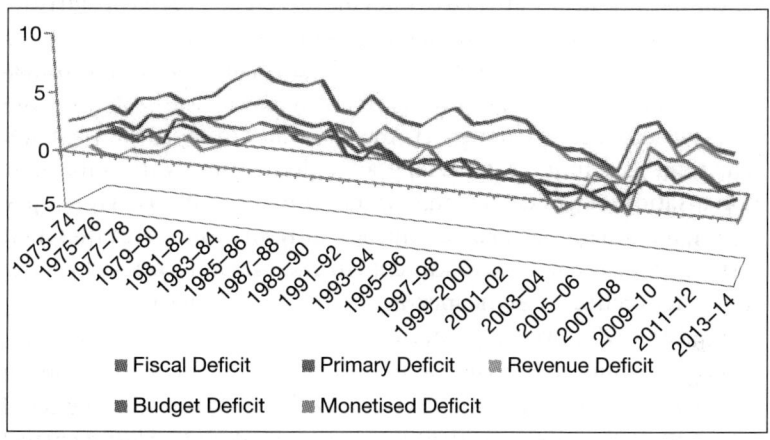

Source: RBI (Basic Data), various years.

Figure 5.2

Financing Pattern of Deficits

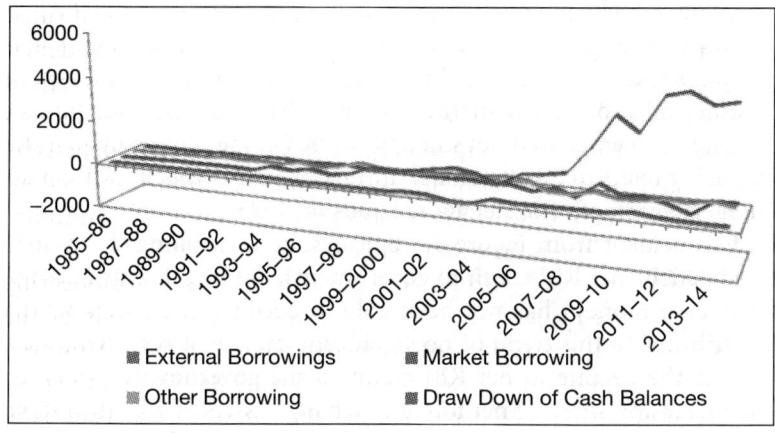

Source: RBI (Basic Data), various years.

Figure 5.2. It is evident from the figure that over the years, the government resorted more to internal financing than to external financing, and market borrowing (bond financing of deficits) has emerged as the most important source of financing of fiscal deficit in India. The rationale behind market borrowing by the central government was to create and widen the investor's base for government securities outside the captive market by attractive rates of interest and thereby to reduce government's dependence on monetisation of deficit.

The deregulation of interest rate in India made market borrowing more expensive because of the sharp rise in the interest rates on government securities. When government's ability to monetise the fiscal deficit became limited, especially after doing away with automatic monetisation of deficit through ad hoc treasury bill on 1st of April 1997, government has been compelled to resort to high-cost market borrowing to finance the fiscal deficit. Increasing recourse to bond financing is reflected in the increase in the share of market borrowing during the 1990s (see Figure 5.2).

It is important in this context to understand the role of fiscal policy in creating seigniorage revenue in India. Historically, the change in reserve money[1] in India is attributed to the conventional *budget deficit* of the government or *deficit financing* (monetisation of fiscal deficit). Ex post to Chakravarty Committee Report (RBI, 1985), the government has made a clear distinction between the overall budget deficit and deficit financing, since their implications on money supply could be entirely different. The overall budget deficit denoted the gap between the expenditure and the receipts under revenue and capital accounts taken together and this budgetary gap was met by the sale of treasury bills (of 91-day maturity period). This conventional budget deficit had been phased out since 1997–98. On the other hand, deficit financing refers to the increment during the year in the net RBI credit to the government (for details, see Rakshit, 1993).

It is evident from Figure 5.3 that despite controlling the monetised deficit (net RBI credit to government), the seigniorage (change in reserve money) has not been able to decline. The factor which contributed to this trend of no significant decline of reserve money, despite the decline in net RBI credit to the government, is due to the increasing share of net foreign exchange assets of RBI in reserve money creation (Figure 5.3). The net RBI credit to the government is on increase recently and it is important to test whether it has implications for seigniorage-deficit linkages.

---

[1] Reserve Money=Net RBI credit to government+RBI credit to commercial sector and other banks+Net FOREX assets of RBI+Government's currency liabilities to the public – RBI's net non-monetary liabilities.

Figure 5.3

Two Significant Components of Seigniorage

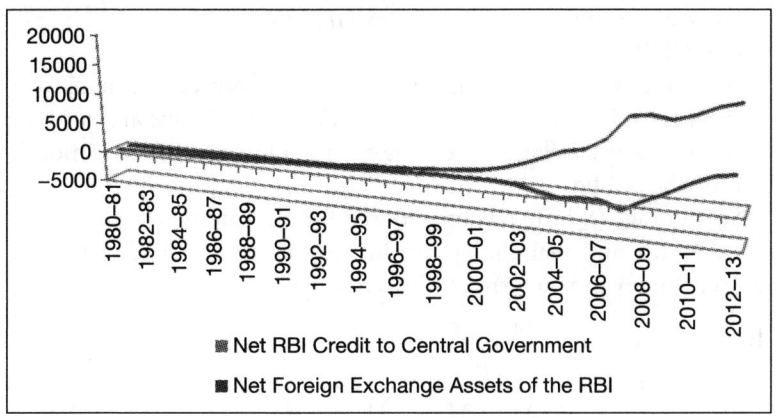

Source: RBI (Basic Data), various years.

5.2 Estimating Monetary Seigniorage

There was an increasing recognition that the seigniorage causes inflation (Buiter, 1990; Dornbusch and Fischer, 1981; Easterly et al., 1994 and Van Wijnbergen, 1989). Seigniorage is defined as the change in the nominal stock of reserve money (Buiter, 2007). The second measure of seigniorage is change in reserve money divided by GDP at current prices. This is the most commonly used definition of seigniorage. It can be expressed in the following equation:

$$S_1 = \frac{\Delta M_t}{Y_t} \qquad (5.1)$$

where S_1 = seigniorage revenue;
ΔM_t = change in reserve money; and
Y_t = GDP at current prices. Equation (5.1) can be rewritten in the following form:

$$S_{rev} = \frac{\Delta M_t}{M_t} * \frac{M_t}{Y_t} \qquad (5.2)$$
$$S_{rev} = \mu_t * m_t$$

where $\mu_t = \Delta M_t / M_t$ and $m_i = M_t / Y_t$

As per Equation (5.2), seigniorage is defined as the product of rate of growth of nominal reserve money (μ_t) and the reserve money per unit of GDP (m_t).

A distinct but related concept of revenue from central bank and seigniorage is inflation tax. Inflation tax and seigniorage are not synonymous always. Inflation tax is the erosion of value of reserve money held by the public.

Seigniorage (S_2) can be decomposed further into two components: inflation tax and real change in the reserve money. The change in reserve money in real term can be written as

$$S_2 = \frac{M_t - M_{t-1}}{P_t}$$

$$S_2 = \frac{M_t}{P_t} - \frac{M_{t-1}}{P_t} + \frac{M_{t-1}}{P_{t-1}} - \frac{M_{t-1}}{P_{t-1}} \quad (5.3)$$

$$S_2 = \frac{M_t}{P_t} + \left(M_{t-1} * \frac{\mu_t}{P_t}\right) - \frac{M_{t-1}}{P_{t-1}}$$

$$S_2 = \dot{m}_t + \mu_t * m_{t-1}$$

where $\pi_t = \frac{(P_t - P_{t-1})}{P_{t-1}}$, $\dot{m}_t = \frac{M_t}{P_t} - \frac{M_{t-1}}{P_{t-1}}$, $m_{t-1} = \frac{M_{t-1}}{P_t}$

Equation (5.3) expresses seigniorage as the sum of increase in the real stock of money $\dot{m}$ and the change in real stock of money that would have occurred with a constant nominal stock because of inflation ($\pi_t * m_{t-1}$) (Agenor and Montiel, 1996). The expression ($\pi_t * m_{t-1}$) of Equation (5.3) is the inflation tax.

As mentioned earlier, inflation tax is not always equal to seigniorage. They are equal only in stationary state, that is, when m_t becomes zero. From Equation (5.3), it becomes clear that inflation tax revenue is a component of seigniorage revenue. Inflation tax, as noted above, is the product of inflation rate (tax rate) and the real monetary base (tax base).

$$I_{tax} = \pi_t * m_{t-1} \quad (5.4)$$

Seigniorage and inflation tax are equal only in stationary state. In other words, seigniorage is defined as change in high-powered money

Figure 5.4

Seigniorage and Inflation Tax

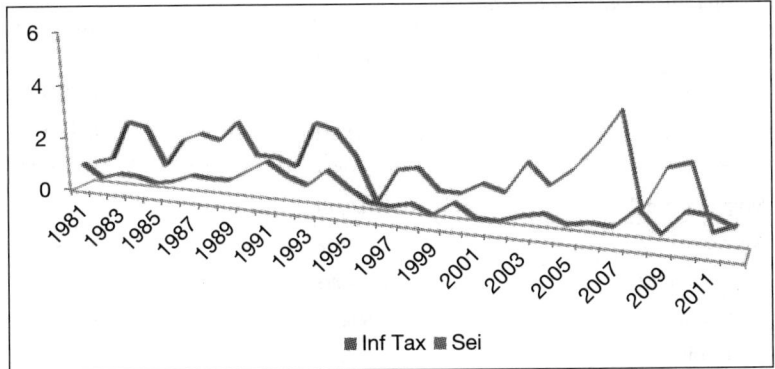

Source: RBI (Basic Data), various years.

to GDP while inflation tax is defined as the product of rate of inflation and high-powered money in period ($t-1$). Figure 5.4 presents the trends in illustrative estimates of seigniorage and inflation tax for India, the trend revealed that the former (seigniorage generation) has not crossed over four per cent of GDP. It can be seen from the figure that there have been wide year-to-year fluctuations in the creation of seigniorage in India during the past three decades.

5.2.1 Robustness in Seigniorage–Inflation Tax Links

The maximum entropy ensemble of bootstrap (MEBOOT) methodology is applied to test the links between seigniorage and inflation tax. The maximum entropy bootstrap is an algorithm that creates an ensemble for time series inference. This method is appealing as it does not cause differencing or detrending of series.

The meboot R-package implements such algorithm. Using MEBOOT, 999 replicas are constructed through algorithms and estimated for the links (for details, see Vinod, 2004, 2006 and 2013; Vinod and Lopez-de-Lacalle, 2009). The bivariate estimation of seigniorage and inflation tax is given in Table 5.1. The results revealed that the relationship is insignificant (Table 5.1).

Table 5.1

Robustness Check of Seigniorage–Inflation Tax Links: Estimates from Maximum Entropy Ensemble of Bootstrapping

	Coefficient	t
α	1.938710	4.2699
β	−0.031222	0.0787
CI (β)	2.5%	97.5%
Simple percentile	−5.160374	5.518575
Asymmetric	−5.151058	5.548626
Boot percentile	−5.171098	5.553167
Boot norm	−1.468227	8.838203
Boot basic	−1.889205	8.835061

Source: RBI (Basic Data), various years.

5.2.2 Seigniorage, Inflation and Fiscal Deficit

The 'orthodox' (monetarist) model of inflation is attempted here to analyse the link between fiscal deficits, money creation and inflation. Using semilogarithmic function for demand for money, now we turn to discuss how fiscal deficit affects the money creation in an economy.[2] This is an empirically relevant specification; its essential property is that seigniorage revenue first increases and then decreases with correctly anticipated inflation (Bruno and Fischer, 1990). Consider semilogarithmic function of demand for money:

$$m_t = \frac{M_t}{P_t} = \exp(-\alpha \pi_t^e) \quad (5.6)$$

where $\alpha > 0$, m_t is real money, and π_t^e is expected rate of inflation, M_t represents real base money stock and P_t the price level. Assume for simplicity that the government cannot issue bonds to public and finances the fiscal deficit (def_t) entirely through seigniorage:

$$def_t = \frac{\dot{M}_t}{P_t} = \mu_t . m_t \quad (5.7)$$

---

[2] The theoretical derivation in this section is based on Cagan (1956), as derived by Bruno and Fischer (1990), Sargent and Wallace (1981) and Agenor and Montiel (1996).

where def_t is fiscal deficit, μ_t is the rate of nominal money growth and m_t is the real balances held by public.

Combining Equations (5.6) and (5.7) implies

$$def_t = \mu_t . \exp(-\alpha \pi_t^e) \qquad (5.8)$$

Equation (5.8) specifies how the fiscal deficit affects the equilibrium rate of growth of money stock, and hence the equilibrium inflation rate. But to the extent that the demand for real money balances is inversely related to the expected rate of inflation, the possibility of multiple solutions to Equation (5.8) arises. In other words, a given amount of seigniorage can be collected at either a high or low rate of inflation.

Sargent and Wallace (1981) and Bruno and Fischer (1990) noted that there might be both high and low inflation equilibrium when government finances the deficit through seigniorage. The dual equilibria—a reflection of Laffer curve—imply that an economy may be stuck in high inflation equilibrium when, with same fiscal deficit as per cent of GDP, it could be at a lower inflation rate. The existence of seigniorage Laffer curve implies that there are two steady-state rates of inflation that generate any given amount of seigniorage. The dual inflation equilibria (low inflation equilibrium and high inflation equilibrium) at any given amount of seigniorage are graphically plotted in Figure 5.5. In the figure, the budget constraint is shown as

Figure 5.5

Seigniorage and Dual Inflation Equilibria

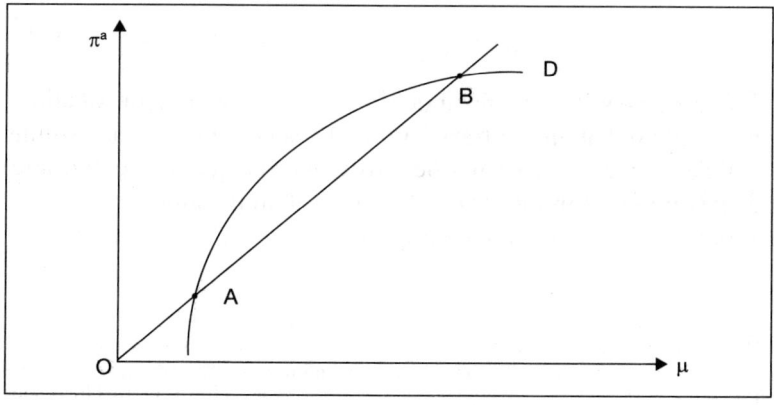

Source: Agenor and Montiel (1996).

the curve D. This curve depicts the positive relationship between the growth rate of monetary base (μ_t) and expected rate of inflation (π_t^e), showing the rate at which the money supply has to be increased to finance the fiscal deficit at each level of π_t^e. Since Equation (5.8) indicates that $def_t = \mu_t$ when the expected inflation rate is zero, the deficit is measured by the distance between the origin and the intercept of the D curve on the μ-axis. Bruno and Fischer (1990) noted that the economy is always on this schedule since the government is arithmetically bound by its budget constraint.

Differentiating Equation (5.6) with respect to time yields, since

$$\dot{m}_t \equiv \frac{\dot{M}_t}{P_t} - m_t \pi_t,$$

$$\mu_t - \pi_t = -\alpha \, \dot{\pi}_t^e \qquad (5.9)$$

so that in the steady state

$$\pi = \pi^e = \mu \qquad (5.10)$$

The steady state relationship shown in Equation (5.10) can be represented by 45° line in Figure 5.5. As depicted in the figure, D curve and 45° line intersect twice. There are, therefore, two potential steady-state points, that is two inflation rates, at which the fiscal deficit is financed through revenue from inflation tax—a low point equilibrium (point A) and a high inflation equilibrium (point B).[3] The inflation rate that maximises steady state seigniorage revenue is equal to $\pi^s = \dfrac{1}{\alpha}$ and the corresponding level of revenue is given by

$$def^s = \exp(-1)/\alpha \qquad (5.11)$$

Assume now that the fiscal deficit that the government wishes to finance is fixed at an arbitrary level d^*. Depending on the size of the fiscal deficit target, there may be zero, one or two equilibria. Because the government cannot obtain more than d^* in the long-run equilibrium, there is no steady state if $d > d^*$. For $d^* = def^s$ or $d^* < 0$, there is

---

[3] At point A the elasticity of the demand for real money balances is less than unity, while at point B it is greater than unity (for details, see Evans and Yarrow, 1981; Agenor and Montiel, 1996).

a unique steady state. If $0 < d^\cdot < def^s$, there are two equilibria or two steady states and the economy may be 'stuck' at the high inflation equilibrium (point B) (for details, see Agenor and Montiel, 1996).

5.2.3 Estimating Monetary Seigniorage Laffer Curve

Sargent and Wallace (1981) and Bruno and Fischer (1990) noted that there might be both high and low inflation equilibrium when government finances the deficit through seigniorage. The dual equilibria—a reflection of Laffer curve—imply that an economy may be stuck in high inflation equilibrium when, with same fiscal deficit as per cent of GDP, it could be at a lower inflation rate. The seigniorage Laffer curve phenomenon depicts the non-linear relationship between revenue from money creation (μ_t) and the inflation rate (π_t). Easterly et al. (1994) noted that econometric estimation of the following quadratic equation statistically confirms the seigniorage Laffer curve.

$$S_{rev} = \alpha + \beta_1 \pi_t + \beta_2 \pi_t^2 + v_t. \tag{5.12}$$

where S_{rev} is seigniorage (fiscal and monetary in separate model specifications) and π_t is the rate of inflation.

The monetary seigniorage is estimated using two data sets; high-frequency data (monthly) for the period ex post to global financial crisis and also using the annual data for the period under study. Using error correction mechanism, the plausibility of monetary seigniorage Laffer curve estimated using the high-frequency data for India is reported in Table 5.2. The estimation revealed that monetary seigniorage Laffer curve exists in the context of India, ex post to global financial crisis period. The squared coefficient is negative and significant, which depicted that the seigniorage revenue creation initially rises and eventually falls with the rise in the rate of inflation, the estimates (π and Π^2) are significant (Table 5.2).

Theoretically, the coefficient of Π^2 provides a seigniorage-maximising inflation rate, which provides the plausible inflation rate where the seigniorage Laffer curve peaks. This model can be extended by incorporating the relevant control variables and the policy dummy to capture the phasing out of monetised deficits in 1997. However, these results are partial and illustrative.

118 FISCAL CONSOLIDATION, BUDGET DEFICITS AND THE MACRO ECONOMY

Table 5.2

High-Frequency Data Estimation of Monetary Seigniorage Laffer Curve: ECM Estimates

	Coefficient	t
α	−0.094	−0.653
		[0.516]
π	1.078	1.638
		[0.108]
Π^2	−0.095*	−1.739
		[0.088]
ECM	−0.645***	−11.545
		[0.000]
R-squared	0.435	

Source: RBI (Basic Data), various years.
Note: Figures in parentheses denote probability.

Table 5.3

Annual Frequency Data Estimation of Monetary Seigniorage Laffer Curve: Error Correction Mechanism Estimates

Variable	Coefficient	t-statistic	Prob.
α	−0.020	−0.217	0.829
π	1.932***	4.614	0.0001
Π^2	−0.500*	−3.118	0.004
ECM	−0.833***	−7.087	0.000
R-squared	0.423		

Source: RBI (Basic Data), various years.

The re-specification of the non-linear monetary seigniorage Laffer curve models with annual frequency data is reported in Table 5.3. The model provided a preliminary evidence for the seigniorage Laffer curve.

5.3 Conclusion and Policy Suggestions

The decision of a shift from seigniorage financing to bond financing of deficits has happened beyond the purview of fiscal rules in India. The fiscal rules have restricted the macroeconomic debates to numerical targets of different concepts of deficits. The evolution of purpose-specific concepts of deficits generated by four pioneering IMF surveys has close linkages of analysing the impact of fiscal policy stance on macroeconomic activity. However, the formulation of fiscal rules—strict on numerical targets—has pre-empted the development of such macroeconomic debates, institutions and policy outcomes.

The shift in the financing pattern of deficits from seigniorage to bond has occurred prior to the deregulation of interest rate regime. However, despite the concerted efforts by the government and the central bank to contain the monetised deficit in India, the seigniorage is not yet on the decline. The seigniorage creation is on the rise, and the major component contributing to the seigniorage is the net Forex assets. Though the net RBI credit to the government (monetised deficit) has been controlled through a significant policy coordination between RBI and the government, recently this component of the reserve money is on the rise.

The estimates of error correction mechanism models suggested a possibility of a monetary seigniorage Laffer curve phenomenon in India. These estimations are partial and illustrative. The plausibility of existence of seigniorage Laffer curve opens the possibilities of monetary and fiscal policy coordination, especially when India is moving towards CBI and new monetary policy framework.

From a public policy perspective, what the fiscal rules have surpassed is that the macroeconomic consequences of deficit emanate not only from the numeric levels of deficit but also from the deficit financing patterns. This has implications in the transitional context from 'discretion' to 'rule' in monetary stance towards inflation targeting. If gen-Next fiscal rules are formulated to attain a striking balance between fiscal sustainability and growth, one cannot surpass the deficit financing rules anymore. The moment we incorporate the macroeconomic channel of fiscal deficit, the rules take the form of not mere fiscal rules, but macro–fiscal rule. To conclude, 'macro–fiscal rule' incorporating monetary–fiscal coordination should be the gen-Next rules-based fiscal policy.

6
Fiscal Seigniorage: Composition of Deficits

Fiscal seigniorage deals with the intertemporal financial composition of public sector deficits. This chapter attempts to examine the linkages between fiscal and monetary policy through constructing fiscal seigniorage. The chapter also presents an econometric investigation of seigniorage and inflation linkages, after arriving at a plausible 'fiscal seigniorage' Laffer curve. In the last chapter, we presented a monetary seigniorage Laffer curve, the construction of fiscal seigniorage using Neumann (1992) methodology is attempted in this chapter.

6.1 The Analytical Framework of Fiscal Seigniorage

The fiscal seigniorage is derived from the intertemporal budget constraint of financing the public sector deficit. In this framework, we try to derive fiscal seigniorage from the central government budget identity as well as from the components of central bank's balance sheet. This derivation of fiscal seigniorage is drawn from Klein and Neumann (1990) and Neumann (1992).

The reserve money or the high-powered money (M) can be created by the central bank by lending credit to the government (A), by lending credit to the private sector (B), by acquiring the net Forex reserves (F) and through OMO by purchasing public debt in open markets

(D). Symbolically, the balance sheet of the central bank for the flows can be as follows:

$$\dot{M} = \dot{A} + \dot{B} + \dot{D} + e\dot{F} + N_M, \quad (6.1)$$

Where dots over variables denote time derivatives, e is the nominal exchange rate and N_M denotes the change in the net balance of all other items.

Klein and Neumann (1990) derived the central bank's profit transfer to the government from the central bank's profit and loss account as follows:

$$R = aA + bB + dD + efF + N_R - V - C \quad (6.2)$$

The central bank's profit transfer to the government (R) can be derived as the difference between total revenues and total costs. The rates of interest on the assets are denoted by a, b, d and f. N_R is the surrogate of all other net revenues of central bank. V represents revaluation losses (or gains, if negative) on net Forex reserves and C denotes the central bank's operating costs.

After incorporating these stylised facts into the intertemporal budget constraint of central government, the equation would transform into an identity of financing public deficits, as follows:

$$G - T + bB_T + aA = \dot{B}_T + \dot{A} + R \quad (6.3)$$

The LHS of this equation denotes the fiscal deficit. The RHS denotes how fiscal deficit can be financed. Fiscal deficit is interpreted in the LHS as an aggregation of primary deficit ($G-T$) and interest payments expenditure. The interest expenditure comprises of two components, the interest payments on all government bonds (bB_T) and those held by the central bank (aA). The RHS reveals that the total public deficit can be financed by issuing bonds, by net credit from the central bank, and by using the profit disbursed by the central bank. B_T denotes the total stock of government bonds.

Consolidating Equations (6.1), (6.2) and (6.3) yields the intertemporal budget constraint identity of the public sector. The term 'public sector' is used in this context as the consolidation of the central government and the central bank (Klein and Neumann, 1990).

$$G = T + (bB_P - \dot{B}_P) = \dot{M} + (dD - \dot{D}) + e(fF - \dot{F}) - V - V - N \quad (6.4)$$

where B_p denotes the government bonds with the public and $N = N_R - N_M$ is a net residual of all other items. Equation (6.4) provides the analytical framework for deriving the fiscal seigniorage. The LHS of Equation (6.4) reflects the accounts of the central government while the RHS reflects the accounts of the central bank.

Fiscal seigniorage can be derived from the above analytical framework. The method of estimating fiscal seigniorage is through central government's intertemporal budget constraint, as follows:

$$S_G = (G - T + aA_o - \Delta A_o)/P \qquad (6.5)$$

where $(G-T)$ is the primary budget deficit or surplus of the central bank and aA_o is the interest payments expenditure on the public debt held outside the monetary system (A_o) (Neumann, 1992). Equation (6.5) denotes that fiscal seigniorage is the portion of the public deficit that is not financed by borrowing from the public (ΔA_o). This translates that fiscal seigniorage contributes to the financing of the primary deficit and of the interest payment expenditures on debt held by the public (outside the purview of central bank).

6.2 Estimating Fiscal Seigniorage: Financial Composition of Deficits

Fiscal seigniorage (S_G) is the government's net monetary finance requirement in output units. It measures that part of seigniorage which the central bank passes on to the government (Klein and Neumann, 1990). Fiscal seigniorage denotes the proper measure of the government's revenue from the creation of money, while monetary seigniorage confines to the fiat money or cost of printing money technically captured by the changes in reserve money.

Fiscal Seigniorage is symbolically, $S_G = (1° + aA_o - \Delta A_o)/P$ where $1°$ is the primary balance, A_o is the interest expenditure incurred outside the purview of central bank. The financing of public deficit through the OMO are deducted to arrive at the estimate of fiscal seigniorage.

The fiscal seigniorage has increased from around three per cent of GDP in the 1970s to a peak of eight per cent of GDP in the late 1980s (Figure 6.1). However since the 1990s, fiscal seigniorage fluctuates within the range of two–five per cent of GDP.

Figure 6.1

Fiscal Seigniorage in India (in Per Cent)

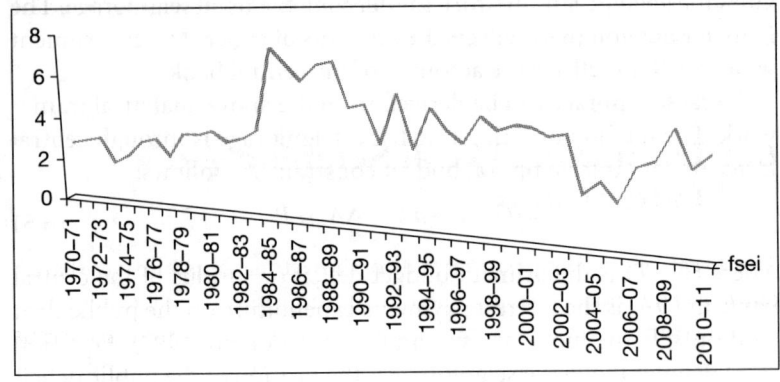

Source: RBI (Basic Data), various years.

Figure 6.2

Co-Movement of Fiscal and Monetary Seigniorage (in Per Cent)

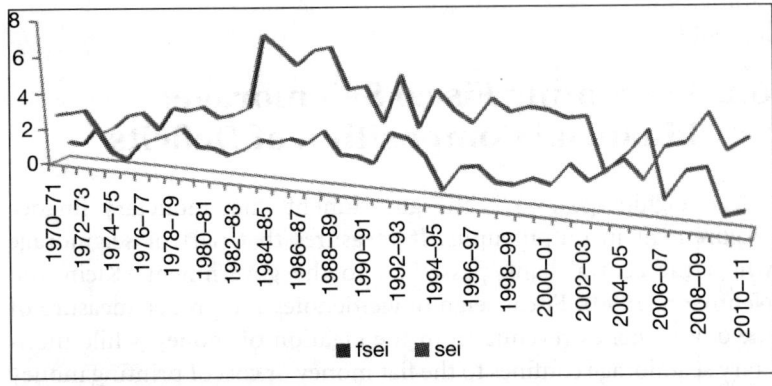

Source: RBI (Basic Data), various years.

Fiscal seigniorage has always been greater than monetary seigniorage except for a crossover in mid-2000 (Figure 6.2). This crossover is not due to the rise in the net RBI credit to the government, but due to rise in net Forex reserves which has increased the high-powered money in the system.

The decadal averages of fiscal and monetary seigniorage suggest that irrespective of the agreement between central government and central bank to control the monetisation of deficits in India signed in 1996–97, the reserve money has not been on the decline due to net foreign exchange assets, which is reflected in the increasing trend of monetary seigniorage in the recent decade (Figure 6.3).

6.2 Estimating Fiscal Seigniorage Laffer Curve

The fiscal seigniorage estimates also showed a plausibility of Laffer curve as the squared term is significant and negative. The seigniorage maximising inflation rate from these preliminary estimations are seemingly not explosive rates and there could a possibility for seigniorage financing at moderate inflation rates (see Table 6.1). However, these estimates are illustrative and need to be read with caution, and these non-linear models need to be further strengthened by incorporating appropriate control variables. These preliminary estimates have policy implications on the current mode of financing public deficits in India, with bond financing as the predominant

Figure 6.3

Fiscal and Monetary Seigniorage in India (in Per Cent): Decadal Averages

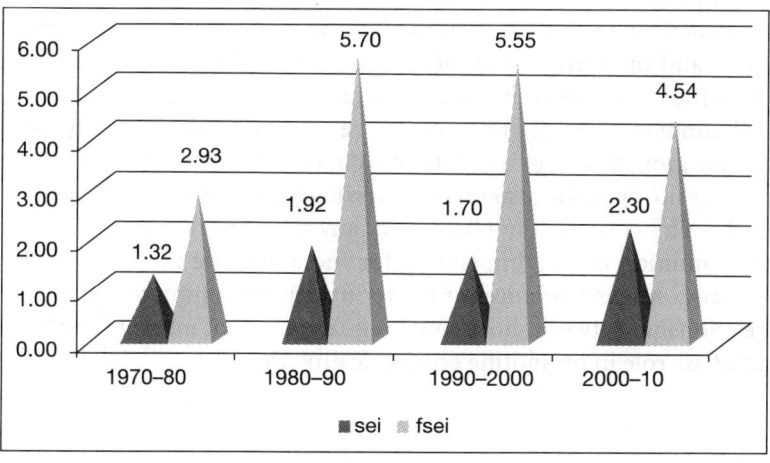

Source: RBI (Basic Data), various years.

Table 6.1

Fiscal Seigniorage Laffer Curve, Annual Frequency Data (1970–71 to 2012–13): Error Correction Mechanism Estimates

Variable	Coefficient	t-statistic	Prob.
α	0.007	0.176	0.861
π	0.872***	3.776	0.0007
Π^2	–0.216**	–3.3823	0.002
ECM	–0.530***	–4.236	0.0002
R-squared	0.330		

Source: RBI (Basic Data), various years.

method. It is interesting to recall heterodox economists' emphasis to seigniorage finance of deficits for public deficits, as they believe it is in technical terms 'free lunch', if the economy has not attained the full employment levels (for details, see Rakshit, 2005 and 2010).

If we take recourse to the original arguments for monetary–fiscal linkages, bond financing of deficits can be flawed even under a fiscal dominance regime. Does bond financing—the dominant source of financing the deficit in India—have an empirical upper bound? If so, does it imply when the rate of interest on government bonds exceed the growth rate of the economy, we need to monetise eventually the deficits through generating seigniorage? The fiscal stance, however, would not be unsustainable soon in India, as the present structure of deficit financing has a negligible share of external financing of debt, and the composition of debt is more of long-term maturities. Still, the assumption that the monetary regime has no influence on the conduct of fiscal policy need a revisit, especially when the economic growth rate (g) is plummeting and the rates of interest (r) have shown no signs for a significant downward trend in recent years in India. This concern is not because of any straightjacket unsustainability condition of $r>g$ impending for India, but the monetary policy stance contains relevance for the term structure of interest rates (the relationship between short- and long-term rates of interest) and has a catalytic role in promoting economic growth.

6.3 Conclusion

Fiscal seigniorage is a wider concept than traditional monetary seigniorage to take into consideration the institutional and policy changes which has direct bearing on government's net monetary finance requirement. The shift in the financing pattern of deficits from seigniorage to bond financing which has occurred prior to the deregulation of interest rate regime in India has implications for the fiscal seigniorage. The estimates of error correction mechanism models suggested a possibility of a fiscal seigniorage Laffer curve phenomenon in India. These estimations are partial and illustrative. The plausibility of existence of fiscal seigniorage Laffer curve opens the possibilities of monetary and fiscal policy coordination, especially when India is moving towards CBI and new monetary policy framework.

7
Fiscal Deficit and Seigniorage Link: Monetary Policy Regimes and Empirical Analysis

The seigniorage financing of fiscal deficit has been excessively controlled by the central banks, based on the perception that seigniorage finance is dangerously inflationary. Over the years, the monetary policy has shifted away from money financing to inflation targeting. Inflation targeting, the process of pegging interest rate based on inflationary expectations, is based on the assumption of CBI. CBI implies the discretion to central banks to decide on the timing and nature of monetary policy intervention and further the transparency in relation to both objectives and strategies. Since the 1990s, there has been a growing literature on central bank autonomy across countries (Brumm, 2000; Forder, 1999; Lin, 1999 and Tambakis, 1999).

It is an empirical question whether seigniorage financing is inflationary and whether deficits cause inflation. The CBI perspective that deficits are inflationary has been criticised from historical, theoretical and empirical angles; and empirically, both panel and single-country time series analysis from a wide range of countries, historical periods and different inflation rates fail to find a statistically significant correlation between fiscal deficits and inflation, regardless of whether deficits are funded via private sector bond purchases or central bank monetisation (Ryan-Collins, 2015). Having said that, historically, the econometric analysis of link between fiscal deficit and money has been inconclusive.

7.1 The Recent Policy Debates: 'Quantitative Easing' versus 'Helicopter Money'

The recent debates on public deficit and reserve money links are eclectic. Since 2008, against the backdrop of global financial crisis, many central banks of developed countries have embarked on 'quantitative easing' (QE), which has led to the record low interest rates. This has also led to a public policy constraint that interest rates are no longer a tool to manoeuvre with regard to stimulating economic revival. This led to the revival of fiscal policy dominance, and monetary policy has been failing as a tool for countercyclical policy. An alternative has been proposed to revive the monetary policy in the postcrisis era for central banks to engage in seigniorage financing of deficits. Ryan-Collins (2015) noted that historically high levels of private and public debts coupled with very low short-term interest rates resulted from 'quantitative easing' has limited the stimulative monetary policy in many advanced economies today, and an option considered to boost demand and relieve debt burdens has been seigniorage financing. Ex post to global financial crisis, many economists have argued that the appropriate role of monetary policy in the postcrisis era is to seigniorage finance the deficits.[1] The creation of seigniorage to finance government deficits is often referred to as 'helicopter money'. This policy has been used in the post-Second World War to reduce debt-to-GDP ratios. Rheinhart and Rogoff (2013) have historically examined the debt-to-GDP ratios of the national governments of developed countries and found that the current level of debt is approaching a two-century high water mark. It is interesting to note that there are parallels to monetary activism in Keynesian tradition, with the Lerner's (1943) 'functional finance' approach, which states that the ultimate source of monetary authority lies with the central bank in a sovereign fiat-currency regime; it does not make sense for governments to 'borrow' via bond financing, rather there should be no limits on a state's ability to fund socially agreed upon objectives, such as full employment via sovereign money creation (Ryan-Collins,

---

[1] These spurts in debates have been published in financial dailies, for instance, Wolf (2013) and Reichlin et al. (2013).

2015). Reinhart and Sbranica (2011) have argued that the current quantitative easing policies should be viewed as a form of financial repression.

The argument against seigniorage financing is that it is fiercely inflationary, and perhaps that has been the prime reason why seigniorage financing has disappeared from the monetary policy realms. It is an empirical question whether seigniorage finance is inflationary. Ryan-Collins (2015) has found that money financing of deficits is not inflationary in the context of Canada. Ex post to global financial crisis, there has been a revisit to monetary activism in catalysing the seigniorage financing of deficits. However, the dominance of 'New Macroeconomic Consensus' policies have given emphasis to 'inflation targeting' as the appropriate role of monetary policy, and such debates led to CBI. In the midst of new debates on CBI and inflation targeting, the revival of 'seigniorage finance' debates did not get adequate attention.

The New Macroeconomic Consensus (NMC) has emphasised on three aspects. As articulated by Arestis and Sawyer (2008): (i) NMC stipulates that the sole task of central bank is to focus on price stability through inflation targeting, (ii) to achieve this, central bank should be operationally and institutionally independent of government and ministries of finance, including being free of any obligation to lend to governments or buy government securities and (iii) engage in indirect methods of monetary policy (in particular, adjustments to interest rates) as opposed to more direct methods of deficit or monetary financing, credit controls (Arestis and Sawyer, 2008; Bernanke and Mishkin, 1997 and Epstein, 2006). Ryan-Collins (2015) further stated that inherent in NMC is a clear dichotomy of monetary and fiscal policy. One of the institutional policies which constitutionally embedded the NMC policy was the Maastricht Treaty in EU, signed in 1992, stipulating fiscal rules to control the deficits, and also prohibiting the direct money financing of deficits by central bank. By the year 2008, around a quarter of central banks adopted inflation targeting advanced and developing countries (Epstein and Yeldan, 2008). However, postcrisis period has revealed the insignificance of using interest rates as a policy tool of countercyclical policy, when the interest rates reached record low and proved ineffective to make an upturn to economic growth or to contain inflationary pressures.

7.2 Evolution of Monetary Framework in India

The objectives of monetary policy in India have broadly been price stability, economic growth and financial stability. There are three major phases in the evolution of monetary policy framework in India: (i) independence to 1985 (no monetary targeting), (ii) 1985–1998 (monetary targeting) and (iii) 1998–present (multiple indicator approach).

7.2.1 Monetary Targeting

The 'monetary targeting' framework suggested by Reserve Bank of India (1985) was against the backdrop of controlling the monetised deficit—net RBI credit to the government—and the phasing out of ad hoc treasury bills. The monetary targeting framework—targeting M_3—became challenging with the deregulation of rates of interest and capital flows, which led to instability in money demand function. With the partial deregulation of interest rates in India in 1991 and the partial opening up of trade and capital account, a move has been seen towards 'multiple indicator approach' from 1998 to present.

7.2.2 Multiple Indicator Approach

The existing monetary framework in India has been a 'multiple indicator approach' since 1998–99, with emphasis on monetary policy transmission channels. This framework has worked significantly well in terms of high economic growth and reasonable inflation till 2008–09. The challenges posed to this framework have begun when the plummeting growth co-existed with persistently high inflation when a plethora of indicators has been criticised for not providing adequate signalling to clear policy decisions. This led to the rethinking for a clearly defined nominal anchor for monetary policy. However, this increasing clarion for monetary policy independence and inflation targeting needs to be co-read with the global tendency of fiscal dominance losing relevance—fiscal policy is not useful as countercyclical instrument—through fiscal rules and an attempt towards monetary policy independence as recently as till 2007 (Feldstein, 2009b).

7.2.3 Rule-Based Monetary Policy

Aftermath of global financial crisis is a story of fiscal re-dominance, when the monetary policy has failed miserably to control the crisis. Despite these developments, there was a renewed debate towards rule-based monetary policy—independent, inflation targeting central bank—has genesis in a series of three reports submitted: Percy Mistry Report (2007), Raghuram Rajan Report (Chakraborty, 2008) and Government of India (2013). These three reports emphatically directed the policy discourse towards price stability as the primary goal of central bank in India, and Urjit Patel Report ultimately formed a part of this camp in terms of new monetary policy framework. The rule-based monetary policy framework throws challenges in terms of theory, empirics and policy implications.

The theoretical framework for rule-based monetary policy narrated in Urjit Patel Report is heavily drawn from the New Keynesian (NK) school of thought, where a monetary policy rule is prescribed (along with other equations/blocks), to set the short-term nominal interest rate on the basis of inflationary expectations and output gap (for details of NK, see Gali and Gertler, 1999).

There is an upcoming literature on the fiscal routes to inflation. Urjit Patel Report, though emphasises on inflation targeting, the theoretical backdrop for their arguments is not 'fiscalist' route, which has underpinnings in the recent *fiscal theories of price determination*. Fiscal theories of price determination is yet another class of policy rules where there exists a unique rational expectations solution that shows that the price level is independent of monetary policy but dependent strictly on fiscal policy. This 'fiscal theory of price level determination' breaks any link between money growth and inflation. The key fiscalist models were developed by Leeper (1991), Sims (1994), Woodford (1994) and Cochrane (1998).

The fiscalist literature argues that price level indeterminacy problems can be solved by having the central bank peg the nominal interest rate at a level consistent with the central bank's desired inflation rate, rather than by controlling the growth rate of the (base) money supply (Sims, 1994 and Woodford, 1990). The report does not take fiscalist route as its theoretical backdrop, rather emphasises on NK framework. This clarity in the conceptual framework of report is worth noting, though it is debatable whether rule-based monetary policy based on price stability is the appropriate monetary framework for India. It is interesting to recall Raghuram Rajan Report where the theoretical backdrop for his recommendations towards single objective of monetary policy as price stability was unclear and his emphasis towards inflation targeting led scholars confused to think whether he pitched on a 'fiscalist route' (Chakraborty, 2008).

7.3 Historical and Empirical Perspectives: Deficit–Money Links

Does existence of high fiscal deficit can always have a tryst with the conduct of monetary policy? The prime mechanism in which fiscal deficit plays a role in the transmission mechanism of monetary policy is via seigniorage. The creation of seigniorage or *high-powered money* through monetisation of fiscal deficits can lead to high rates of monetary growth causing higher rates of inflationary pressures in the economy. If these assertions were true, the implications of fiscal deficit for the conduct of monetary policy would be serious.

The analysis of the effects of fiscal deficit on the conduct of monetary policy is a multifold procedure by examining the interlinkages between fiscal deficit, seigniorage, money supply and inflation in an iterative manner. It is to be noted that even if a positive functional relationship exists between seigniorage and fiscal deficit, it does not naturally ensure a link between deficits and money supply. In other words, there is no simple relationship between the growth of high-powered money and the growth of money supply and therefore, between money supply and fiscal deficit (Gupta, 1992). The behaviour of money multipliers can to a great extent determine the extent of relationship between seigniorage and money supply. If money multipliers are stable, there may be a relationship between seigniorage and money supply and in turn, money supply and deficit. When it comes to the relationship between seigniorage, fiscal deficit, money supply and inflation, it should be noted that apart from the generally agreed principle of increased money supply caused by the monetisation of deficit can lead to higher rates of inflation, it is also argued that fiscal deficit contribute directly to such inflationary pressures (Gupta, 1992). This section analyses whether the fiscal deficit affects seigniorage and the following chapter analyses the subsequent link between fiscal deficit and inflationary pressures in the economy.

Apart from Cagen's model, other major hypotheses in the theoretical and empirical literature on the link between fiscal deficit and money are Unpleasant Monetary Arithmetic (UMA) theory of Sargent and Wallace (1981), Buchanan and Wagner hypothesis, the 'interest-targeting hypothesis' of Dornbusch and Fischer (1990) and the 'self-perpetuating' hypothesis of inflation-induced deficits and deficits-induced inflation or the Oliveria-Tanzi effect. Fiscal dominance hypothesis of UMA implies that monetary policy cannot be manipulated independently (exogeneously) when the growth path of government expenditures and tax structure are both fixed. Moreover, Sargent and Wallace (1981) maintained that the only choice available to the central bank is not whether to monetise a government deficit but when—now or later (Darby, 1984). Under this coordination scheme of fiscal dominance, the ability of monetary authority to meet price stability would be lessened than in a monetary authority in the first coordination scheme, which implies that *tighter money now can mean higher inflation eventually*. Thus, the key argument of Sargent and Wallace (1981) is that a permanently higher government deficit must eventually be monetised (Gupta, 1992). Yet another dimension of this argument is embodied in Buchanan and Wagner (1977) proposition that the political pressures impacts monetary policy stance. They pointed out that monetary authorities are required to monetise the deficits due to political pressures to stabilise the interest rates, independent policy action is not an option. They further pointed out that monetarist proposition that deficits are inflationary can result only when there is an increase in supply of money relative to supply of goods. That is, when deficits are financed by money creation, and if and only if an increase in money supply is greater than increase in the supply of goods, then inflation would be the outcome. In other words, inflationary pressures result in the economy only when productivity/

economic growth does not increase as much as the increase in the money supply. Thus, they validate that inflation can be one possible consequence of budget deficits. Dornbusch and Fischer (1990) put succinctly the possible links between deficits and money growth. This link between deficits and growth in money supply works out under a regime where monetary authorities aim at *interest rate targeting*. In such a policy regime of interest rate targeting, the monetary authorities are compelled to monetise deficits to defend the interest rate targets, resulting in the inflationary pressures in the economy. This is also known as *validation hypothesis*. This hypothesis is on the strong assumption that interest rate stability is the prime concern of the central bank than the growth of money. In other words, the hypothesis rests on the assumption that central bank favours nominal interest rate stability over the rate of growth of money stock; which implies a direct link between treasury (government) borrowing and the central bank's open market purchases. Under this scenario, central bank is said to 'monetise the deficits' whenever it purchases a part of the debt sold by treasury to finance the debt purchase.

Under the scenario of 'interest rate targeting', concerns over private capital market stability lead the central bank to ease the credit control in an attempt to mitigate the pressure exerted by the increased government borrowing on rate of interest and therefore they argued that central bank encourages money supply growth when deficits are high and vice versa when deficits are low. The self-perpetuating hypothesis explained by Aghveli and Khan (1978) pointed out that an increase in central bank financing the deficit can lead to an increase in money supply and in turn create inflationary pressures in the economy. And at the same time, inflation can induce divergent effect on revenue and expenditure, which can lead to the widening of fiscal deficit, which is also known as Oliveria-Tanzi effect.

Historically, the empirical evidences have shown that link between fiscal deficit and money supply is inconclusive (see Tables 7.1 and 7.2). While some studies showed that deficits do not lead to growth of money supply (Ahking and Miller, 1985; Barnhart and Darrat, 1988; Barro, 1978; Demopoulas et al., 1987; Dornbusch and Fischer, 1981; Dwyer, 1982; Hamburger and Zwick, 1981[2]; Niskanen, 1978

---

[2] For the sub-period 1954–74.

Table 7.1
Historical and Empirical Evidences against Central Bank Independence (No Deficit–Money Links)

Author Period (Frequency) Country	Econometric Model	Variables	Results
Niskanen (1978) 1947–76 (Annual) US	Single Equation Model	Deficit = f{Inflation} Expenditure = f{Inflation}	Federal deficits (levels and first differences) do not impact on inflation, either through or independent of the rate of money growth
Barro (1978) 1941–76 and 1946–76 (annual) US	Single Equation Model	Money Supply [M1/M3] = f{Money Supply (t–1), Unemployment rate, Real Federal Expenditure relative to normal, Nominal Federal Surplus/GNP deflator as relative to the trend value of real GNP}	Departure of federal spending from normal rather than federal surplus per se positively impact money creation (and hence rate of inflation)
Hamburger and Zwick (1981) 1954–74 and 1961–74 (annual) US	Single Equation Model	Estimated Barro's function Instead of Barro's federal surplus variable, they used *Federal Deficit* variable Instead of Barro's real federal expenditure relative to normal, they used *real federal expenditure*	Supports Barro's hypothesis that government expenditure rather than federal deficits increase money growth *for the period 1954–74*
Dwyer (1982) US	VAR model	Xt = {first differenced price level, level of nominal income, nominal money, interest rate on three-months Treasury bills, nominal government debt held by the Federal Reserve and the nominal quantity of government debt held by public}	No evidence of deficit leading to rising money supply, interest rates and prices
Catao and Terrones (2005)	panel		No link between fiscal deficit and inflation
Lin and Chu (2013)	panel		No link between fiscal deficit and inflation

Source: RBI (Basic Data), various years.

and Protopapadakis and Siegel, 1987), some studies found strong evidence for Buchanan-Wagner conjecture of significant link between fiscal deficit and inflation (Aghveli and Khan, 1977, 1978; Allen and Smith, 1983; Darrat, 1986; Dutton, 1971; Frenkel, 1977; de Haan and Zelhorst, 1990; Hoffman et al., 1983; Jadhav, 1994; Levy, 1981; Mcmillan and Beard, 1980; Sargent and Wallace 1973 and Sarma, 1982). The historical analysis of these models across developed and developing countries is presented in Table 7.2. In the context of India, empirical literature validated the self-perpetuating process of deficit-induced inflation and inflation-induced deficits (Jadhav, 1994 and Sarma, 1982). The general assertion in the historical empirical evidences is that monetisation of fiscal deficits is one of the principal reasons for the creation of seigniorage in the economy. The methodology incorporated Barro's model, quantity theory-based models and eclectic models for specifying money function across countries. We would opt out for strictly specifying the model using either Barro's money function or quantity theory-based models in the context of India, as both models are too narrow to explain the multiplicity of interactive objectives of monetary policy in India. As we discussed, Barro's model confined only to the question whether fiscal deficit creates money creation in a single equation model; while quantity theory confines to price level and output.[3]

7.4 An Eclectic Paradigm or New Macroeconomic Consensus?

The model specification for our study emanates from an eclectic approach due to the constraints cited above with respect to historical Barro or Cagan paradigms. Levy (1981) has also used an eclectic paradigm by not following the specific models (based on quantity theory of money) in determining money growth. The conduct of monetary policy is too complex a phenomenon to be analysed with 'tidy' or

---

[3] Barro's specification: $M = a + bM_{t-1} + c\ SUR + d\ UN + e\ PUB$; where M is money, SUR is budget surplus (deficit), UN is unemployment rate and PUB is real expenditure relative to normal; and a–e are parameters.

Quantity theory-based models: $\log M = a + b\ \log P + c\ \log Y$ where M is money, P is price level, Y is output; and a, b and c are the parameters.

Table 7.2

Historical and Empirical Evidences for Central Bank Independence (Deficit–Money Links)

Author Period (Frequency) Country	Model	Model and Variables	Results
Hamburger and Zwick (1981) 1954–76 and 1961–74 (annual) US	Single Equation Model; Barro's model	Estimated Barro's function Instead of Barro's federal surplus variable, they used *Federal Deficit* variable Instead of Barro's real federal expenditure relative to normal, they used *real federal expenditure*	For the period 1961–74, study supports deficit impacts money supply; hence validates Buchanan Wagner conjecture
Allen and Smith (1983) 1954:1 to 1980:4 (quarterly) US	Single Equation Model; Barro's model	Estimated Barro's Model Instead of Barro's Federal Surplus variable *Real trend value of change in Federal DEBT* is used. Instead of Barro's Money Supply variable *Monetary base is used*	Positive and Significant impact of debt on monetary base
Mcmillan and Beard (1980) 1953:1–1976:4 (quarterly, seasonally adjusted) US	Iterative Three Stage Least Square Method Estimated Linear Variant of ISLM model	Federal reserve behaviour is treated as exogenous so that effect of fiscal policy on money supply is entirely due to private sector response Federal reserve is made endogenous by incorporating a reaction function into ISLM model, so that the effect of fiscal policy on money supply is due to both private and Federal Reserve response	Substantial impact of fiscal expansion on money supply

Study	Model	Variables/Approach	Findings
Hoffman, Low and Reinberg (1983) 1960–74 and 1977–80 (monthly)	Single equation model	Regressed money growth on future and past deficits (i) Examined the extent to which the Federal Reserve accommodates Treasury financing activities by effectively monetising newly issued debt, that is central bank increases money supply to finance the deficit	Strong relationship between deficits and money growth
Ahking and Miller (1985) 1947:1 to 1980:111 (quarterly) US	Trivariate Autoregressive Model	X_t = {deficit, base money growth, inflation}	Bi directional Causality between deficit and inflation
Darrat (1986) 1960–80 (quarterly) North African countries (Tunisia, Libya and Morocco)	Cointegration and Causality	Inflation = {Money supply, GDP, Foreign rate of interest}	Inflation is significantly a monetary phenomenon, and partly due to external factors like foreign rate of interest
Sarma (1982) 1979–80 (annual) India	3-sector Macroeconomic Model	Self-perpetuating process of deficit induced inflation and inflation induced deficits	Confirms the validity of inflation induced deficit hypothesis for India
Jadhav (1994) 1970–71 to 1987–88 (annual) India	4 sector-Macroeconomic Model	Self-perpetuating process of deficit induced inflation and inflation induced deficits	Confirms the validity of inflation induced deficit hypothesis for India.

Source: RBI (Basic Data), various years.

precise models.[4] Moreover, in India, there is a revival in debate for reviving monetary activism (via monetisation of fiscal deficit) and redesigning the conduct of monetary policy (Rao, 2003; Rakshit, 2000). It is argued that monetisation of fiscal deficit is not inflationary when economy is demand-constrained (Patnaik, 2001) and that maximising seigniorage revenue may, in fact, be optimal in a situation when budget constraint is hard (Rakshit, 2000).

As McCallum (2001) emphasised, the key stumbling block for monetary policy formulation is the limited knowledge of the way the macroeconomy functions, results that are confined to a particular model are of limited use. In India, as mentioned, through a historic agreement between central government and RBI, monetisation of deficits through seigniorage has been contained in the late 1980s. Till the late 1980s, monetised deficit remained to be one of the major components of reserve money during this period. Due to the unanticipated increase in the fiscal deficits, actual increase in the money supply was much higher than its projected increase. Efforts were made to reduce monetisation by trying to create a demand for government securities outside the captive market so that government's dependence on RBI support through monetisation declines. Other specific measures were doing away with automatic monetisation of deficits through ad hoc treasury bills in the year 1997. Monetary policy of 1990s has undergone entirely new experiments in India.[5] In the late 1990s, for the first

---

[4] Often 'tidy models' or 'precise' models focus too specifically on one dimension of the conduct of monetary policy, to the point that it becomes dominant and assume away some important features of the phenomenon in order to make the problem tractable and to achieve their ostensibly precise results. The drawback of 'tidy' or 'precise' models is that the results achieved through these models are at the cost of severe simplification of reality that limits their usefulness as a basis for either empirical testing or policy prescription. It is important to note that our analysis of money creation and implications have relied on eclectic paradigm to serve as a general analytic framework. Inclusion of all the determinants, which act on the conduct of monetary policy in a single model, which yields a precise solution, is impossible because variables are too numerous and their effects can be inconsistent intertemporally. Even if it were possible to produce a definitive money reaction function, the model would be so general and would not be operational in the sense of either being subject to empirical test or useful for policy prescription. In empirical literature on international finance, Dunning's (1979) eclectic paradigm is often used for modeling, integrating the existing strands of economic theory to explain the phenomenon.

[5] With the changed institutional context of new economic policies and financial sector reforms, the upsurge of capital flows contributed to the sharp increase in FOREX reserve from $9.2 billion in March 1992 to $25.1 billion in March 1995, for the first time RBI endeavoured into the reference of exchange rate stability in the conduct of monetary policy (Rangarajan, 2001).

time, external sector became the main cause of expansion of money supply. RBI actively intervened in the Forex market to stabilise the currency and regulated money supply through sterilisation. In order to neutralise the expansionary impact of capital flows, RBI conducted OMO extensively. With this policy initiative, there has been a growing debate on the autonomy of Central Bank in India.

New transmission channels of monetary policy opened up with the progressive dismantling of the administered interest rate structure and the evolution of a regime of market determined interest rate on government securities. As part of the financial sector reforms and because of the anticipated decline in the gross fiscal deficit (after the control of monetisation of fiscal deficit) of the central government, the Statutory Liquidity Ratio (SLR) on incremental deposit liabilities was reduced to 30 per cent from 38.5 per cent. With the reduction of SLR and other policy initiatives mentioned above, stage was set to introduce several financial sector reforms. The major policy initiatives have been to develop government securities market. The reform measures in this area included the introduction of 364-day treasury bills and 91-day treasury bills on auction basis, auctions of dated securities and Repo auctions. All these changes in the monetary policy realm have led to recent 'inflation targeting framework'. Urjit Patel Committee (2013) recommendations have clearly argued for CBI and inflation targeting in India. The recent new Monetary Framework signed by Government of India and central bank in February 2015 has endorsed the inflation targeting framework. Given these eclectic developments in policy realms, it is clear that historically the monetary policies of 1980s and 1990s in India reinforced that apart from price stability, RBI deals with a range of interactive objectives in the conduct of monetary policy. Incorporating these policy concerns, we specify an eclectic model for seigniorage in the context of India rather than a 'rule based' monetary framework in India which was introduced only recently.

The NK macroeconomics has transformed into what we now label as NCM (Arestis, 2009). The major policy implications of the NCM paradigm are particularly important for inflation management. The NCM pitches that price stability can be achieved through monetary policy since inflation is a monetary phenomenon; as such it can only be controlled through changes in the rate of interest. It is, thus, agreed that monetary policy is effective as a means of inflation control

(Arestis, 2009). This is controversial in the context of developing countries like India, as inflation is not strictly monetary process. The conceptual framework of inflation targeting in the context of India raises concern, and therefore we use an eclectic paradigm.

7.5 Econometric Model: Deficit–Money Linkages

The econometric model specified in an eclectic paradigm is as follows:

$$M_t = \alpha + \beta_1 M_{(t-1)} + \beta_2 DEF_t + \beta_3 \pi_t^e + \beta_4 OGAP_t + \beta_5 REER_t + D93 + \mu$$

where M_t = seigniorage
DEF_t = fiscal deficit GDP ratio
π^e_t = inflationary expectations
$OGAP_t$ = output gap
$REER_t$ = real effective exchange rate
$D93$ = dummy for financial deregulation

The fiscal deficit is expected to be positively related to monetary base. As discussed earlier, in the face of rising fiscal deficits, central bank may be forced to monetise a portion of it and in turn may create seigniorage and money supply. In other words, this variable will test the popular assertion that deficits contribute to growth in money creation. The inflationary expectations enter into monetary base equation to reflect the price stability objective of the central bank. The inclusion of expected inflation rather than actual inflation is based on the assumption that central bank forms expectations of inflation and respond to those expectations. The output gap is included in the reaction function to reflect the concern of monetary authority with the cyclical fluctuations in the economy.[6] This variable is included in the monetary base model also to portray whether monetary policy is

---

[6] In certain studies, unemployment rate variable is included instead of GAP (deviation of actual GDP from potential). Levy (1981) noted that unemployment rate is primarily an indicator of labour market tightness, and is a less comprehensive measure of economic utilisation than the GNP GAP. We used output gap in the model and the variable is constructed as the deviation of actual from potential GDP expressed as ratio of actual GDP.

Table 7.3

Unit Root Test Results

Macrovariables	Lags	t-statistics	Mc Kinnon Critical Value	Order of Integration
Seigniorage	0	−4.419979	−4.284580	$I \sim (1)$ c^*, t^* at 1%
Fiscal deficit	0	−5.731913	−4.284580	$I \sim (1)$ c, t^* at 1%
Output gap	0	−3.729007	−3.661661	$I \sim (1)$ c at 1%
Expected inflation	0	−10.29430	−4.296729	$I \sim (1)$ c^*, t^* at 1%
Real effective exchange rate	0	−7.296329	−4.284580	$I \sim (1)$ c, t at 1%

Source: Handbook of Statistics on Indian Economy (Basic Data), RBI (various years).

pro-cyclical or anticyclical in nature. The lagged monetary base or lagged money supply variable is included as a continuity variable. The coefficient of lagged variable of monetary base/money supply measures the extent to which the RBI follows a continuous policy rather than one characterised by abrupt changes. The variable real effective exchange rate is included in the model to capture the impact of external sector with the surge of capital flows on the conduct of monetary policy. A dummy is introduced in the model to capture the effects of financial deregulation on the conduct of monetary policy.

7.5.1 Econometric Estimation and Results

The econometric estimation is done in four steps, as in the case of earlier chapters. As a first step, we verified the order of integration of the macrovariables since the causality tests are valid if the variables have same order of integration (Table 7.3). We use ADF test to detect the presence of unit roots. The second step involves testing for cointegration using the Johansen Maximum Likelihood approach (Johansen, 1988; Johansen and Juselius, 1990 and 1992). The Johansen–Juselius estimation method is based on the error correction representation of the VAR model with Gaussian errors. The third step in the econometric estimation is to find out the causal relationship between the variables in Hsiao's VAR framework. And the final step in the econometric estimation is the error correction equation of the model which implies the changes in the dependent variable is a function of the level of disequilibrium in the cointegrating relationship, captured by the error correction term (ECM), as well as changes in the other explanatory variables to capture all short-term relationships among variables.

The unit root test results showed that all variables are integrated of order 1. After checking for unit roots, we turn to find out where the variables are cointegrated using Johansen Maximum Likelihood method. The order of VAR in the cointegration tests is 1 and we include linear trends in the model. The results from maximum eigenvalue and likelihood trace tests detect two cointegrating vectors. After detecting the cointegrating relationships, now we turn to estimate the causality in Hsiao's VAR framework. The order of one-dimensional autoregressive process of seigniorage is determined to be one, using the FPE criterion. The next step in the process is to examine the relative importance of the set of multiple causal variables for seigniorage in entering the model. The order in which the causal variables such as inflationary expectations, output gap, gross fiscal deficit and real effective exchange rate enter the model is determined by defining the specific gravities of the multiple causal variables. The specific gravity of a causal variable is the inverse of the FPE computed for the multivariate autoregressive model. In order of decreasing specific gravity, the causal variables of seigniorage are ranked and stagewise causality detection is applied to determine the causal relationships of the variables.

In other words, we first constructed the optimal univariate AR model using FPE criterion for seigniorage, which is determined to be one. Then we included the multiple causal variables of seigniorage, one at a time, according to their causal ranks and use FPE criterion to determine the optimal orders of the model at each step. As per the specific gravity criterion, fiscal deficit, output gap, real effective exchange rate and expected inflation entered the model sequentially. The optimal parametrisation of these variables detected through FPE criterion is determined to be one for all the variables. Simultaneously, while getting the optimal ordered multivariable AR model of seigniorage against its causal variables, the stagewise causality detection has also been performed.

This result is in confirmation with the fact that fiscal deficit does not cause seigniorage in India, due to the attempts by the government to bring down the monetisation of deficit (Table 7.4). The output gap

Table 7.4
Seigniorage Model: Results from Asymmetric VAR

Controlled Variable	Manipulated Variables	Optimum Lags of Manipulated Variable	Final Prediction Error	Causality Inference
$(sei)_{t\ [1]}$	–	–	1.044012043	
$(sei)_{t\ [1]}$	(DEF_t)	1	1.091425562	$(DEF_t) \neq (sei)_t$
$(sei)_{t\ [1]}$	$(DEF_t)\ O_g$	1	1.046297903	$O_g \neq (sei)_t$
$(sei)_{t\ [1]}$	$(DEF_t)\ O_g\ (e_r)_t$	2	1.041209916	$(e_r)_t \Rightarrow (sei)_t$
$(sei)_{t\ [1]}$	$(DEF_t)\ O_g\ (e_r)_t\ \pi_t$	1	1.124808834	$\pi_t \neq (sei)_t$

Source: Handbook of Statistics on Indian Economy (Basic Data), RBI, various issues.

and inflationary expectations also do not cause seigniorage in India. The seigniorage is caused by the net Forex reserves, which is captured through the exchange rate in the equation. This result is in confirmation with the fact that although government has reduced the monetised deficit to control the reserve money in the system, the rising component of net Forex reserves has spiraled the reserve money upwards, in the period under study.

7.6 Fiscal Deficit–Money Supply Links

It has already been noted that an analysis of the effects of fiscal deficit on the conduct of monetary policy is a multifold procedure. It examines the interlinkages between fiscal deficit, seigniorage, money supply and inflation in an iterative manner. Also, a relationship between high-powered money or seigniorage and the fiscal deficit does not necessarily mean a stable relationship between high-powered money and money growth and therefore, between money supply and fiscal deficit. However, our results refute the links between deficits and seigniorage, any plausible links between deficits and money supply, if any, would not be a link through reserve money creation.

The behaviour of money multipliers can to a great extent determine the relationship between seigniorage and money supply. In other words, if money multipliers are stable, there may be a relationship between seigniorage and money supply and in turn, money supply and deficit. The determination of money supply is, thus, a process of determination of sources of variations in reserve money and the money multiplier. This section analyses the relationship between money supply and fiscal deficit.

Since the money multipliers, M1/M0 and M3/M0, consist of the ratio of currency to demand deposits and that of bank reserves to demand deposits, it follows that the determinants of the money multiplier implies specifying the determinants of these ratios (Gupta, 1992). Since these ratios are the outcome of the portfolio behaviour of the non-bank public and banks, we need to specify models determining such behaviour. Once we have done that, we can combine the analysis of the relationship between fiscal deficit and money supply. This is a huge task beyond the scope of the present study. So our approach instead is to directly estimate the relationship between money supply and fiscal deficits. This is also the approach, which has been commonly used in literature (Barro, 1978; Demopoulos et al., 1987; Dornbush and Fischer, 1981; Gupta, 1992; Hamberger and Zwick, 1981; Levy, 1981 and Niskanen, 1978). The evidence from data analysis showed that money multipliers may not be stable in Indian economy for the period 1980–81 to 2014–15, and the possibility of links through money multipliers can also be prima facie refuted. The subperiod-wise buoyancy estimates showed that the money multiplier coefficients are broadly unstable (Table 7.5). The estimation is illustrative to capture money multipliers.

The Hsiao's estimates from asymmetric VAR model also refuted any links of fiscal deficit to money supply. This is in confirmation with the analysis that neither seigniorage nor money multipliers proved to a channel of effectiveness of seigniorage to money supply. The deviation of potential GDP from actual GDP can cause changes in money supply.

The results from Hsiao's asymmetric VAR models showed that it is not the fiscal deficit; the output gap (proxy for the economic activity cycles), inflationary expectations and REER cause money supply in India (Table 7.6).

Table 7.5

Stability of Money Multipliers: Evidence from Buoyancy Estimates

	M0	M1
	1980–90	1980–90
c	0.96*	0.32
	(5.56)	(2.57)
b	0.99*	1.10*
	(36.08)	(54.59)
AR(1)	0.02	0.10
	(0.05)	(0.30)
R^2	0.99	0.99
DW	1.90	1.72
	1990–2000	1990–2000
c	−1.11	−0.15
	(−1.28)	(−0.19)
b	1.29*	1.16*
	(11.37)	(11.25)
AR(1)	0.89	0.62
	(2.63)	(2.23)*
R^2	0.98	0.99
DW	2.02	1.64
	2000–13	2000–13
c	0.83	0.51
	(1.31)	(0.86)
b	1.06*	1.08*
	(15.18)	(16.63)
AR(1)	0.54	0.81
	(1.63)	(2.17)
AR(2)	–	−0.20
		(−0.52)
R^2	0.99	0.99
DW	1.63	2.02

Source: Handbook of Statistics on Indian Economy (Basic Data), RBI (various years).

Table 7.6

Money Supply – Deficit – Asymmetric VAR Model

Controlled Variable	Manipulated Variables				Optimum Lags of Manipulated Variable	Final Prediction Error	Causality Inference
$(Ms)_{t\,[1]}$	–	–	–	–	–	0.000566023	
$(Ms)t$	πe_t	–	–		1	0.000561719	$\pi e_t \Rightarrow (Ms)_t$
$(Ms)t$	πe_t	O_g	–		1	0.000533976	$O_g \Rightarrow (Ms)_t$
$(Ms)t$	πe_t	O_g	$(e_r)_t$		1	0.000549402	$(e_r)_t \Rightarrow (Ms)_t$
$(Ms)t$	πe_t	O_g	$(e_r)_t$	(DEF_t)	1	0.000593181	$(DEF_t) \neq (Ms)_t$

Source: Handbook of Statistics on Indian Economy (Basic Data), RBI (various years).

7.7 Fiscal Deficit and Reserve Money: High-Frequency Data Analysis

This section explores the link between fiscal deficit, creation of reserve money and inflation using the high-frequency data for the recent years in India. As data on GDP is not available on monthly basis, we use the montly data on Index of Industrial Production (IIP) to construct the output gap. Using HP filter, the potential GDP is arrived at Figure 7.1.

The high-frequency data analysis of money multipliers showed that M3/M0 have shown greater variation than M1/M0 in the post-deregulated financial regime of India (Figure 7.2). It is also noted that M3/M0 is higher than M1/M0 (Figure 7.2).

The extent of variability is more for M3/M0 (standard deviation 0.41) than M1/M0 (standard deviation 0.06) (see Table 7.7). The M1/M0 ranged between 1.15 to 1.41 during the period between 2006:04 and 2015:07; while M3/M0 ranged between 4.32 and 5.82 during the same period.

The movements of the variables under high frequency regime is shown in Figure 7.3. The unit root tests revealed that all macrovariables under concern are stationary series in the high-frequency data series, and technically speaking, they are $I \sim (0)$. The results were presented in earlier chapter under high-frequency regime. Now we turn to estimate the sequential autoregressive model to understand

Figure 7.1

Cyclical and Trend Components of Index of Industrial Production

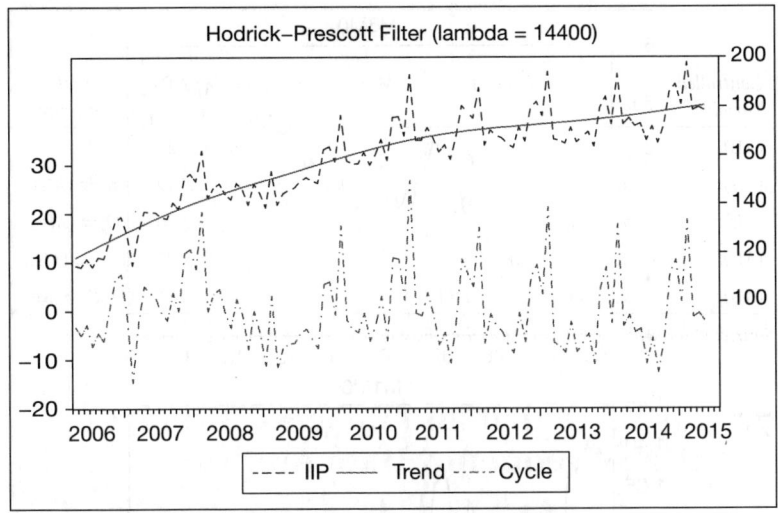

Source: RBI (Basic Data), various years.

whether there is any link between fiscal deficit and change in reserve money in the high-frequency regime. Seigniorage is defined as a change in reserve money in the high-frequency estimations. The results showed that in the high-frequency regime, fiscal deficit does not affect change in reserve money (see Table 7.8). Thus the shift in the financing pattern of fiscal deficit away from seigniorage financing to bond financing has considerably reduced the potential of fiscal deficit to create reserve money in the economy.

The point to be noted here is that despite the decline in the monetisation of deficit, the reserve money has not declined simultaneously. The factor which contributed to this trend of no significant decline of reserve money, despite the decline in net RBI credit to the government is due to the increasing share of net foreign exchange assets of RBI in reserve money creation. This trend is precisely captured in the results of sequential autoregressive model that real effective exchange rate is found to be a significant causal factor of reserve money creation in the deregulated financial regime. The significance of this result is that it is in conformity with the determinants of recent monetary stance in India; that external sector became the main cause of expansion of money supply.

Figure 7.2

Trends in Money Multipliers: High-Frequency Data

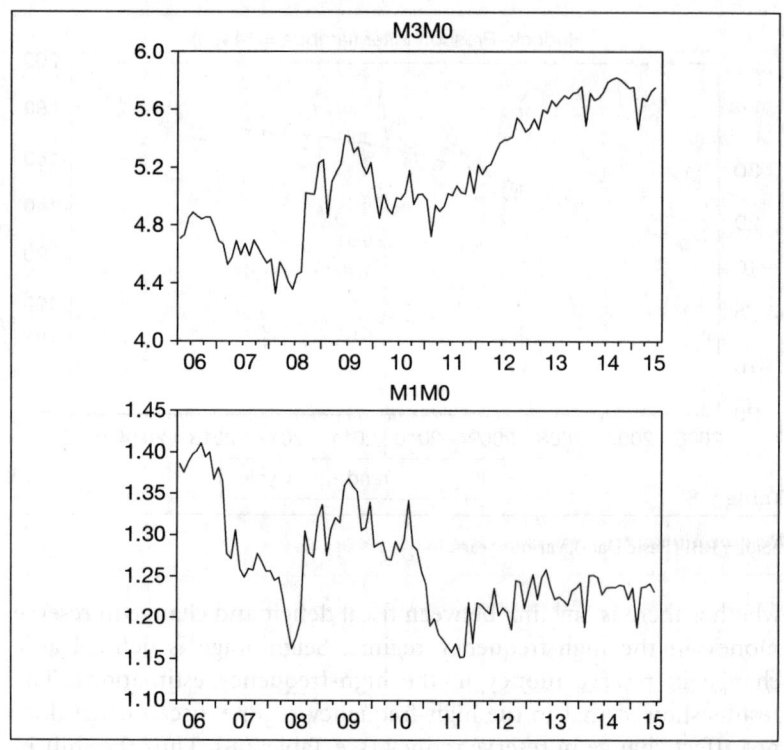

Source: *Handbook of Statistics on Indian Economy* (Basic Data), RBI, various years.

7.8 Conclusion

The existence of unstable money multipliers provided a prima facie evidence for lack of relationship between money supply and fiscal deficit. Instead of confining to the quantity theory-based model (where money is a function of only price level and output), we have developed a comprehensive reaction function for money in India, taking into account the historical and institutional perspectives of interactive objectives of monetary policy. The causality detection in the sequential VAR framework deciphered that fiscal deficit does not cause money in India. The analysis of deregulated financial regime revealed that fiscal deficit does not induce creation of reserve money;

Fiscal Deficit and Seigniorage Link 151

Table 7.7

Descriptive Statistics of Money Multipliers

	M3M0	M1M0
Mean	5.15	1.26
Median	5.10	1.25
Maximum	5.82	1.41
Minimum	4.33	1.15
Std. Dev.	0.41	0.06
Skewness	−0.01	0.61
Kurtosis	1.90	2.76
Jarque-Bera	5.56	7.11
Probability	0.06	0.03
Sum	571.60	139.96
Sum Sq. Dev.	18.88	0.44

Source: Handbook of Statistics on Indian Economy (Basic Data), RBI (various years).

Table 7.8

Reserve Money Model in High-Frequency Data Regime

Controlled Variable	Manipulated Variables	Optimum Lags of Manipulated Variable	Final Prediction Error	Causality Inference
$(sei)_t$ [1]			1.084182127	
$(sei)_t$ [1]	O_g	1	1.103869922	$O_g \neq (Ms)_t$
$(sei)_t$ [1]	O_g $(e_r)_t$	1	1.014230362	$(e_r)_t \Rightarrow (Ms)_t$
$(sei)_t$ [1]	O_g $(e_r)_t$ π_t	1	1.090693377	$\pi_t \neq (Ms)_t$
$(sei)_t$ [1]	O_g $(e_r)_t$ π_t (DEF_t)	1	1.897936447	$(DEF_t) \neq (Ms)_t$
$(sei)_t$ [1]	O_g $(e_r)_t$ π_t (DEF_t) $(i_r-\pi)_t$	1	1.913004534	$(i_r-\pi)_t \neq (Ms)_t$

Source: Handbook of Statistics on Indian Economy (Basic Data), RBI (various years).

which is in conformity with the shift in the financing pattern of fiscal deficit away from seigniorage financing to bond financing. The factor which contributed to this trend of no significant decline of reserve money, despite the decline in net RBI credit to the government is due to the increasing share of net foreign exchange assets of RBI in reserve money creation. This trend is precisely captured in the results of sequential autoregressive model that real effective exchange rate is

Figure 7.3

Movements of Macrovariables in High-Frequency Regime

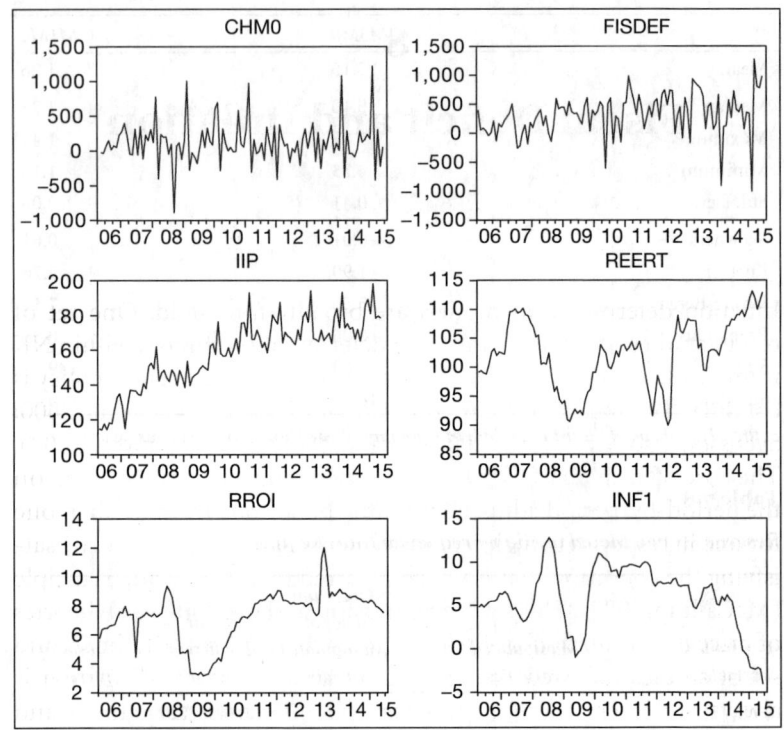

Source: RBI (Basic Data), various years.

found to be a significant causal factor of reserve money creation in the high-frequency data regime. The significance of this result is that it is in conformity with the determinants of recent monetary stance in India; that external sector became the main cause of expansion of money supply.

Though fiscal deficit does not induce high-powered money, this result by itself is not sufficient to conclude that fiscal deficit does not have inflationary potential. These results only reflect the partial explanation that monetary roots of inflation may be insignificant in India. Therefore, in the next chapter we will turn to analysing whether the determinants of inflationary expectations in India contain direct fiscal roots.

8
Fiscal Deficit and Inflation

Inflation determination models are broadly three-fold. One set of recent studies provide the inflation determination models within NK framework, which is based on the assumption that monetary policy is conducted by means of central bank policy rule (Clarida, et al., 2000; Svensson and Woodford, 2005; Taylor, 1999 and Woodford, 2003). The core of such analysis is the rule-based monetary stance based on the period-by-period adjustment of the policy rate by more than one for one in response to incipient movements in inflation—thereby satisfying the condition that is widely referred to as the Taylor Principle (McCallum, 1988). This set of research forms the recent 'fiscal theories of price determination' or fiscalist approaches. In contrast, the second set of studies followed the Friedman's famous axiom—'inflation is always and everywhere a monetary phenomenon' (Friedman and Schwartz, 1963). Such research, which attributed the root cause of inflationary pressures to expansionary monetary policies (the growth in the money supply) has what become to be known as the 'monetarist' tradition (Friedman, 1968 and Friedman and Schwartz, 1963). The third set of empirical models relate to inflation being termed as eclectic, or can be referred to as untidy models as it cannot adhere to the strict theoretical framework of monetarism, and it incorporates structural parameters along with monetary and fiscal variables. The inflationary phenomenon in India is complex, and it is highly inconclusive to adhere to fiscalist path or monetarist adage to determine inflation, especially in the deregulated financial regime. It is untidy in India in the sense that it cannot be determined within the neat monetarist models as monsoon failures or oil shocks can trigger inflation. The structuralist models of inflation, emphasising on the supply side factors, were found relatively relevant in the context of India (Balakrishnan, 1991).

In India, there is still a widespread debate with regard to the factors that cause inflation and their respective strengths. In this chapter, we shall try to incorporate all the relevant factors that can possibly effect inflation within the theoretical framework of Lucas (1973), which perceives aggregate price level as a result of a comprehensive interaction of aggregate supply and aggregate demand factors; and shall empirically test it using the official data from the Handbook of Indian Statistics, RBI and Ministry of Statistics and Policy Implementation, Government of India.

This chapter is all the more relevant having been developed against the backdrop of a New Monetary Framework between the RBI and the central government giving the RBI more autonomy to pursue a policy of inflation-targeting. The aim of this chapter is to bring forth the relationship between the supply-side factors and the other parameters of inflation with respect to India during the financially deregulated regime.

8.1 Conceptual Backdrop and Empirical Literature

The RBI and the central government signed an agreement in February 2015, devising a New Monetary Framework that agrees to give greater autonomy to the RBI with regard to its monetary policy. Against the backdrop of the new monetary policy framework agreement between the Government of India and the RBI in February 2015, this chapter empirically investigates the determinants of inflation in India. As per the new monetary framework, the objective of the monetary policy would predominantly be to maintain price stability while keeping growth in mind. Is inflation strictly a monetary phenomenon in India? There are equally convincing discourses which highlight that supply-side shocks determine inflation, in addition to the monetary determinants. However, the new monetary policy framework indicated a shift from discretion to rule-based monetary policy—inflation targeting—in the context of India, and to peg the policy rates based on inflationary expectations and output gap (RBI, 2014). This also calls for CBI, and suggests a move towards the NMC, which we have discussed in the earlier chapter. However, a large section of economists and policymakers still have their reservations about the use of inflation-targeting monetary policy in a developing country like India (Mahajan et al., 2014 and Sheel, 2014).

One of the hypothetical reasons could be that if the central bank is not independent, government engages in seigniorage financing of deficit and in turn increases money supply and inflationary pressures in the economy. However, such kind of deficit financing had been contained, taking cue from the seminal Chakravarty Committee Report to review the working of the monetary system, 1985 in controlling monetised deficits. What independence central bank seeks, hence, attains a new dimension in the backdrop of fiscal rules. With the shift from seigniorage financing to bond financing of fiscal deficits, the indication towards inflation targeting and CBI take a different perspective. This perspective may be linked to the hypothetical situation of a 'fiscal dominance' scenario of unsustainable debts through bond financing and the eventual monetisation of deficits, termed as UMA by Sargent and Wallace (1975), that inflation today or tomorrow is the only flexible policy option.

Inflation determination in the context of a developing country, such as India, is complex. Existing models such as the Phillips Curve model, monetarist model, supply-side model or structuralist model alone cannot explain the inflationary phenomenon in the context of developing economies. India has a large pool of unorganised sector. A study by the National Commission for Enterprises in the Unorganized Sector (NCEUS) in 2005 estimated that out of the 485 million persons employed in India, 86 per cent or 395 million worked in the unorganised sector, generating 50.6 per cent of the country's GDP. Therefore, as stated by Bhattacharya (1984), the Philips Curve model is not strictly applicable to India because the organised labour market is only a minor segment of total labour market, and in unorganised sector wage rate has no direct relationship with labour productivity, and therefore not a significant determinant of commodity price level.

The monetarists have, however, argued that developing economies are constrained by supply-side bottlenecks, and therefore inflationary pressures are created in the developing economies due to the excess money supply. Because of supply-side bottlenecks, excess money supply cannot generate output through technological advancements and real resources cannot be augmented by a mere expansion of money supply (Bhattacharya and Lodh, 1990). They also ruled out the trade-off between inflation and economic growth.

On the other hand, the supply-side economists have argued otherwise. They have laid great amount of stress on the structural disequilibrium in the growth process. Moreover, in pure *supply-side* models, inflation can occur without rise in money supply but in modified *supply-side* model, money supply expands along with price level but the direction of causality can either be from money to price or vice versa (Ibid., 1990). It is also noted that in *supply-side school*, there is a trade-off between growth and inflation which was ruled out by the monetarists as noted earlier, but the trade-off occurs not due to Phillips Curve type wage-unemployment relationship but due to differential growth of output and demand between sectors. The study also noted that the Rational Expectations model appear to be invalid for developing countries. They argued that for expectations to be rational there should be perfect information to all economic agents. But in developing countries, information is asymmetric. The presence of vast informal sector is a major obstruction to the free flow of information. The empirical studies on inflation based on Rational Expectations model in the context of developing countries is almost non-existent as the assumptions of homogeneous market or homogeneous production behaviour and perfect information appear to be practically irrelevant. This auger well when looked in the context of India that has a major part of its population working in the informal sector.

In the context of developing countries, studies by Siddique (1989), Saini (1982), Nachane and Nadkharni (1985), Dornbusch and Fischer (1981), Ramachandran (1983), Bhalla (1981), Aghveli and Khan (1978), Darrat (1986), Onis and Ozmucur (1990) and Minhas (1987) have broadly conducted empirical experiments to determine the direction of causality between inflation and money supply, with some of these studies specifying structural models of inflation while others draw inferences about causality using data exploratory and diagrammatic representations. The empirical evidences from India have shown that inflation modeling is broadly based on elements of both monetarist and supply-side model together rather than going strictly by either monetarist models or supply-side models. The inflation models developed in the context of India by Ahluwaliah (1979), Bhattacharya (1984), Pandit (1978) and Bhalla (1981) combined the elements of structural, monetarist, Keynesian, cost-push theories and Lewis model.

Balakrishnan (1991) has provided a comprehensive and coherent analysis of inflationary phenomenon in India within the framework of structuralist model for Indian economy for the period between 1950 and 1980 and he has also compared the explanatory power of the model based on structuralist framework with that of a simple version of a model based on monetarist framework and found statistical evidence in favour of structuralist model. His results have attributed excess demand as the reason for inflation. In Bayesian econometric framework, Balakrishnan et al. (1994) analysed the price behaviour in the context of India and the statistical evidence favoured structuralist model to monetarist model.

Some of the studies on inflation have also incorporated fiscal policy variable. Bhattacharya (1984) had stressed on the fiscal policy impact on inflation. Aghveli and Khan (1978) found a feedback relationship between money and prices in the context of Brazil, Columbia, Dominican Republic and Thailand. He explained his results in the structural model that monetary supply shock leads to increase in prices via the quantity theory mechanism, the increase in inflation leads to an increase in government expenditure (but not to a corresponding increase in revenues), thus creating a budget deficit, which is financed by money creation, which then leads to a further increase in prices and so on.

Bhalla (1981) and Saini (1982) estimated augmented versions of monetarist models by inclusion of additional variables into the monetarist model. Dornbusch and Fischer (1981) estimated an equation derived from standard IS-LM-AS model which includes budget deficit and money growth as causal factors of inflation. In three countries of their sample—Gautemala, Israel and Sri Lanka—monetary growth did not provide an adequate explanation for inflationary pressures in the economy. As for the budget deficit, it was found positive and significant in Israel. The results of Bhalla (1981) showed that in developing countries, such as India, Malaysia, Pakistan, Philippines, Sri Lanka, Thailand and Taiwan, there exists some indirect effects of budget deficit on inflation through the coefficients of lagged monetary growth. Sadanand Prusty (2012) concluded that a major cause of inflation in India is the increase in the fiscal deficit (especially revenue deficit) of not only the central government but also the state governments. To add to the earlier argument, a paper by Kumar and Mitra (2012) had stated that a restrictive monetary policy alone is insufficient to control inflation unless accompanied by a coordinated reduction in budget deficits.

The paper by Mohanty and Klau (2001) concluded that first, the output gap is a significant determinant of inflation in all countries, though the precise influence is difficult to establish. Second, supply-side factors seem to play more than a passing role in the inflation process. The results by Dua and Gaur (2009) showed that the supply-side factors do affect inflation in agrarian economies. Mishra and Roy (2011) explained inflation in India with a focus on food price inflation. They stated that food price inflation is typically higher than non-food inflation. Mohanty and Joice (2014) stated that monetary policy impact on inflation has remained broadly unchanged. Their paper underscores the role of monetary policy and fiscal policy in the reduction of inflation irrespective of the nature of shock.

As discussed in earlier studies on inflation model in the context of India, the monetarist approach is highly inadequate to explain the inflationary phenomenon in India. In the next section, we try to identify the key determinants of inflationary process in the context of developing countries, incorporating both demand-side and supply-side factors.

8.2 Inflation: Analytical Framework

The analytical framework of the inflation model for this chapter is derived from Lucas (1973), where he viewed aggregate price level as a result of interaction of aggregate supply and aggregate demand factors. The aggregate supply schedule depends on the deviation of actual output from potential output in the economy. We can start by specifying Lucas (1973) aggregate supply function:

$$\pi_t^* = p_t - p_{t-1} = \alpha + \beta_1(y_t - y^*) \tag{8.1}$$

where current inflation depends on the current output gap, and y^* is the potential output.

As Lucas (1973) argued, the aggregate demand function is drawn up by the set of demand-shift variables like monetary and fiscal policies and variations in the external sector. The aggregate demand thus can be can be specified as follows:

$$y_t = y_{t-1} + \beta_2 sei_t + \beta_3 i_t + \beta_4 def_t + \beta_5 k_t \qquad (8.2)$$

sei_t is the seigniorage, i_t is the real rate of interest, DEF_t is fiscal deficit and K_t is capital flows.

Deducting y^* from both sides of the Equation (8.2), and applying it to Equation (8.1), we get

$$\pi_t^* = \alpha + \varphi_1(y_t - y^*) + \varphi_2 sei_t + \varphi_3 def_t + \varphi_4 i_t + \varphi_5 k_t + \varphi_6 og_t + v_t \qquad (8.3)$$

It is to be noted that the variable GAP (the deviation between potential output and actual output scaled to actual output) alone may not be a powerful variable to capture the supply-side effects on inflation when compared to rainfall in the context of India. Balakrishnan (1991) has highlighted the role of food grains in the inflation model of India. They noted that no models of inflationary process in India have found it possible to do without 'money' as a statistically significant variable. Therefore, it does suggest that money plays a role, although certainly not an exclusive role, in determining the dynamics of price movements. The food grain price is in turn highly correlated with rainfall. Therefore we used rainfall to proxy the supply-side variable in the equation. In the light of above discussions, we re-modified the inflation equation using supply-side variable along with output gap.

$$\pi_t^* = \alpha + \varphi_1 ss_t + \varphi_2 sei_t + \varphi_3 def_t + \varphi_4 i_t + \varphi_5 k_t + \varphi_6 og_t + v_t \qquad (8.4)$$

The period of estimation is the financially deregulated regime. The process of financial deregulation started in India since 1991. The highlights of financial deregulation are interest rate deregulation, a phased reduction of cash reserve requirement and SLR, simplifying directed credit programmes, development of money markets, etc. The administered interest rates were simplified since 1992–93 (Chakraborty, 2002 and 2010). The deregulation of interest rates has been accompanied by the introduction of new instruments like 14-day and 182-day auction treasury bills in addition to the 91-day and 364-day auction treasury bills.

The WPI inflation rate in India fell to a low of −2.65 per cent in April 2015, the sixth successive month of deflating prices. Inflation rates in India are quoted as changes in the WPI or CPI for all commodities. The variables that have been included in the model are output gap, seigniorage, gross fixed deficit, supply-side variables, real rate of interest and capital flows. Seigniorage is defined as the change in the nominal stock of reserve money. To study the effects of the supply-side, we have used the amount of rainfall in the month of July. The rainfall effects the food grains production significantly in India, and therefore acts as a good proxy for the supply-side factors. The capital flows contain both the foreign direct investment as well as the foreign institutional investments.

8.3 Inflation-Econometric Model Specification and Results

The inflation function to be empirically tested in the chapter is stated in the following form, and all variables are in log form.

$$\pi_t^* = \alpha + \varphi_1 ss_t + \varphi_2 sei_t + \varphi_3 def_t + \varphi_4 i_t + \varphi_5 k_t + \varphi_6 og_t + v_t \qquad (8.5)$$

where ss_t denotes the amount of rainfall in July, sei_t is the seigniorage, def_t is fiscal deficit, i_t is the real rate of interest, k_t is the capital flows and og_t is the output gap.

Having checked for the pretests, now we turn to causality procedure using Hsiao's sequential autoregressive modeling for inflation. The FPE of fitting one-dimensional autoregressive process for inflation is computed with upper bound of lag length (L^*) assumed equal to 5. First, we have considered inflation as controlled variable, holding the order of its autoregressive operator to one as per FPE criterion, we sequentially added the lags of the manipulated variables such as change in money supply, food grain prices, real rate of interest and real effective exchange rate upto the L^* of 5 and found respective order which gives the smallest FPE.

The order in which variable enter into the equation is based on *specific gravity criteria* (Caines et al., 1981). The results showed that

Table 8.1

Inflation Model: Detection of Optimal Lags of the Manipulated Variables and FPE

Controlled Variable	Manipulated Variables				Optimum Lags of Manipulated Variable	Final Prediction Error	Causality Inference
$(\pi)_{t[1]}$	–	–	–	–	–	0.368807601	
$(\pi)_t$	Jrf_t	–	–	–	1	0.361957313	$Jrf_t \Rightarrow \pi_t$
$(\pi)_t$	Jrf_t	Ms	–	–	1	0.365955894	$Ms \Rightarrow \pi_t$
$(\pi)_t$	Jrf_t	Ms	$(e_r)_t$	–	1	0.400278576	$(e_r)_t \neq \pi_t$
$(\pi)_t$	Jrf_t	Ms	$(e_r)_t$	$(i_r - \pi)_t$	1	0.414860016	$(i_r - \pi)_t \neq \pi_t$
$(\pi)_t$	Jrf_t	Ms	$(e_r)_t$	$(i_r - \pi)_t$ DEF_t	1	0.344305380	$(DEF_t) \Rightarrow \pi_t$

Source: Handbook of Statistics on Indian Economy (Basic Data), RBI (various years).

Table 8.2

Inflation Model: High-Frequency Regime

Controlled Variable	Manipulated Variables					Optimum Lags of Manipulated Variable	Final Prediction Error	Causality Inference
$(\pi)_t$	–	–	–	–	–	–	1.004271343	
$(\pi)_t$	(DEF_t)					1	1.002135986	$(DEF_t) \Rightarrow \pi_t$
$(\pi)_t$	(DEF_t)	$(e_r)_t$				1	1.002202642	$(e_r)_t \Rightarrow \pi_t$
$(\pi)_t$	(DEF_t)	$(e_r)_t$	$(i_r - \pi)_t$			1	1.027656226	$(i_r - \pi)_t \neq \pi$
$(\pi)_t$	(DEF_t)	$(e_r)_t$	$(i_r - \pi)_t$	Ms		1	1.002353684	$(Ms)_t \Rightarrow \pi_t$
$(\pi)_t$	(DEF_t)	$(e_r)_t$	$(i_r - \pi)_t$	Ms	Og	1	1.003084615	$Og \Rightarrow \pi_t$

Source: Handbook of Statistics on Indian Economy (Basic Data), RBI (2001).

July rainfall, change in money supply and fiscal deficit cause inflation (Table 8.1).

The unit root tests for high-frequency data regime revealed that the macrovariables under concern are $I(0)$. The results from the asymmetric VAR model revealed that for the period under study, fiscal deficit determine inflation (Table 8.2).

The real effective exchange rates are also found causal variables in determining the rate of inflation in the high-frequency regime.

8.4 Conclusion

As we found no link between money supply and deficit, the potential question arising is whether fiscal deficit is inflationary. It should be noted that apart from the generally agreed principle of increased money supply leading to higher rates of inflation, it is also argued that fiscal deficit contribute directly to inflationary pressures. We developed the structure of inflation model derived from Lucas (1973), where he viewed aggregate price level is a result of interaction of aggregate supply and aggregate demand factors. The results from sequential autoregressive causality detection showed that money does cause inflation in India, although not an exclusively role. The supply-side factors also found significant in the dynamics of price determination in India. Moreover, fiscal deficit does cause inflationary pressures in the economy. The analysis of recent high-frequency data regime also revealed that fiscal deficit does induce inflationary pressures along with supply-side factors. The output gap, REER and money supply are also found to be the significant causal factors of inflation in recent regime.

9
Policy Takeaways: The Revival of Fiscal Activism

It is interesting to set this study against 'the rise and fall of fiscal activism'. As recently as till 2007, there was a widespread consensus among economists that fiscal policy is not useful as a countercyclical instrument. However, after the crisis, the governments in Washington and around the world were developing massive fiscal stimulus packages, supported by a wide range of economists in universities, governments and businesses (Feldstein, 2009). Prior to financial crisis, there was an increasing consensus among the (NK) economists to use monetary policy as countercyclical policy, as they visualised that monetary policy could be adjusted more rapidly through interest rate changes and could be effective in manoeuvring aggregate demand. The NK economists projected entirely a different view about the efficacy of fiscal policy, drawing partial conclusions from their retrospective analysis on Great Depression and the subsequent recovery. The prominent among these studies was Romer (1992), where it was suggested that monetary policy was central for the recovery, and the significance of fiscal policy—the employment creation through New Deal—stood only next to monetary policy.

In 1990s, this view on the weak role of fiscal policy generated a new consensus among economists to move towards fiscal austerity— rule-based fiscal economics and fiscal consolidation, or controlling fiscal deficits by rising taxes and reducing public expenditure. Certain studies had gone even a step ahead—Giavazzi and Pagano (1990)— indicating that contractionary fiscal policy—fiscal austerity—has positive effects on economic growth. Feldstein (2002) had sensed this widespread consensus among economists about the detrimental effects of fiscal policy based on conclusions related to fiscal and monetary multipliers. This new consensus is based on the controversial assumption that money is endogenous and the central bank controls rate of interest. However, monetary policy failed as a tool during global financial crisis; altering interest rates could not arrest the recession as the roots of recession was not linked to interest rate changes but underpricing the risks (Feldstein, 2009). When Feldstein failed to control the recession from monetary policy stance, US has announced fiscal stimulus packages, begun with a temporary one-time tax rebate, gaining a bipartisan support and it was implemented quickly (for details, see Feldstein, 2009).

The policy backdrop of the emergence of revival of fiscal dominance was when Obama's Economic Advisor Christina Romer suggested that fiscal multiplier from stimulus could be 1.5 (Romer and Bernstein, 2009). This was a hurricane in macroeconomic policy discourse by putting dignity back to fiscal policy space. This needs to co-read especially against the context of fiscal space (and its effectiveness on the output as a countercyclical tool) has been losing relevance as recently as till 2007, and a plethora of fiscal rules had been designed to tighten the fiscal stance, and nations across globe diligently started implementing the rules-based fiscal management and controls.

Till 2007, the macroeconomic policy discourse had been catalysed towards deficit thresholds, fiscal rules and public expenditure ceilings. Fiscal consolidation became the single most significant agenda, implemented diligently mostly through expenditure cuts than tax revenue rise. It was increasingly fed from the multilateral agencies, such as IMF, that fiscal consolidation has expansionary impacts on output, and any rise on fiscal deficit would crowd out private investment. Empirical literature in the context of emerging economies tried to take head on with these assertions, and tried to empirically analyse whether public investment crowd out private investment. It is interesting to recall here the metamorphosis happened in the policy thinking within the multilateral agencies, especially IMF, over the period aftermath to recession and led them to revise their stands that public investment need not crowd out corporate investment in times of recession, and reinforced the significance of public investments—infrastructure investment—during downturn. The qualifier was that fiscal consolidation is required to be strengthened only when a country collapses in terms of investor's confidence in sovereign bond market, and not from any macroeconomic consequences of fiscal deficit. Yet another roll back of plausible argument about bad macroeconomic consequence of fiscal deficit was its pressure on interest rates. This argument too was refuted by many empirical studies in the context of emerging economies including India (Chakraborty, 2002, 2007 and 2012; Vinod et al., 2014). However, the revisions of thoughts within multilateral agencies may be acknowledging this fact too that deficits could not exert pressure on interest rates especially in the context of global integration of financial markets. This acknowledgement may look normal aftermath to recession, and the evolutions happened in the macroeconomic policy thought process. However, till 2007, these arguments of negative consequences of fiscal deficit have always been on the forefront with assertions, which intimidated the researchers, especially those belong to the heterodox school of thought. The empirical studies, however, proved it inconclusive due to the methodological irregularities as well as the variations in model specifications. Having said this, India has fiscal consolidation agenda still on the forefront at the subnational and national levels. The subnational governments have achieved reasonable levels in terms of fiscal deficit thresholds, while the national government is still grappling with the fiscal consolidation. The path towards consolidation is equally significant as achieving targets, as the measures adopted to reach the target should not have negative impacts on economic growth in the long turn. If fiscal consolidation is by curbing capital spending, it affects investment and delay supply responses that are required for inflation containment. The curbing of capital spending also decreases potential output, making monetary policy easing difficult (RBI, 2012). Needless to say we derived these fiscal rules from the Maastricht Treaty of EU. However, the EU nations have realised the significance of a roll back from 'austerity' moves and the excessive deficit procedures (EDP), and a doctrinal shift towards the realisation of negative consequences of such moves on output in the long run, if it has been achieved through aggressive capital spending cuts. The renewed clarion is tax reforms path for fiscal consolidation.

9.1 India: Policy Takeaways

Fiscal deficit containment has been the raison d'être of macroeconomic adjustment in India, especially during the past two decades.

Excessive fiscal deficit has often indicted for macroeconomic tribulations, namely, rise in rate of interest, crowding out of private capital formation, creation of seigniorage and rise in inflation. Our analysis in this book looked into the impact of fiscal deficit of the central government on selected macroeconomic variables in India, namely, private capital formation, rate of interest, seigniorage, money supply and rate of inflation over the period between 1980–81 and 2014–15; and also the high-frequency data analysis of recent years.

As a prelude to the econometric analysis of macroeconomic impacts of fiscal deficit, we surveyed the existing macroeconomic paradigms discussing the impact of fiscal deficit. The Neoclassicals envisioned that economic agents are farsighted and rational who make appropriate intertemporal decisions with respect to consumption and income within finite horizon; thus, fiscal deficits raise total lifetime consumption by shifting taxes to future generations. This necessarily implies decreased savings and eventual crowding out of private capital formation through rise in rate of interest. While Keynesians argued that significant proportion of economic agents are myopic or liquidity-constrained and have high propensity to consume out of their current disposable income. This assumption implies that aggregate demand is responsive to changes in disposable income, and Keynesians believed that an appropriately timed fiscal deficit can have beneficial consequences through stimulating national income, savings and capital formation.

Apart from these two diametrically opposite views lies the much-debated RET. RET envisioned that rational economic agents can see through the intertemporal veil and realise that deficits merely postpone taxes to future generations. In the RET, increase in deficits will be offset by an equivalent increase in private savings in anticipation of future increased taxes to be levied by the government, to repay the borrowing. This implies that tax financing and bond financing of fiscal deficit can have no effect on aggregate demand. The important restatement of RET under the rubrics of debt neutrality and ultra rationality explained that macroeconomic impact of fiscal deficit is measured wholly by the size and content of the deficit, regardless of the mode of financing fiscal deficit. It is to be noted that the macroeconomic effects of fiscal deficit depend not only on the levels of fiscal deficit but also on the modes of financing the deficit.

Policy Takeaways: The Revival of Fiscal Activism 167

We derived the theoretical framework of the study from the intertemporal budget constraint, where fiscal deficit is defined and linked to its various modes of financing. As mentioned earlier, excessive use of any particular mode of financing the fiscal deficit has adverse macroeconomic consequences, namely, seigniorage financing of fiscal deficit can create inflationary pressures in the economy, bond financing of fiscal deficit can lead to rise in interest rates and in turn can crowd out private investment and the external financing of fiscal deficit can spill over to balance of payments crisis and appreciation of exchange rates. The study looked into the macroeconomic impact of fiscal deficit within this theoretical framework in the context of India.

As an orientating data exploration, we extensively delved into the trends in deficits and its financing pattern over the years and also the movement of fiscal deficit in relation to selected macroeconomic variables, namely, private capital formation, rate of interest, seigniorage, money supply and inflation using simple statistical methods.

The analysis of financing pattern of fiscal deficit over the past decades revealed that monetisation of fiscal deficit has shown wide fluctuations and has been brought down through deliberate OMO, especially in the deregulated financial regime. It is argued that a shift in the financing pattern of fiscal deficit from seigniorage financing to bond financing may exert upward pressures on rate of interest, which can crowd out the interest-sensitive components of private spending. Also, the recourse to external financing of fiscal deficit has become negligible over the years. Among the various sources of finance, government's dependence on the market borrowing and other contractual liabilities in the public account (namely, small savings and provident funds) has increased heavily over the years. The analysis of short-run and long-run rates of interest in the intertemporal scale adjusted for inflationary expectations showed that even in the administrated interest rate regime, all real rates of interest have shown considerable variations. The statistical properties of the rate of interest revealed that among all rates of interest, call money market rate remained highly volatile, while bank rate in nominal terms showed a sticky trend. The movement of fiscal deficit with real and nominal rates of interest does not reveal a definite pattern; and the correlation coefficients between the two revealed that fiscal deficit and rate of interest (real and nominal) are generally weakly correlated.

Apart from analysing the movement of gross capital formation and rates of interest vis-à-vis fiscal deficits, we have delved into the data exploration for preliminary evidence of link between fiscal deficit, seigniorage, money supply and inflation. Seigniorage (defined as the ratio of change in reserve money/high-powered money to GDP) has shown wide fluctuations over the past three decades. Seigniorage per se cannot spill over into growth of money supply. The transmissions through which seigniorage affect money supply are money multipliers. If the money multipliers are stable, there is a possibility that creation of seigniorage will lead to an increase in money supply. The money multipliers (defined as ratios of narrow money to monetary base (M1/M0) and broad money to monetary base (M3/M0)), are found to be not stable over the period of time, which in turn give an indication of the non-existence of the link between fiscal deficit and money supply. The correlation coefficient too suggested that both macro series are weakly correlated. On the basis of the preliminary data exploration and tentative inferences drawn from Chapter 2, we investigated the exact nature of the relationship between fiscal deficit and the macrovariables econometrically in the following chapters.

Subsequently, we looked into the link between fiscal deficit and private capital formation and the phenomenon of crowding out. As identified in theoretical literature, taxonomy of real (or direct) and financial (or indirect) crowding out is considered to be important in the present context. Real crowding out/in refers to the substitution/complementary relationship between public and private spending that occur irrespective of the mode of financing of fiscal deficit. In other words, real crowding out occurs when public investment displaces private investment broadly on a *dollar-for-dollar* basis (Blinder and Solow, 1973). Financial (indirect) crowding out occurs as the consequences of government actions that affect private sector behaviour via changes in the rate of interest. Thus, the taxonomy of crowding out suggested that high fiscal deficit is affecting capital formation in the economy both by reducing private investment through increase in public sector's own investment and also through an increase in the rate of interest arising out of high fiscal deficit. The investment vacuum, if any, created by fiscal deficit would depend on the nature of relationship between private and public investment.

We specified a model for private investment focusing on fiscal policy and tried to derive an explicit relationship between public and private investment. The AVAR results suggest that there is crowding in rather than crowding out in India. One of the plausible reasons for no crowding out could be the increase in the financial resources raised through capital markets, which give an indication that private corporate sector on the aggregate, did not face any shortage in the availability of investible resources. The interest rate sensitivity of private investment itself does not indicate *financial* crowding out. The evidence for *financial* crowding out can only be established after checking whether real rates of interest rise is induced by fiscal deficit. This is because ad hoc configurations of demand for and supply of loanable funds in the market are affected by various factors and these factors may have their respective role in the determination of the rate of interest. But from the perspective of *financial* crowding out hypothesis, what is relevant is the extent to which the rate of interest rise is induced by the fiscal deficit.

Based on a theoretical model (Sargent, 1969) we have estimated the relationship between fiscal deficit and rate of interest in a multivariate framework. Using the asymmetric VAR estimates, we have found no evidence of *financial* crowding out for both administered and deregulated interest rate regime. No evidence of relationship between fiscal deficit and rate of interest was found in both the regime, which is quite contrary to the popular belief that increase in fiscal deficit induces the rate of interest. The 91-day treasury bill rate adjusted for inflationary expectations is selected as the reference rate and analysed the link between the two. The PLR was also considered for the analysis, the overwhelming conclusion drawn from both the analysis is that rate of interest is affected by inflationary expectations.

The impact of fiscal deficit on seigniorage and the conduct of monetary policy is analysed. Though the prime channel through which fiscal deficit affects the conduct of monetary policy is seigniorage; it is to be noted that even if a positive functional relationship exists between seigniorage and fiscal deficit, it does not naturally ensure a link between deficit and money supply. As a prelude to the analysis of interlinkages between fiscal deficit, seigniorage and inflation, we have estimated the revenue generated by the government through seigniorage and also inflation tax. The estimates showed that seigniorage revenue as a percentage of GDP has shown fluctuations. However, the potential question arises whether fiscal deficit itself is inflationary. It should be noted that apart from the generally agreed principle of increased money supply leading to higher rates of inflation, it is also argued that fiscal deficit contributes directly to inflationary pressures. The recent *fiscal theories of price determination* argued that the problems of price level indeterminacy can be solved if the central bank peg the nominal interest rate at a level consistent with the central bank's desired inflation rate, rather than by controlling the growth of (base) money supply. It is also to be noted that the fiscal policy has enormous influence on the price level because the central bank is forced to accommodate fiscal tendencies.

Against the backdrop of analysis in this study, the important question is *Unpleasant Monetarist Arithmetic* or a switching over to *Unpleasant Fiscal Arithmetic* an appropriate policy step. Unpleasant Fiscal Arithmetic visualise to reverse the order of adjustment as assumed in Unpleasant Monetarist Arithmetic, that is to transfer the first mover advantage from fiscal agencies to the monetary authorities by introducing strict fiscal policy rules, through which fiscal agencies are obliged to adjust to the anti-inflationary policies of the independent central bank. Thus, central bank autonomy is at the heart of Unpleasant Fiscal Arithmetic. While the Unpleasant Monetary Arithmetic envisages a *fiscal dominance* with bond financing as the predominant source of financing the deficit, the eventual monetisation of deficits happens under this UMA regime only if debt is found unsustainable. The recent agreement between Government of India and central bank in March 2015 towards CBI and inflation targeting is a consensus towards Unpleasant Fiscal Arithmetic regime. There is a tilt in the power equations towards monetary independence from the existing fiscal dominance regime. Given that fiscal deficit per se has no adverse macroeconomic consequences, has the move from discretion to rules—both fiscal rules and inflation targeting rules—been a transformation of macroeconomic policies towards an New Macroeconomic Consensus in India?

Bibliography

Adams, C. and D.T. Coe. 1990. 'A Systems Approach to Estimating the Natural Rate of Unemployment and Potential Output for the United States'. *IMF Staff Papers*, 37(2): 232–93.
Agenor, R.P. and P.J. Montiel. 1996. *Development Macroeconomics*. Princeton, NJ: Princeton University Press.
Aghion, P., I. Marinescu, R.J. Caballero and A.K. Kashyap. 2007. 'Cyclical Budgetary Policy and Economic Growth: What Do We Learn from OECD Panel Data?' *NBER Macroeconomics Annual*, 22: 251–93 and 295–97.
Aghveli, B.B. 1977. 'Inflationary Finance and Economic Growth'. *Journal of Political Economy*, 85: 1295–307.
Aghveli, B.B. and M.S. Khan. 1977. 'Inflationary Finance and Dynamics of Inflation: Indonesia 1951–72'. *The American Economic Review*, 67: 390–403.
———. 1978. 'Government Deficits and the Inflationary Process in Developing Countries'. *IMF Staff Papers*, 25(3): 383–415.
Ahamad, M. 1994. 'The Effects of Government Budget Deficits on Interest Rates: A Case Study of a Small Open Economy'. *Economia Internazionale*, 47(1): 1–6.
Ahking, F.W. and S.M. Miller. 1985. 'The Relationship between Government Deficits, Money Growth and Inflation'. *Journal of Macroeconomics*, 7(4): 447–67.
Ahluwaliah, I.J. 1979. *Behaviour of Prices and Output in India: A Macroeconometric Approach*. Delhi: Macmillan.
Akaike, H. 1969. 'Fitting Autoregressive Models for Prediction'. *Annals of the Institute of Statistical Mathematics*, 21(2): 243–47.
Alesina, A. and R. Perotti. 1995. 'The Political Economy of Budget Deficits'. *IMF Staff Papers*, 42(1): 1–31.
Alesina, A., R. Perotti and J. Tavares. 1998. 'The Political Economy of Fiscal Adjustments'. *Brookings Papers on Economic Activity*, 1(1): 197–248.
Alesina, A., S. Ardagna, R. Perotti and F. Schiantarelli. 2002. 'Fiscal Policy, Profits and Investment'. *The American Economic Review*, 92(3): 571–89.
Alexandre, F., J. Driffill and F. Spagnolo. 2002. 'Inflation Targeting, Exchange Rate Volatility and International Policy Coordination'. *The Manchester School*, 70(4): 546–69.
Allen, S.D. and D.L. McCrickard. 1988. 'Deficits and Money Growth in the United States: A Comment'. *Journal of Monetary Economics*, 21(1): 143–53.
Allen, S.D. and M.L. Smith. 1983. 'Government Borrowing and Monetary Accommodation'. *Journal of Monetary Economics*, 21(4): 605–16.
Arango, S. and M.I. Nadiri. 1981. 'Demand for Money in Open Economies'. *Journal of Monetary Economics*, 7(1): 69–83.
Arestis, P. 2009. 'New Consensus Macroeconomics: A Critical Appraisal'. Economics Working Paper Archive_564, New York: The Levy Institute of Bard College.

Arestis, P. and M. Sawyer. 2008. 'A Critical Reconsideration of the Foundations of Monetary Policy in the New Consensus Macroeconomics Framework'. *Cambridge Journal of Economics*, 32(5): 761–79.
Aschauer, D.A. 1989. 'Does Public Capital Crowd Out Private Capital'. *Journal of Monetary Economics*, 24(2): 171–88.
Auerbach, A.J. (ed.). 1997. *Fiscal Policy: Lessons from Economic Research*. Cambridge, MA and London: The MIT Press.
Auernheimer, L. 1974. 'The Honest Government's Guide to the Revenue from the Creation of Money'. *Journal of Political Economy*, 92(3): 598–606.
Baba, Y., D.F. Hendry and M.S. Ross. 1992. 'The Demand for M1 in the USA, 1960–1988'. *Review of Economic Studies*, 59(1): 25–61.
Bagchi, A. 2001. 'Perspectives on Correcting Fiscal Imbalance in the Indian Economy: Some Comments'. *ICRA Bulletin Money and Finance* (January–June): 76–89.
Bagchi, A. and N. Stern. 1994. *Tax Policy and Planning in Developing Countries*. New Delhi: Oxford University Press.
Bailey, M.J. 1956. 'The Welfare Cost of Inflationary Finance'. *Journal of Political Economy*, 64(2): 788–802.
Balakrishnan, P. 1991. *Pricing and Inflation in India*. New Delhi: Oxford University Press.
Balakrishnan, P., K.S. Rao and B.P. Vani. 1994. 'The Determinants of Inflation in India: Bayesian and Classical Analyses'. *Journal of Quantitative Economics*, 10(2): 325–36.
Balkan, E. and U. Balkan. 1995. 'Country Risk and International Portfolio Diversification'. *EconomiaInternazionale*, 48(1): 1–12.
Banerjee, A., J. Dolado, W. Galbrith and D.F. Henry. 1994. *Cointegration, Error Correction and the Econometric Analysis of Non-Stationary Data*. Oxford: Oxford University Press.
Barnhart, S.W. and A.F. Darrat. 1988. 'Budget Deficits, Money Growth and Causality: Further OECD Evidence'. *Journal of International Money and Finance*, 7(2): 231–42.
Barro, R.J. 1974. 'Are Government Bonds Net Wealth?' *Journal of Political Economy*, 82(6): 1095–117.
———. 1977. 'Unanticipated Money Growth and Unemployment in the United States'. *The American Economic Review*, 67(2): 101–15.
———. 1978. 'Comment from an Unreconstructed Ricardian'. *Journal of Monetary Economics*, 4 (3): 569–81.
Barro, R.J. and X. Sala-i-Martin. 1990. 'World Real Interest Rates'. In *NBER Macroeconomics Annual*, edited by O. J. Blanchard and S. Fischer. Cambridge, MA: MIT Press.
Baxter, M. and R.G. King. 1993. 'Fiscal Policy in General Equilibrium'. *The American Economic Review*, 83 (3): 315–34.
Bayomi, T. and C. Towe. 1998. 'Macroeconomic Developments and Prospects'. IMF Staff Country Report No. 98/113. Washington, D.C.: International Monetary Fund.
Belongia, M.T. 1996. 'Measurement Matters: Recent Results from Monetary Economics Reexamined'. *Journal of Political Economy*, 104 (5): 1065–83.
Berheim, B.D. 1989. 'A Neo-classical Perspective on Budget Deficits'. *Journal of Economic Perspectives*, 3(2): 55–71.
Bernanke, B.S. and F.S. Mishkin. 1997. 'Inflation Targeting: A New Framework for Monetary Policy?'. NBER Working Paper No. 5893. Cambridge, MA: NBER.
Berndt, Antje, Hanno Lustig and Şevin Yeltekin. 2012, January. 'How Does the US Government Finance Fiscal Shocks?' *American Economic Journal: Macroeconomics*, 4 (1): 69–104.

Bhalla, S.S. 1981. 'The Transmission of Inflation into Developing Economies'. In *World Inflation and the Developing Countries*, edited by W.R. Cline and Associates. Washington, D.C.: The Brookings Institution.

Bhattacharya, B.B. 1984. *Public Expenditure, Inflation and Growth: A Macroeconometric Analysis for India*. New Delhi: Oxford University Press.

Bhattacharya, B.B. and M. Lodh. 1990. 'Inflation in India: An Analytical Survey'. *ArthaVijnana*, 32(1): 25–68.

Blanchard, O.J. 1985. 'Debt, Deficits, and Finite Horizons'. In *Fiscal and Monetary Policy* (Volume 1), edited by T. Mayer and S.M. Sheffrin. Aldershot: International Library of Critical Writings in Economics.

Blanchard, O.J. and S. Fischer. 1989. *Lectures on Macroeconomics*. Cambridge, MA: The MIT Press.

Blanchard, O.J. and R. Perotti. 1999. 'An Empirical Investigation of the Dynamic Effects of Changes in Government Spending and Revenues on Output'. Working Paper No. 7269, National Bureau of Economic Research, Cambridge, MA.

Blejer, M.I. 1978. 'Black Market Exchange Rate Expectations and the Domestic Demand for Money: Some Empirical Results'. *Journal of Monetary Economics*, 4(4): 768–74.

Blejer, M.I. and Adrienne Cheasty. 1991. 'The Measurement of Fiscal Deficits: Analytical and Methodological Issues'. *Journal of Economic Literature*, 29 (4): 1644–78.

———. 1993. '*How to Measure the Fiscal Deficit*'. Washington, D.C.: International Monetary Fund.

Blejer, M.I. and K.Y. Chu. 1988. 'Measurement of Fiscal Impact: Methodological Issues'. IMF Occasional Paper No. 59, International Monetary Fund, Washington, D.C.

Blejer, M.I. and M.S. Khan. 1984. 'Government Policy and Private Investment in Developing Countries'. *IMF Staff Papers*, 31(2): 379–403.

Blinder, A.S. and R. Solow. 1973. 'Does Fiscal Policy Matter'? *Journal of Public Economics*, 2(4): 319–37.

———. 1974. 'Analytical Foundations of Fiscal Policy'. In *The Economics of Public Finance*, edited by A.S. Blinder, Robert M. Solow, George F. Break, Peter O. Steiner and Dick Netzer. Washington, D.C.: Brookings Institution.

Borpujari, J. and T.M. Teresa. 1973. 'The Weighted Budget Balance Approach to Fiscal Analysis: A Methodology and Some Case Studies'. *IMF Staff Paper*, 20(3): 801–31.

Boskin, M.J. 1982. 'Federal Government Deficits: Some Myths and Realities'. *The American Economic Review*, 72(2): 296–303.

———. 1988. 'Concepts and Measures of Federal Deficits and Debt and Their Impact on Economic Activity'. In *The Economics of Public Debt*, edited by K.J. Arrowand M.J. Boskin. New York: St. Martin Press.

Boughton, J.M. 1984. 'Exchange Rate Movements and Adjustment in Financial Markets: Quarterly Estimates for Major Currencies'. *IMF Staff Papers*, 31(3): 445–68.

Brainard, W.C. and J. Tobin.1968. 'Pitfalls in Financial Model-building'. *The American Economic Review*, 58(2): 99–122.

Brumm, H.J. 2000. 'Inflation and Central Bank Independence: Conventional Wisdom Redux'. *Journal of Money, Credit and Banking*, 32(4): 807–19.

Bruno, M. and W. Easterly. 1996. 'Inflation's Children: Tales of Crises that Beget Reforms'. *The American Economic Review*, 86(2): 213–17.

———. 1998. 'Inflation Crises and Long-run Growth'. *Journal of Monetary Economics* 41(1): 3–26.

Bruno, M. and S. Fischer. 1990. 'Seigniorage, Operating Rules and the High Inflation Trap'. *Quarterly Journal of Economics*, 105(2): 353–74.
Buchanan, J.M. 1958. *'Public Principles of the Public Debt'*. Illinois: Homewood.
———. 1976. 'Barro on the Ricardian Equivalence Theorem'. *Journal of Political Economy*, 84(2): 337–42.
Buchanan, J.M. and R.E. Wagner. 1977. *Democracy in Deficit: The Policy Legacy of Lord Keynes*. New York: Academic Press.
Buiter, W.H. 1977. 'Crowding Out and the Effectiveness of Fiscal Policy'. *Journal of Public Economics*, 7(3): 309–28.
Buiter, W.H. 1990. *Principles of Budgetary and Financial Policy*. New York: Harvester Wheatsheafhm.
———. 1999. 'The fallacy of the fiscal theory of the price level'. Working Paper No. 7302, National Bureau of Economic Research.
———. 2007. 'Seigniorage'.Working Paper No. 12919, National Bureau of Economic Research. Cambridge, MA: NBER.
Burnside, C., M. Eichenbaum and J.D.M. Fischer. 2000. 'Assessing the Effects of Fiscal Shocks'.Working Paper No. 7459, National Bureau of Economic Research. Cambridge, MA: NBER.
Cagan, P. 1956. 'The Monetary Dynamics of Hyperinflation'. In *Studies in the Quantity Theory of Money*, edited by M. Friedman. Chicago, IL: University of Chicago Press.
———. 1972. 'The Channel of Monetary Effects on Interest Rates'. NBER General Series Working Paper No. 97. London: Columbia University Press.
Caines, K.C., W. Keng and S.P. Sethi. 1981. 'Causality Analysis and Multivariate Autoregressive Modeling with an Application to Supermarket Sales Analysis'. *Journal of Economic Dynamics and Control*, 3(3): 267–98.
Calvo, G. and M. King. 1998. *The Debt Burden and its Consequences for Monetary Policy*, Proceedings of a Conference held by International Economic Association at the Deutsche Bundesbank, Frankfurt, Germany.
Cargil, T.F. and R.A. Meyer.1981. 'Revealed Preferences in Macroeconomic Policy Decisions'. *Journal of Macroeconomics*, 3(2): 205–26.
Carlson, A.J. 1977. 'Short-term Rates as Predictors of Inflation: Comment'. *The American Economic Review*, 67(3): 469–75.
Carlson, J.B., D.L. Hoffman, B.D. Keen and R.H. Rasche. 2000. 'Results of a Study of the Stability of Cointegrating Relations Comprised of Broad Monetary Aggregates'. *Journal of Monetary Economics*, 46(2): 365–83.
Carson, S., E. Charles and D. Claudia. 2002. *Statistical Implications of Inflation Targeting: Getting the Right Numbers and Getting the Numbers Right*. Washington, D.C.: Statistics Department, International Monetary Fund.
Catao, L.a.V. and M.E. Terrones. 2005. 'Fiscal deficits and inflation'. *Journal of Monetary Economics*, 52(3): 529–54.
Cebula, R.J. 1978. 'An Empirical Analysis of the "Crowding Out" Effect of Fiscal Policy in the United States and Canada'. *Kyklos*, 3(3): 424–36.
———. 1988. 'Federal Government Deficits and Interest Rates: An Empirical Analysis of United States, 1955–1984'. *Public Finance*, 43(3): 206–10.
———. 1990. 'Federal Government Borrowing and Interest Rates in United States: An Empirical Analysis Using IS-LM Framework'. *EconomiaInternationale*, 43(2): 159–64.
———. 1997a. 'Structural Budget Deficits and the Ex Ante Real Long Term Interest Rate: An Analysis of the Direction of Causality'. *Public Finance*, 52(1): 36–49.

Cebula, R.J. 1997b. 'The Impact of Federal Budget Deficits on Long-term Nominal Interest Rates in the U.S.: New Evidence and an Updating Using Cointegration and Granger-causality Tests, 1973.2–1993.3'. *EconomiaInternazionale*, 50(1): 49–60.

Central Statistical Organisation. 2001. *National Accounts Statistics Back Series: 1950–51 to 1996–97*. Ministry of Statistics and Programme Implementation, Government of India. New Delhi: CSO, Ministry of Statistics and Programme Implementation.

———. 2001. *National Accounts Statistics 2001*. Ministry of Statistics and Programme Implementation, Government of India. New Delhi: CSO, Ministry of Statistics and Programme Implementation.

Chakraborty, Lekha. 2002. 'Fiscal Deficit and Rate of Interest Link in India: An Econometric Analysis of Deregulated Financial Regime'. *Economic and Political Weekly*, 37(19): 1831–38.

———. 2006. 'Fiscal Deficit and Selected Rates of Interest Link in India: An Analysis of Period between 1970–71 and 1999–2000'. In *State Level Fiscal Reforms in the Indian Economy* (Volume 1), edited by D.K. Srivastava and M. Narasimhulu. New Delhi: Deep and Deep.

———. 2007. 'Fiscal Deficit, Capital Formation and Crowding Out in India: Evidence from an Asymmetric VAR Model'. Economics Working Paper Archive, Levy Economics Institute.

———. 2008. 'Analyzing Raghuram Rajan Committee Report on Financial Sector Reforms'. *Economic and Political Weekly*, 43(25): 11–14.

———. 2012. 'Interest Rate Determination in India: Empirical Evidence from Fiscal Deficit-rate of Interest Linkages and Financial Crowding Out' Working Paper 110, National Institute of Public Finance and Policy, New Delhi (also published as Working Paper No. 731, The Levy Economics Institute, New York).

Chakraborty, Pinaki. Forthcoming. 'Federalism Fiscal Space and Public Investment Spending: Does Fiscal Rule Impose Hard Budget Constraints?' ADBI Working Paper, Japan: Asian Development Bank Institute.

Chakraborty, Pinaki and B.B. Dash. 2013. 'Fiscal Reforms, Fiscal Rule and Development Spending: How Indian States have Performed?' National Institute of Public Finance and Policy Working Paper: 2013-122.

Chakraborty, Pinaki and Lekha Chakraborty. 2008. 'Is Fiscal Policy Contra Cyclical in India: An Empirical Analysis' (co-authored), in *Policy Innovations*. New York: The Carnegie Council (also published as MPRA Working Paper No. 7604, Munich University, Munich).

Chakravarty, S. 1977. *Behaviour of Prices in India: 1952–1970*. New Delhi: The Macmillan Company of India Limited.

———. 1987. *Development Planning: The Indian Experience*. Oxford: Clarendon Press.

Chambers, M.J. and R.E. Bailey.1996. 'A Theory of Commodity Price Fluctuations'. *Journal of Political Economy*, 104(5): 924–57.

Christ, C. 1979. 'On Fiscal and Monetary Policies and the Government Budget Restraint'. *The American Economic Review*, 69(4): 526–38.

Christiano, L.J. 1981.'A Survey of Measures of Capacity Utilization'. *IMF Staff Papers* 28(1): 144–29.

Clarida, R., J. Gali and M. Gertler. 1999. 'The Science of Monetary Policy: A New Keynesian Perspective'. *Journal of Economic Literature*, 37(2): 1661–707.

Clark, J.M. 1917. 'Business Acceleration and the Law of Demand: A Technical Factor in Economic Cycles'. *Journal of Political Economy*, 25(3): 217–35.

Clark, P.K. 1979. 'Investment in the 1970s: Theory, Performance and Prediction'. *Brookings Papers on Economic Activity*, 1(1): 73–124.
Claude, G., P. Richardson, D. Roseveare and P. Van den Noord. 1995. 'Potential Output, Output Gaps and Structural Budget Balances'. *OECD Economic Studies*, 24: 167–209.
Cochrane, J.H. 1998a. 'What Do the VARs Mean? Measuring the Output Effects of Monetary Policy'. *Journal of Monetary Economics*, 41(2): 277–300.
———. 1998b. 'A Frictionless View of US Inflation'. In *NBER Macroeconomics Annual*, edited by B. Bernanke and J. J. Rotemberg. Cambridge, MA: MIT Press.
Collignon, S. 2012. 'Fiscal Policy Rules and the Sustainability of Public Debt in Europe'. *International Economic Review*, 53 (2, May), 539–67.
Congdon, T. 1998. 'Did Britain Ever hada Keynesian Revolution'. In *Debt and Deficits: A Historical Perspective*, edited by J. Maloney. Cheltenham, UK: Edward Elgar.
———. 1998. 'Did Britain Have a Keynesian Revolution? Fiscal Policy Since 1941'. In *Debt and Deficits: An Historical Perspective*, edited by J. Maloney. Cheltenham, UK: Edward Elgar.
Corden, W.M. 1988a. 'Debt Relief and Adjustment Incentives'. *IMF Staff Papers*, 35(4): 628–43.
———. 1988b. 'An International Debt Facility?' *IMF Staff Papers*, 35(3): 401–21.
Correia, N.J. and L. Stemitsiotis. 1995. 'Budget Deficit and Interest Rates: Is There a Link? International Evidence'. *Oxford Bulletin of Economics and Statistics*, 57(4): 425–49.
Correia, I., J. C. Neves and S. T Rebelo. 1995. 'Business Cycles in a Small Open Economy', *European Economic Review*, 39: 1089–13.
Cottrell, A. 1994. 'Endogenous Money and the Multiplier'. *Journal of Post Keynesian Economics*, 17(1): 111–20.
Crosby, M. 1998. 'Central Bank Independence and Output Variability'. *Economic Letters*, 60(1): 67–75.
Dalamagas, B.A. 1987. 'Government Deficits, Crowding Out, and Inflation: Some International Evidence'. *Public Finance*, 42(1): 65–84.
Dalton, H. 1954. *Principles of Public Finance* (Fourth Edition). London: Routledge and Kegan Paul.
Darby, M. 1984. 'Some Unpleasant Monetarist Arithmetic'. *Quarterly Review Federal Reserve*, 9(1): 15–20.
Darrat, A.F. 1986. 'Money, Inflation and Causality in the North African Countries: An Empirical Investigation'. *Journal of Macroeconomics*, 8(1): 87–103.
deHaan, J. and D. Zelhorst. 1990. 'Financial-market Effects of Federal Government Budget Deficits: Comment'. *Weltwirtschaftliches Archiv*, 126(2): 388–92.
Delong, J. Bradford, H. Summers Lawrence, Martin Feldstein and Valerie A. Ramey. 2012. 'Fiscal Policy in a Depressed Economy'. *Brookings Papers on Economic Activity*, Spring 44(1): 233–97.
Demopoulas, G., D. Katsimbris, M. George and S.M. Miller. 1987. 'Monetary Policy and the Central Bank Financing of Government Budget Deficits: A Cross Country Comparison'. *European Economic Review*, 31(5): 1023–50.
Diamond, P. 1965. 'National Debt in a Neoclassical Growth Model'. *The American Economic Review*, 55(5): 1126–50.
Dickey, D.A. and W.A. Fuller. 1981. 'The Likelihood Ratio Statistics for Autoregressive Time Series with a Unit-root'. *Econometrica*, 49(4): 1057–72.
Dickey, D.A., D.W. Jansen and D.L. Thornton. 1994. 'A Primer on Cointegration with an Application to Money and Income'. In *Cointegration for Applied Economist*, edited by B.B. Rao. London: The Macmillan Press Ltd.

Dixit, A. and R. Pindyk. 1994. *Investment Under Uncertainty*. Princeton, NJ: Princeton University Press.
Dolmas, J., G. Huffman and M.A. Wynne. 2000. 'Inequality, Inflation, and Central Bank Independence'. *Canadian Journal of Economics*, 33(1): 271–87.
Dornbusch, R. 1986. *Dollar, Debts and Deficits*. Cambridge, MA: MIT Press.
———. 1988. 'Doubts about the McKinnon Standard'. *Journal of Economic Perspectives*, 2(1): 105–12.
———. 1998. 'Debt and Monetary Policy: The Policy Issues'. In *The Debt Burden and Its Consequences for Monetary Policy*, edited by G. Calvo and K. Mervyn; Proceedings of a conference held by the International Economic Association at the Deutsche Bundesbank, Frankfurt, Germany.
Dornbusch, R. and S. Fischer. 1981. 'Budget Deficits and Inflation'. In *Development in an Inflationary World*, edited by J. Flanders and A. Razin. New York: Academic Press.
———. 1990. *Macroeconomics* (Fifth Edition). Singapore: McGraw Hill.
———. 1999. *Macroeconomics*. Singapore: Tata McGraw Hill.
Doyle, C. and M. Weale. 1994. 'Do We Really Want an Independent Central Bank?' *Oxford Review of Economic Policy*, 10(3): 61–77.
Driscoll, M.J. and A.K. Lahiri. 1983. 'Income Velocity of Money in Agricultural Developing Economies'. *Review of Economics and Statistics*, 65(4): 393–401.
Dua, Pami and Upasna Gaur. 2009. 'Determinants of Inflation in an Open Economy Phillips Curve Framework: The Case of Developed and Developing Asian Countries'. Working Paper No. 178. Delhi: Centre for Development Economics, Delhi School of Economics.
Duck, N.W. 1993. 'Some International Evidence on the Quantity Theory of Money'. *Journal of Money, Credit and Banking*, 25(1): 1–12.
Dunning, J.H. 1979. 'In Defence of the Eclectic Theory'. *Oxford Bulletin of Economics and Statistics*, 41(4): 269–95.
Dutkowsky, D.H. and H.S. Atesoglu. 2001. 'The Demand for Money: A Structural Econometric Investigation'. *Southern Economic Journal*, 68(1): 92–106.
Dutton, D.S. 1971. 'A Model of Self-Generating Inflation: The Argentine Case'. *Journal of Money, Credit and Banking*, 3(2): 245–62.
Dwyer, G. 1982. 'Inflation and Government Deficits'. *Economic Enquiry*, 20(3): 315–29.
Easterly, W. and K. Schimdt-Hebbel. 1993. 'Fiscal Deficits and Macroeconomic Performance in Developing Countries'. *The World Bank Research Observer*, 8(2): 211–37.
Easterly, W., A. Rodriguez and K. Schmidt-Hebbel (eds.) 1994. *Public Sector Deficits and Macroeconomic Performance*. Oxford and New York: Oxford University Press for the World Bank.
Eatwell, J., Murray Milgate and Peter Newman. 1999. *The New Palgrave Dictionary on Money*. London, New York: The Macmillan Press.
———.1996. 'And Now the Primary Deficit'. Editorial Note. *Economic and Political Weekly*, 31(11): 635–36.
Eggertsson, G.B. and B. Gauti. 2011. 'What Fiscal Policy Is Effective at Zero Interest Rates?' *NBER Macroeconomics Annual*, 25 (1, January): 59–112.
Eisner R. and P.J. Pieper. 1984. 'A New View of the Federal Debt and Budget Deficits'. *The American Economic Review*, 74(1): 11–29.
Enders, W. 1995. *Applied Econometric Time Series*. New York: John Wiley and Sons, Inc.
Engle, R.F. and C.W.J. Granger. 1987. 'Co-integration and Error Correction: Representation, Estimation, and Testing'. *Econometrica*, 55(2): 251–76.
EPW Research Foundation. 1997. 'National Accounts Statistics of India: 1950–51 to 1995–96'. *Economic and Political Weekly*.

Erenburg, S.J. 1993. 'The Real Effects of Public Investment on Private Investment'. *Applied Economics*, 25(6): 831–37.
Erenburg, S.J. and M.E. Wohar. 1995. 'Public and Private Investment: Are There Causal Linkages?' *Journal of Macroeconomics*, 17(1): 1–30.
Epstein, G. 2006. 'Central Banks as Agents of Economic Development. UNU-WIDER Research Paper No. 2006/54. Helsinki: UNU/Wider.
Epstein, G. and E. Yeldan. 2008. 'Inflation targeting, employment creation and economic development: assessing the impacts and policy alternatives'. *International Review of Applied Economics*, 22(2): 131–44.
Estrella, A. and F.S. Mishkin. 1997. 'Is There a Role for Monetary Aggregates in the Conduct of Monetary Policy?'. *Journal of Monetary Economics*, 40(2): 279–304.
Evans, P. 1985. 'Do Large Deficits Produce High Interest Rates?' *The American Economic Review*, 75(1): 68–87.
Evans, J. and G. Yarrow. 1981. 'Some Implications of Alternative Expectation Hypothesis in the Monetary Analysis of Hyperinflation'. *Oxford Economic Papers*, 33(1): 61–80.
Faini, Riccardo, Duranton Gilles and Hau Harald. 2006. 'Fiscal Policy and Interest Rates in Europe'. *Economic Policy*, 21 (47, July): 443, 445–89.
Fama, E. 1975. 'Short-term Rates as Predictors of Inflation'. *The American Economic Review*, 65(3): 269–82.
Faraglia,Elisa, Albert Marcet and Andrew Scott. 2008, March. 'Fiscal Insurance and Debt Management in OECD Economies'. The Economic Journal, 118(527): 363–86.
Feldstein, A. 1984. 'Financial Crowding Out: The Theory with Application to Australia'. *IMF Staff Papers*, 33(1): 60–90.
Feldstein, Martin. 2002. 'Economic and Financial Crises in Emerging Market Economies: Overview of Prevention and Management'. NBER Working Paper No. 8837, National Bureau of Economic Research, Inc. Chicago and London: University of Chicago Press.
———. 1976. 'Inflation, Income Taxes and Interest Rates: A Theoretical Analysis'. *The American Economic Review*, 66(5): 809–20.
———. 1988. 'Thinking about International Economic Coordination'. *Journal of Economic Perspectives*, 2(2): 3–14.
———.2009a.'Rethinking the Role of Fiscal Policy'. *The American Economic Review*, 99 (2, May): 556–59.
———. 2009b. 'Rethinking the Role of Fiscal Policy'. NBER Working Papers No. 14684, National Bureau of Economic Research, Inc. Cambridge MA: NBER.
Feldstein, M. and O.H. Eckstein. 1970. 'The Fundamental Determinants of the Interest Rate'. *Review of Economics and Statistics*, 52 (4): 363–75.
Fisher, I. 1930. *The Theory of Interest*. New York: McMillan.
Fischer, S. 1977. 'Long-term Contracts, Rational Expectations and the Optimal Money Supply Rule'. *Journal of Political Economy*, 85 (1): 191–205.
———. 1981. 'Relative Shocks, Relative Price Variability, and Inflation'. *Brookings Paper on Economic Activity*, 2 (2): 381–431.
———. 1982. 'Seigniorage and the Case for a National Money'. *Journal of Political Economy*, 90 (2): 295–313.
Forder, J. 1999. 'Central Bank Independence: Reassessing the Measurements'. *Journal of Economic Issues*, 33 (1): 23–40.
Frenkel, J. 1977. 'The Forward Exchange Rate, Expectations and the Demand for Money: The German Hyperinflation'. *The American Economic Review*, 67 (4): 653–70.

Friedman, B.M. 1978. 'Crowding Out or Crowding In?: Economic Consequences of Financing Government Deficits'. *Brooking Papers on Economic Activity*, 9(3): 593–654.
———. 1988. 'Lessons on Monetary Policy from the 1980s'. *Journal of Economic Perspectives*, 2(3): 51–72.
Friedman, M. and A. Schwartz. 1963. *A Monetary History of the United States, 1867–1960*. Princeton, N.J.: Princeton University Press.
Friedman, B.M. and K.N. Kuttner. 1993.'Another Look at the Evidence on Money Income Causality'. *Journal of Econometrics*, 57(1–3): 279–304.
———. 1942. 'Discussion on the Inflationary Gap'. *The American Economic Review*, 32(2): 308–14; Reprint. *Essays in the Positive Economics*, University of Chicago Press.
———. 1968. 'The Role of monetary policy'. *The American Economic Review*, 58(1): 1–7.
Friedman, M. (ed.). 1968. 'Inflation: Causes and Consequences'. In *Dollars and Deficits*. Englewood Cliffs, NJ: Prentice Hall.
———. 1971. 'Government Revenue from Inflation'. *Journal of Political Economy*, 79(4): 846–56.
Friedman, M. and R.D. Friedman. 1980. *Free to Choose*. New York: Harcourt Brace Jovanovich.
Friedman, M. and A.J. Schwartz. 1982. *Monetary trends in UK and US: Their Relation to Income, Prices and Interest Rates: 1867–1975*.Chicago, IL: University of Chicago Press for the National Bureau of Economic Research.
Fry, M.J. 1980. 'Money, Inflation and Growth in Turkey'. *Journal of Monetary Economics*, 6(4): 535–45.
Fry, M., D. Julius, L. Mahadeva, S. Roger and G. Sterne. 2000. 'Key Issues in the Choice of Monetary Policy Framework'. In *Monetary Frameworks in a Global Context* L. Mahadeva and G. Sterne. London: Routledge.
Fuller, W. A. 1976. *Introduction to Statistical Time Series*. New York: Wiley and Sons.
Fullwiler, Scott T. 2007. 'Interest Rates and Fiscal Sustainability'. *Journal of Economic Issues*, 41 (4 December): 1003–42.
Gale, William G. and Peter R. Orszag. 17 December 2002. 'The Economic Effects of Long-Term Fiscal Discipline'. Urban-Brookings Tax Policy Center Discussion Paper.
Gali, J. and M. Gertler. 1999. 'Inflation Dynamics: A Structural Econometric Analysis'. *Journal of Monetary Economics*, 44(2): 195–222.
Genberg, H., M.K. Salemi and A. Swoboda.1987. 'The Relative Importance of Foreign and Domestic Disturbances for Aggregate Fluctuations in the Open Economy, Switzerland: 1964–1981'. *Journal of Monetary Economics*, 19(1): 45–67.
Giannitsarou, Chryssi, Andrew Scott, and Eric M. Leeper. 2006. 'Inflation Implications of Rising Government Debt'. *NBER International Seminar on Macroeconomics*, 393–439.
Giavazzi, F, and M. Pagano. 1990. 'Can Severe Fiscal Contractions be Expansionary? Tales of two Small European Countries'. In *NBER Macroeconomics Annual* 1990, edited by O.J. Blanchard and S. Fischer. Cambridge, MA: MIT Press.
Giavazzi, F., T. Jappelli and M. Pagano.2000. 'Searching for Non-linear Effects of Fiscal Policy: Evidence from Industrial and Developing Countries'. *European Economic Review*, 44(7): 1259–89.
Gibson, W.E. 1970. 'Price Expectations Effects on Interest Rates'. *Journal of Finance*, 25(1): 19–34.
Giorno, C., P. Richardson and P. Van den Noord. 1995. 'Estimating Potential Output, Output Gaps and Structural Budget Balances'. OECD Economics Department Working Paper 24, Paris.

Girton, L. and D. Nattress. 1985. 'Monetary Innovations and Interest Rates'. *Journal of Money, Credit, and Banking*, 17(3): 289–97.
Gonzalo, J. 1994. 'Five Alternative Methods of Estimating Long-run Relationships'. *Journal of Econometrics*, 60(1–2): 203–33.
Goodhart, C. 1989. 'Has Moore Become Too Horizontal?' *Journal of Post Keynesian Economics*, 12(1): 29–34.
Government of India. 2001a. *Prime Minister's Economic Advisory Council Report*. New Delhi.
Government of India. 2001b. *Economic Survey*. New Delhi: Ministry of Finance.
Goyal, Rajan. 22 May 2004. 'Does Higher Fiscal Deficit Lead to Rise in Interest Rates? An Empirical Investigation'. *Economic and Political Weekly*, XXXIX(21): 2128–33.
———. 2013. 'Report of the Financial Sector Legislative Reforms Commission'. New Delhi: Government of India.
Granger, C.W.J. 1969.'Investigating Causal Relations by Econometric Models and Cross-Spectral Methods'. *Econometrica*, 37(3): 424–38.
———. 1988. 'Some Recent Developments in a Concept of Causality'. *Journal of Econometrics*, 39(1–2): 199–211.
———. 1988. 'Causality, Cointegration and Control'. *Journal of Economic Dynamics and Control*, 12(2–3): 551–59.
Granger, C.W.J. and P. Newbold. 1974. 'Spurious Regression in Econometrics'. *Journal of Econometrics*, 2(2): 111–20.
Greene, J., and V. Delano. 1990. 'Private Investment in Developing Countries: An Empirical Analysis'. IMF Working Paper No. 90/40, International Monetary Fund, Washington, D.C.
Grier, K.B. 1986. 'A Note on Unanticipated Money Growth and Interest Rate Surprises: Mishkin and Makin Revisited'. *Journal of Finance*, 41(4): 981–85.
Guhan, S. 1991. 'Fiscal Deficit and Public Enterprises'. *Economic and Political Weekly*, 26(49): 2840.
Gulati, I. S. 1991. 'Reducing the Fiscal Deficit: Soft and Hard Options'. *Economic and Political Weekly*, 26(29): 1721–22.
———. 1994. 'Calculating the Fiscal Deficit: A Note on Certain Capital Receipts'. *Economic and Political Weekly*, 29(21): 1297.
Gupta, K.L. 1984. *Finance and Economic Growth in Developing Countries*. London: Croom Helm.
———. 1990. 'Nominal vs Real Adjustment in Demand for Money Functions'. *Applied Economics*, 22(1): 5–12.
———. 1991. Dynamic Specification and the Long-run Effect of Budget Deficits on Interest Rates'. *Public Finance*, 46(2): 208–21.
———. 1992. *Budget Deficits and Economic Activity in Asia*. London: Routledge.
Gupta, K.L. and B. Moazzami. 1989. 'Demand for Money in Asia'. *Economic Modelling*, 6(4): 467–73.
———. 1996. *Interest Rate and Budget Deficit: A Study of the Advanced Economies*. Routledge Studies in Modern World Economies. London: Routledge.
Hadri, K., B. Lockwood and J. Maloney. 1998. 'Does Central Bank Independence Smooth the Political Business Cycle in Inflation? Some OECD Evidence'. *Manchester School*, 66(4): 377–95.
Hafer, R.W. and D. Jansen. 1991. 'The Demand for Money in the US: Evidence from Cointegration Tests'. *Journal of Money, Credit and Banking*, 23(2): 155–68.

Hallman, J.J., R.D. Porter and D.H. Small. 1991. 'Is Price Level tied to the M2 Monetary Aggregate in the Long-run?'. *The American Economic Review*, 81(4): 841–58.

Hamburger, M.J. 1977.'The Demand for Money in an Open Economy Germany and the United Kingdom'. *Journal of Monetary Economics*, 3(1): 25–40.

Hamburger, M.J. and B. Zwick. 1981. 'Deficits, Money and Inflation'. *Journal of Monetary Economics*, 7: 141–50.

Hansen, B. 1973. 'On the Effects of Fiscal and Monetary Policy: A Taxonomic Discussion'. *The American Economic Review*, 63(4): 546–71.

Harris, R. 1995. *Using Cointegration Analysis in Econometric Modelling*. Prentice Hall and Harvester Wheatsheaf. London; New York: Prentice Hall/Harvester Wheatsheaf.

Hasan, M. 1999. 'Monetary Growth and Inflation in China: A Re-examination'. *Journal of Comparative Economics*, 27(4): 669–85.

Havrilesky, T. and J. Granato. 1993. 'Determinants of Inflationary Performance: Corporatist Structures vs. Central Bank Autonomy'. *Public Choice*, 76(3): 249–61.

Heller, P.S. 1980. 'Impact of Inflation on Fiscal Policy in Developing Countries'. *IMF Staff Papers*, 27(4): 712–48.

Heller, P., Richard Haas and Ahsan S. Mansur. 1986. 'A Review of the Fiscal Impulse Measure'. IMF Occasional Paper No. 44. Washington, D.C: IMF.

Hendry, D., R. Engle and J.L. Richard. 1983. 'Exogeneity'. *Econometrica*, 51(2): 227–304.

Ho, M.S. and B.E. Sorensen. 1996. 'Finding Cointegration Rank in High Dimensional Systems Using the Johansen Test'. *The Review of Economics and Statistics*, 78(4): 726–32.

Hodrick, R.J. and E.C. Prescott. 1997. 'Postwar U.S. Business Cycles: An Empirical Investigation'. *Journal of Money, Credit and Banking*, 29(1): 1–16.

Hoffman, D. and H.R. Robert.1991. 'Long-run Demand and Interest Elasticities of Money Demand in the US'. *Review of Economics and Statistics*, 73(1): 665–74.

Hoffman, D.L., S.A. Low and H.H. Reinberg. 1983. 'Recent Evidence on the Relationship between Money Growth and Budget Deficits'. *Journal of Macroeconomics*, 5(2): 223–31.

Hoffman, D., H.R. Robert and M.A. Tieslau. 1995. 'The Stability of Long-run Money Demand in Five Industrial Countries'. *Journal of Monetary Economics*, 35(2): 317–39.

Hondroyiannis, G. and E. Papaetrou. 2001. 'An Investigation of the Public Deficits and Government Expenditure Relationship: Evidence for Greece'. *Public Choice*, 107(1): 169–82.

Hsiao, C. 1981. 'Autoregressive Modeling and Money Income Causality Detection'. *Journal of Monetary Economics*, 7(1): 85–106.

Hume, D. (1955) 1752a. 'Of Money'. In *Political Discourses*, edited by E. Rotwein. Reprint. Edinburgh: Nelson.

———. (1955) 1752b. 'Of Interest'. In *Political Discourses*, edited by E. Rotwein. Reprint. Edinburgh: Nelson.

Husain, A.M. 1992. 'Sovereign Debt Relief Schemes and Welfare'. IMF Working Paper WP/92/25.

International Monetary Fund. 2000. *World Economic Outlook*. Washington, D.C.: IMF.

International Monetary Fund. 2001. *World Economic Outlook*. Washington, D.C.: IMF.

Ireland, P. 1996. 'The Role of Countercyclical Monetary Policy'. *Journal of Political Economy*, 104(4): 704–21.

Iversen, T. 1999. 'The Political Economy of Inflation: Bargaining Structure or Central Bank Independence?' *Public Choice*, 101(3–4): 285–306.

Jadhav, M. 1994. *Monetary Economics for India*, Macmillan India Ltd, New Delhi.

Jasperson Z.F., H.A. Aylward and A.M. Sumlinski. 1995. 'Trends in Private Investment in Developing Countries: Statistics for 1970–94'.International Finance Corporation Discussion Paper Number No. 28, World Bank, Washington, D.C.
Jean-Louis, Combes, Xavier Debrun, Alexandru Minea and René Tapsoba. 2014. 'Inflation Targeting and Fiscal Rules: Do Interactions and Sequencing Matter?' IMF Working Paper No. WP/14/89. Washington, D.C: IMF.
Jha, R. 2001. 'Economic Reforms: A Decadal Stocktaking'. *Economic and Political Weekly*, 36(51): 4704–706.
Johansen, S. 1988. 'Statistical Analysis of Cointegration Vectors'. *Journal of Economic Dynamics and Control*, 12(2–3): 231–54.
Johansen, S. and K. Juselius. 1990. 'Maximum Likelihood Estimation and Inference on Cointegration—With Application to the Demand for Money'. *Oxford Bulletin of Economics and Statistics*, 52(2): 169–210.
———. 1992. 'Testing Structural Hypotheses in a Multivariate Cointegration Analysis of the PPP and the UIP for the UK'. *Journal of Econometrics*, 53(1–3): 211–44.
John, C. 1977. 'Short-term Rates as Predictors of Inflation: Comment'. *The American Economic Review*, 67(3): 469–75.
Jones, J.D. and D. Joulfaian. 1991. 'Federal Government Expenditures and Revenues in the Early Years of the American Republic: Evidence from 1792–1860'. *Journal of Macroeconomics*, 13(1): 133–55.
Jorgenson, D.W. 1963. 'Capital Theory and Investment Behaviour'. *The American Economic Review*, 53(2): 247–59.
———.1971. 'Econometric Studies on Investment Behaviour: A Survey'. *Journal of Economic Literature*, 9(4): 1111–47.
Joshua, Greene and Delano Villanueva. 1991. 'Private Investment in Developing Countries: An Empirical Analysis'. *Staff Papers (International Monetary Fund)*, 38 (1) (Mar., 1991): 33–58.
Keating, J.W. 2000. 'Macroeconomic Modeling with Asymmetric Vector Autoregression'. *Journal of Macroeconomics*, 21(1): 1–28.
Keynes, J.M. 1923. *A Tract on Monetary Reforms*. London: Macmillan.
Khan, A.H. and Z. Iqbal. 1991. 'Fiscal Deficit and Private Sector Activities in Pakistan'. *EconomiaInternationale*, 44(2–3): 182–90.
Khan, M.S. 1980. 'Monetary Shocks and the Dynamics of Inflation'. *IMF Staff Papers*, 27(2): 250–84.
Khan, M.S. and M.S. Kumar. 1997. 'Public and Private Investment and the Growth Process in Developing Countries'. *Oxford Bulletin of Economics and Statistics*, 1(2): 261–77.
Khan, M.S. and C.M. Reinhart. 1990. 'Private Investment and Economic growth in Developing Countries'. *World Development*, 18(1): 19–27.
Khundrakpam, J.K. 1996. 'Alternate Measures of Deficit and Inflation Impact'. Reserve Bank of India Occasional Papers, 17(1), March.
King, D. and Y. Ma. 2001. 'Fiscal Decentralization, Central Bank Independence, and Inflation'. *Economic Letters*, 72(1): 95–98.
Kirsanova,Tatiana, Campbell Leith, Simon Wren-Lewis 2009. 'Monetary and Fiscal Policy Interaction: The Current Consensus Assignment in the Light of Recent Developments'. *The Economic Journal*, 119 (541, November): F482–96.
Klein, R. 1975. *Inflation and Priorities*. London: Centre for Studies in Social Policy.
Klein Martin and Manfred J.M. Neumann. 1990. 'Seigniorage: What Is It and Who Gets It?' I4&twirtschaftlichea Archiv (Heft 2/1990): 205–21.

Kopits, G. and Symansky, S. 1998. 'Fiscal Policy Rules'. IMF Occasional Paper No. 162, Washington, D.C: IMF.
Kormendi, R.C. 1983. 'Government Debt, Government Spending and Private Sector Behaviour'. *The American Economic Review*, 73 (5): 783–92.
Kotlikoff, L.J. 1984. 'Economic Impact of Deficit Financing'. *IMF Staff Papers* 31(3): 549–82.
Krishna, K.L. (ed.) 1997. *Econometric Applications in India*. New Delhi: Oxford University Press.
Krishnamurty, K. 1985. 'Inflation and Growth: A Model for India'. In *Macro-econometric Modeling of Indian Economy: Studies on Inflation and Growth*, edited by K. Krishnamurty and V.N. Pandit. New Delhi: Hindustan Publishers.
Krugman, P. 1988. 'Financing vs. Forgiving a Debt Overhang'. *Journal of Development Economics*, 29(3): 253–68.
Kulkarni, G.K., and J.U. Balders. 1998. 'An Empirical Study of the Crowding Out Hypothesis: A Case of Mexico'. *Prajnan*, 27(3): 263–79.
Kulkarni, G.K., and L.E. Erickson. 1994. 'Is Crowding-out Hypothesis Evident in LDCs?: A Case of India'. *Prajnan*, 22(1): 11–24.
Kulkarni, G. Kishore, and Erick lee Erickson. 1996. 'Is Crowding out Hypothesis Evident in LDCs? A Case of India'. *Indian Economic Journal*, 43(1): 116–26.
Kumar, Pankaj and Pratik Mitra. 2012. 'Fiscal Stance, Credibility and Inflation Persistence in India'. Working Paper No. 13. Mumbai: Reserve Bank of India Publications.
Lahiri, A.K. 1991. 'Money and Inflation in Yugoslavia'. *International Monetary Fund Staff Papers*, 38(4): 751–88.
Lahiri, A., and R. Kannan. 2001. 'India's Fiscal Deficits and their Sustainability in Perspective'. Paper Presented at *World Bank-NIPFP Seminar on Fiscal Policies for Growth*. Mumbai: RBI.
Laubach, Thomas. 2009. 'New Evidence on the Interest Rate Effects of Budget Deficits and Debt'. *Journal of the European Economic Association*, 7 (4, June): 858–85.
———. 2011. 'Fiscal Policy and Interest Rates: The Role of Sovereign Default Risk'. *NBER International Seminar on Macroeconomics*, 7 (1, May): 7–30.
Lavhari, D. and D. Patinkin. 1968. 'The Role of Money in a Simple Growth Model'. *The American Economic Review*, 75(4): 828–35.
Leeper, E.M. 1991. 'Equilibria under Active and Passive Monetary and Fiscal Policies'. *Journal of Monetary Economics*, 27(1): 129–47.
Lerner, A.P. 1943. 'Functional Finance and the Federal Debt'. *Social Research*, 10(1): 38–51.
Levy, M.D. 1981. 'Factors Affecting Monetary Policy in an Era of Inflation'. *Journal of Monetary Economics*, 8(3): 351–73.
Limosani, M. 2000. 'Crowding In or Crowding Out in a Tobinian Model: A Note on the Economic Consequences of Financing Government Deficits when Money Supply is Endogenous'. *EconomiaInternazionale (International Economics)*, 53(3): 359–70.
Lin, X. 1999. 'Central-Bank Independence, Economic Behavior, and Optimal Term Lengths: Comment'. *The American Economic Review*, 89(4): 1056–62.
Lin, H.Y. and H.P. Chu. 2013. 'Are fiscal deficits inflationary?' *Journal of International Money and Finance*, 32: 214–33.
Litterman, R.B. 1986. 'Forecasting with Bayesian Vector Autoregressions: Five Years of Experience'. *Journal of Business and Economic Statistic*, 4(1): 25–38.
Little, I.M.D., and V. Joshi. 1994. *India: Macroeconomics and Political Economy*. Washington, D.C.: The World Bank.

Lothian, J. 1985. 'Equilibrium Relationships between Money and Other Economic Variables'. *The American Economic Review*, 75(4): 828–35.

Lucas, R.E., Jr. 1973. 'Some International Evidence on Output Inflation Trade-off'. *The American Economic Review*, 63(3): 326–34.

———. 1980. 'Two Illustrations of the Quantity Theory of Money'. *The American Economic Review*, 70(3): 1005–14.

———. 1996. 'Nobel Lecture: Money Neutrality'. *Journal of Political Economy*, 104(4): 661–82.

Lybek, T. 1998. 'Central Bank Autonomy, and Inflation and Output Performance in the Baltic States, Russia, and Other Countries of the Former Soviet Union, 1995–97'. IMF Working Paper No. WP/99/04. Washington, D.C: IMF.

MacKinnon, J.G. 1991. 'Critical Values of Cointegration Tests'. In *Long-run Economic Relationships: Readings in Cointegration*, edited by R.F. Engle and C.W.J. Granger. New York: Oxford University Press.

Madalgi, S.S. 1976. 'Trends in Monetisation in the Indian Economy: 1961–62 to 1974–75'. RBI Occasional Paper No. 1–2. Mumbai: RBI.

Mahajan S., S.K. Saha and C. Singh. 2014. 'Inflation Targeting in India'. Working Paper No. 449. Bangalore: Indian Institute of Management.

Majumdar, T. (ed.) 1993. *Nature, Man and the Indian Economy*. New Delhi: Oxford University Press.

Makin, J. 1983. 'Real Interest, Money Surprises, Anticipated Inflation and Fiscal Deficits'. *Review of Economics and Statistics*, 65(3): 374–84.

Maloney, J. (ed.). 1998. *Debt and Deficits: A Historical Perspective*. Cheltenham, UK: Edward Elgar Publishing Ltd.

Manasse, Paolo. 2007. 'Deficit Limits and Fiscal Rules for Dummies'. *IMF Staff Papers*, 54(3): 455–73.

Martijn, J.K. and H. Samiei. 1999. 'Central Bank Independence and the Conduct of Monetary Policy in the United Kingdom'. IMF Working Paper No. WP/99/170. Washington, D.C: IMF.

Marty, A.L. 1967. 'Growth and Welfare Cost of Inflationary Finance'. *Journal of Political Economy*, 75(1): 71–77.

McCallum, B.T. 1996. 'Crucial Issues Concerning Central Bank Independence'. National Bureau of Economic Research Working Paper No. 5597. Cambridge, MA: NBER.

McCallum, Bennett T. 1988. 'Robustness Properties of a Rule for Monetary Policy'. Carnegie-Rochester Conference Series on Public Policy (Autumn 1988, 29): 173–203.

———. 2001. 'Indeterminacy Bubbles, and Fiscal Theory of Price Determination'. *Journal of Monetary Economics*, 47(1): 19–30.

McKinnon, R.I. 1973. *Money and Capital in Economic Development*. Washington, D.C.: The Brookings Institution.

McKinnon, R.I. 1988. 'Monetary and Exchange Rate Policies for International Financial Stability: A Proposal'. *Journal of Economic Perspectives*, 2(1): 83–104.

Mcmillin, W.D., and T.D. Beard. 1980. 'The Short-run Impact of Fiscal Policy on the Money Supply'. *Southern Economic Journal*, 47(1): 97–109.

McMillin, W.D. and F. Koray. 1989. 'An Empirical Analysis of the Macroeconomic Effects of Government Debt: Evidence from Canada'. *Applied Economics*, 21(1): 113–24.

Mervyn, K. (eds.). The Debt Burden and Its Consequences for Monetary Policy, Proceedings of a Conference held by the International Economic Association at the Deutsche Bundesbank, Frankfurt, Germany.

Meyer, J. and E. Kuch. 1957. *The Investment Decision*. Cambridge, MA: Harvard University Press.
Minhas, B.S. 1987. 'The Planning Process and the Annual Budgets: Some Reflections on Recent Indian Experience'. *Indian Economic Review*, 22(2): 115–47.
Mino, K. 1989. 'Implications of Endogenous Money Supply Rules in Dynamic Models with Perfect Foresight'. *Journal of Macroeconomics*, 11(2): 81–97.
Mishkin, F. 1982. 'Does Anticipated Monetary Policy Matter? An Econometric Investigation'. *Journal of Political Economy*, 90(1): 22–51.
———. 1997. 'Strategies for Controlling Inflation'. NBER Working Paper No. 6122. Cambridge, MA: NBER.
Mishra, Prachi and Devesh Roy. 2011. 'Explaining Inflation in India: The Role of Food Prices'. Presentation at the Brookings Institution – National Council of Applied Economic Research India Policy Forum, New Delhi.
Mistry, Percy. 2007. High Powered Expert Committee (HPEC) on Mumbai as an International Financial Centre (MIFC), by Sage Publications.
Modigliani, F. 1961. 'Long-run Implications of Alternative Fiscal Policies and the Burden of the National Debt'. *Economic Journal*, 71(284): 730–55.
Modigliani, F. and M. Miller. 1958. 'The Cost of Capital, Corporate Finance and the Theory of Investment'. *The American Economic Review*, 58(3): 261–97.
Mody, R.J. 1991. 'On defining the Fiscal Deficit'. *Economic and Political Weekly*, 26(38): 2223–24.
———. 1992. 'Fiscal Deficit and Stabilisation Policy'. *Economic and Political Weekly* 27(7): 325–26.
———. 1994. 'Calculating the Fiscal Deficit'. *Economic and Political Weekly*, 29(38): 2507–08.
Mohanty, M.S. 1995. 'Budget Deficits and Private Savings in India: Evidence on Ricardian Equivalence'. *RBI Occasional Papers*, 16(1): 1–26.
Mohanty, M.S. and M. Klau. 2001. 'What Determines Inflation in Emerging Market Countries?' BIS Papers No. 8, Modeling Aspects of the Inflation Process and Monetary Transmission Mechanism in Emerging Market Countries.
Mohanty, Deepak and John Joice. 2014. 'Determinants of Inflation in India'. *Journal of Asian Economics*, 36(c): 86–89.
Molho, L. 1986. 'Interest Rates, Saving and Investment in Developing Countries: A Re-examination of the McKinnon-Shaw Hypothesis'. *IMF Staff Papers*, 33(1): 90–116.
Moore, B.J. 1988. 'The Endogenous Money Supply'. *Journal of Post Keynesian Economics* 10(3): 372–85.
Morgan, D.R. 1979. 'Fiscal Policy of Oil Exporting Countries, 1972–78'. *IMF Staff Papers*, 26(1): 55–86.
Moroney, J.R. 2002. 'Monetary Growth, Output Growth and Inflation: Estimation of a Modern Quantity Theory'. *Southern Economic Journal*, 69 (2): 398–413.
Mountford, Andrew and Harald Uhlig. 2009. 'What Are the Effects of Fiscal Policy Shocks?'. *Journal of Applied Econometrics*, 24(6, September–October): 960–92.
Mukherjee, C., W. White and M. Wuyts. 1998. *Econometrics and Data Analysis for the Developing Countries*. London: Routledge.
Mundell, R.A. 1965. 'Growth, Stability and Inflationary Finance'. *Journal of Political Economy*, 73(2): 97–109.
Mundle, S. 1999. 'Fiscal Policy and Growth: Some Asian Lessons for Asia'. *Journal of Asian Economics*, 10(1): 15–36.

Mundle, S. and H. Mukhopadhyay. 1993. 'Stabilization and the Control of Government Expenditure in India'. In *Development and Change: Essays in Honour of K. N. Raj*, edited by P. Bardhan, M. Dutta Chowdhury, and T.N. Krishnan. New Delhi: Oxford University Press.

Naastepad, C.W.M. 1999. *The Budget Deficit and Macroeconomic Performance: A Real-financial Computable General Equilibrium Model for India*. USA: Oxford University Press.

———. 2002. 'Effective Supply Failures and Structural Adjustment: A Real-financial Model with reference to India'. *Cambridge Journal of Economics*, 26(5): 637–58.

Nachane, D.M. and R.M. Nadkharni. 1985. 'Empirical Testing of Certain Monetarist Propositions Via Causality Theory: The Indian Case'. *Indian Economic Journal* 1(1): 13–41.

Nachane, D.M., R.M. Nadkarni and A.V. Karnik. 1988. 'Cointegration and Causality Testing of the Energy-GDP Relationship: A Cross-country Study'.*Applied Economics*, 20(11): 1511–31.

Nachane, D.M., A.V. Karnik and N.R. Hatekar. 1997. 'The Interest Rate Imbroglio: Monetary and Fiscal Dimensions'. *Economic and Political Weekly*, 1167–74.

Neumann. 1992. 'Seigniorage in the United States: How Much Does the U. S. Government Make from Money Production?' *Federal Reserve Bank of St Louis Review*, 74(2): 29–40.

Niskanen, W.A. 1978. 'Deficits, Government Spending and Inflation: What is the Evidence?' *Journal of Monetary Economics*, 4(3): 591–602.

Nugent, J.B. and C. Glezakos. 1979. 'A Model for Inflation and Expectations in Latin America'. *Journal of Development Economics*, 6(3): 431–46.

Onis, Z. and S. Ozmucur. 1990. 'Exchange Rates, Inflation and Money Supply in Turkey'. *Journal of Development Economics*, 32(1): 133–54.

Ostrosky, A. 1979. 'An Empirical Analysis of the Crowding-out Effect of Fiscal Policy in the United States and Canada: Comments and Extensions'. *Kyklos* 32(4): 813–16.

Otto, G. and G.M. Voss. 1994. 'Public Capital and Private Sector Productivity'. *Economic Record*, 70(209): 121–32.

———. 1996. 'Public Capital and Private Production in Australia'. *Southern Economic Journal*, 62(3): 723–38.

Pandit, V. 1978. 'An Analysis of Inflation in India, 1950–1975'. *Indian Economic Review*, 23(2): 89–115.

———. 1985. 'Macroeconomic Adjustments in a Developing Economy: A Medium term model of output and prices in India'. In *Macroeconometric Modelling of the Indian Economy: Studies on Inflation and Growth*, edited by K. Krishnamurtyand V. Pandit. New Delhi: Hindustan PC.

Park, Y.C. 1973. 'The Role of Money in Stabilization Policy in Developing Countries'. *IMF Staff Papers*, 20(2): 379–418.

Parker, K. 1995.'The Behaviour of Private Investment'. IMF Occasional Paper No. 134, International Monetary Fund, Washington, D.C.

Patinkin, D. 1965.*Money, Interest and Prices*. New York: Harper and Row.

Patnaik, P. 2001. 'On Fiscal Deficits and Real Interest Rates'. *Economic and Political Weekly*, 36(14): 1160–63.

———. 2007. 'Budgetary Policy in the Context of Inflation'. *Economic and Political Weekly*, 42 (14, April): 1260–62.

Pattnaik, R.K., Amaresh Samantaraya. 2006. 'Indian Experience of Inflation: A Review of the Evolving Process'. *Economic and Political Weekly*, 41 (4, January–February): 349 and 351–357.
Pattnaik, R.K., S.M. Pillai and S. Das. 1999. *Budget Deficit in India: A Primer on Measurement*. Mumbai: Department of Economic Analysis and Policy, RBI Staff Studies.
Perotti, R. 1999. 'Fiscal Policy in Good Times and Bad'. *Quarterly Journal of Economics*, 114(4): 1399–436.
Perron, P. 1989. 'The Great Crash, the Oil Price Shock and the Unit-root Hypothesis'. *Econometrica*, 57(6): 1361–401.
Phelps, E. and J.B. Taylor. 1977. 'Stabilising Powers of Monetary Policy under Rational Expectations'. *Journal of Political Economy*, 85(1): 163–90.
Phillips, P.C.B. and P. Perron. 1987. 'Testing for a Unit-root in Time Series Regression'. *Biometrika*, 75(2): 335–46.
Pillai, S.M., S. Chatterjee, B. Singh, S. Das and A. Gupta. 1997. 'Fiscal Policy: Issues and Perspectives'. Reserve Bank of India Occasional Paper No. 18. Mumbai: RBI.
Pindyck, R. and A. Solimano. 1993. 'Economic Instability and Aggregate Investment'. *NBER Macroeconomics Annual*. Cambridge, MA: MIT Press.
Pindyk, R. 1988. 'Irreversible Investment, Capacity Choice and the Value of the Firm'. *The American Economic Review*, 78(5): 969–85.
Pinell Siles, Armando. 1979. 'Determinants of Private Industrial Investment in India'. World Bank Staff Working Paper No. 333. Washington, D.C.: The World Bank.
Poole, W. 1988. 'Monetary Policy Lessons of Recent Inflation and Disinflation'. *Journal of Economic Perspectives*, 2(3): 73–100.
Pradhan, B.K., D.K. Ratha and Atul Sarma. 1990. 'Complementarity between Public and Private Investment in India'. *Journal of Development Economics*, 33(1): 101–16.
Protopapadakis, A. and J. Siegel. 1987. 'Are Monetary Growth and Inflation Related to Government Deficits? Evidence from Ten Industrialised Countries'. *Journal of International Money and Finance*, 6(1): 31–48.
Prusty, Sadananda. 2012. 'State Fiscal Policy and Inflation in India'. World Review of Business Research, 2(4): 103–14.
Rakshit, M. 1987. 'On the Inflationary Impact of Budget Deficit'. *Economic and Political Weekly*, 22(19): AN35-AN37+AN39-AN42.
―――. 1993. 'Money, Credit and Monetary Policy'. In *Nature, Man and the Indian Economy*, edited by T. Majumdar. Delhi: Oxford University Press and New York and Toronto: Oxford.
―――. 2000. 'On Correcting Fiscal Imbalances in the Indian Economy—Some Perspectives'. *ICRA Bulletin, Money and Finance*, July–September: 19–58.
―――. 2005. 'Budget Deficit: Sustainability, Solvency and Optimality'. In *Readings in Public Finance*, edited by A. Bagchi. New Delhi: Oxford University Press.
―――. 2006. 'Budgetary Rules and Plan Financing: Revisiting the Fiscal Responsibility Act'. *Economic and Political Weekly*, 41 (43–44, November): 4547–53.
―――. 2010. 'Fiscal Consolidation and Inclusive Growth: The Finance Commission Approach'. *Economic and Political Weekly*, 45(48): 56–63.
Rakshit, M.K. 1994. 'Money and Public Finance under Structural Adjustment: The Indian Experience'. *Economic and Political Weekly*, 29(16–17): 923–37.
Ramachandran, V.S. 1983. 'Direction of Causality between Monetary and Real Variables in India: An Empirical Result'. *Indian Economic Journal*, 30 (1): 65–74.

Ramirez, M. 1994. 'Public and Private Investment in Mexico, 1950–90: An Empirical Analysis'. *Southern Economic Journal*, 61(1): 1–17.
Rangarajan, C. 2001. 'Some Critical Issues in Monetary Policy'. *Economic and Political Weekly*, 36(24): 2139–46.
Rangarajan, C. and R. Arif. 1990. 'Money, Output and Prices: A Macroeconometric Model'. *Economic and Political Weekly* (April), 25(16): 852–73.
Rangarajan, C. and M.S. Mohanty. 1997. 'Fiscal Deficit, External Balance and Monetary Growth—A Study of Indian Economy'. Reserve Bank of India Occasional Papers, 18(4): 583–653.
Rangarajan, C. and A. Singh. 1984. 'Reserve Money: Concepts and Policy Implications for India'. *RB I Occasional Papers*, 5(1): 1–26.
Rangarajan, C., A. Basu and N. Jadhav. 1989. 'Dynamics of Interaction between Government Deficit and Domestic'. *RBI Occasional Papers*, 10(3): 163–220.
Rao, M.G. 1998. 'Accommodating Public Expenditure Policies: The Case of Fast Growing Asian Economies'. *World Development*, 26(4): 673–94.
Rao, M.J. 1992. 'Operating Procedures for Conducting Monetary Policy'. *Indian Economic Journal*, 39(3): 162–84.
———. 1997. 'Monetary Economics: An Econometric Investigation'. In *Econometric Applications in India*, edited by K.L. Krishna. New Delhi: Oxford University Press.
———. 2000. 'On Some Unpleasant Monetarist Arithmetic'. *Indian Economic Journal*, 48(1): 56–60.
———. 2003. 'Science of Monetary Policy: Some Perspectives on the Indian Economy'. *Economic and Political Weekly*, 38(8): 809–20.
Rao, M.J. and R. Nallari. 1996. *Macroeconomics Stabilization and Adjustment*. New Delhi: Oxford University Press.
Reichlin, L., A. Turner and M. Woodford. 2013, August 21. 'Helicopter Money as a Policy Option'. *VoxEU.org*. Available at: http://www.voxeu.org/article/helicopter-money-policy-option (accessed on 26 February 2016).
Reinhart, C.M. and M.B. Sbrancia. 2011. 'The liquidation of government debt'. NBER Working Paper No. 16893. Cambridge, MA: NBER.
Reinhart, M.C. and M.K. Rogoff. 2013. 'Financial and sovereign debt crises: Some lessons learned and those forgotten', *IMF Working Papers*, 13(226). Washington DC
Reserve Bank of India. 1977. *Report of the Second Working Group on Money Supply*. Bombay: RBI.
———. 1985. *Report of the Committee to Review the Working of the Monetary System (Sukhamoy Chakravarty Report)*. Mumbai: RBI.
———. 1999a. *Budget Deficit in India: A Primer on Measurement*, Mumbai: RBI Staff Studies, Department of Economic Analysis and Policy, Reserve Bank of India.
———. 1999b. *Report on Currency and Finance*. Mumbai: RBI.
———. 2000. *Handbook of Statistics 2001*. Mumbai: RBI.
———. 2001. *Handbook of Statistics on Indian Economy*. Mumbai: RBI.
———. 2002. *Report on Currency and Finance, 2000–01*. Mumbai: RBI.
———. 2012. *The Report of Currency and Finance*. Mumbai: RBI.
———. 2014. The Report of the Expert Committee to Revise and Strengthen the Monetary Policy Framework (Urjit Patel Report). Mumbai: RBI.
———. 2015. *Hanbook of Statistics of Indian Economy*. Mumbai: RBI.
Ricardo, David. 1821. *On the Principles of Political Economy and Taxation*. London: John Murray.

Rochon, Louis-Philippe, and Mark Setterfield. 2007. 'Interest Rates, Income Distribution, and Monetary Policy Dominance: Post Keynesians and the 'Fair Rate' of Interest'. *Journal of Post Keynesian Economics*, 30(1): 13–42.
Rodney, J.L. 1977. 'Hyperinflation and the Supply of Money'. *Journal of Money, Credit and Banking*, 9(1): 387–403.
Rolnick, A.J. and E.W. Warren. 1995. 'Money, Inflation and Output under Fiat and Commodity Standards'. *Journal of Political Economy*, 105(6): 1308–21.
Romer, Christina D. 1992. 'What Ended the Great Depression?' *Journal of Economic History*, 52 (December): 757–84.
Romer, Christina and Jared Bernstein. 8 January 2009. 'The Job Impact of the American Recovery and Reinvestment Plan'.
Ryan-Collins. 2015. 'Is Monetary Financing Inflationary? A Case Study of the Canadian Economy'. Levy Economics Institute Working Paper No. 848, New York: 1935–75.
Sachs, J.D. 1988. 'International Policy Coordination: The Case of the Developing Country Debt Crisis'. In *International Economic Cooperation. NBER Conference Report Series*, edited by Feldstein, M. Chicago, IL and London: University of Chicago Press.
Saini, K.G. 1982. 'The Monetarist Explanation of Inflation: The Experience of Six Asian Countries'. *World Development*, 10(10): 871–84.
Sankar, D. 1997. *Private Corporate Investment in India: An Analysis of its Relationship with Public Investment*. Unpublished M. Phil. Thesis, Centre for Development Studies, Thiruvananthapuram.
Saracoglu, R. 1984. 'Expectations of Inflation and Interest Rate Determination'. *IMF Staff Papers*, 31(1): 141–78.
Sargent, Thomas and Neil Wallace. April 1975. '"Rational" Expectations, the Optimal Monetary Instrument'. *Journal of Political Economy*, 83(2): 241–54.
Sargent, Thomas J. 1976. 'The demand for money during hyperinflations under rational expectations: II'. Working Papers 60, Federal Reserve Bank of Minneapolis.
———. 'Commodity Price Expectations and the Interest Rate'. *Quarterly Journal of Economics*, 83(1): 127–40.
———. 1993. *Rational Expectations and Inflation* (Second Edition). New York: Harper Collins and College Publishers.
Sargent, T.J. and N. Wallace. 1973. 'Rational Expectations and the Dynamics of Hyperinflation'. *International Economic Review*, 2(2): 328–50.
———. 1981. 'Some Unpleasant Monetary Arithmetic'. *Federal Reserve Bank of Minneapolis Quarterly Review*, Fall, 5(3): 1–7.
Sarma, Y.S.R. 1982. 'Government Deficit, Money Supply and Inflation in India'. *Reserve Bank of India Occasional Papers*, 3(1): 56–67.
Sawyer, Malcolm. 2009. 'Fiscal and Interest Rate Policies in the 'New Consensus' Framework: A Different Perspective'. *Journal of Post Keynesian Economics*, 31(4): 549–65.
Schaechter, A., T. Kinda, N. Budina and A. Weber. 2012. *Fiscal Rules in Response to the Crisis—Toward the "Next-Generation" Rules*. A New Dataset, International Monetary Fund Working Paper No. WP/12/187.
Shafik, N. 1992. 'Modeling Private Investment in Egypt'. *Journal of Development Economics*, 39(2): 263–77.
Shariff, K. 1990. *Macroeconomic Policy, Performance and Private Investment*. Washington DC: World Bank, Country Economics Department.
Shaw, E.S. 1973. *Financial Deepening in Economic Development*. New York: Oxford University Press.

Sheeley, E.J. 1980. 'Money, Income and Prices in Latin America: An empirical Note'. *Journal of Development Economics*, 7(3): 345–57.

Sheel, Alok. 2014. 'The Unraveling of Inflation Targeting'. *Economic and Political Weekly*, 49(20): 15–19.

Shiller, R.J. 1979. 'The Volatility of Long-term Interest Rates and Expectations Models of the Term Structure'. *Journal of Political Economy*, 87(6): 1190–219.

Siddique, A. 1989. 'The Causal Relation between Money and Inflation in a Developing Economy'. *International Economic Journal*, 3(2): 79–96.

Sidney, L. 1991. 'The Macroeconomic effects of Government Debt in a stochastic Growth Model'. *Journal of Monetary Economics*, 38(1): 25–45.

Sidrauski, M. 1967. 'Inflation and Economic Growth'. *Journal of Political Economy*, 75(1): 796–810.

Sims, C. 1972. 'Money, Income and Causality'. *The American Economic Review*, 62(4): 540–52.

———. 1980. 'Macroeconomics and Reality'. *Econometrica*, 48(1): 1–48.

———. 1994. 'A Simple Model for Study of the Determination of the Price Level and the Interaction of Monetary and Fiscal Policy'. *Economic Theory*, 4(3): 381–99.

Singh, Kanhaiya. 2006. 'Inflation Targeting: International Experience and Prospects for India'. *Economic and Political Weekly*, 41 (27–28 July): 2958–61.

Smith, Adam. 1776. *An Inquiry into the Nature and Causes of the Wealth of Nations*, London: W. Strahan and T. Cadell.

Spaventa, L. 1987. 'Public Debt and Monetary Growth: An Exercise in Monetarist Arithmetic'. In *Monetary Theory and Economic Institutions*, edited by M. de Cecco and J.P. Fitoussi. London: Macmillan Press; Proceedings at Internal Economic Association, Florence, Italy.

Srivastava, D.K. 1987. 'Policy Simulation with a Macroeconomic Model of the Indian Economy'. *Journal of Policy Modeling*.

———. 2006. 'FRBM Act and Eleventh Plan Approach Paper'. *Economic and Political Weekly*, 41 (43–44, November): 4553–59.

Stein, J.L 1969. 'Neoclassical and Keynes-Wicksell Monetary Growth Models'. *Journal of Money, Credit and Banking*, 1(2): 153–71.

———. 1976. *Monetarism*. Amsterdam, Oxford: North Holland Publishing Company.

Steindl, F.G. 1990. 'Interest Rates, Inflationary Expectations and Endogenous Money Finance in a Growth Model with a Government Budget Restraint'. *Southern Economic Journal*, 57(1): 1–13.

Stigliz, J. and A. Weiss. 1981. 'Credit Rationing in Markets with Imperfect Information'. *The American Economic Review*, 71(2): 399–404.

Stock, J.H., and M.H. Watson. 1989. 'Interpreting the Evidence on Money-income Causality'. *Journal of Econometrics*, 40(1): 161–81.

———. (eds.). 1993a. 'Business Cycles, Indicators, and Forecasting'. In *NBER Studies in Business Cycles* (Volume 28). Chicago, IL and London: University of Chicago Press.

———. 1993b. 'A Simple Estimator of Cointegrating Vectors in Higher Order Integrated Systems'. *Econometrica*, 61(4): 783–820.

Sturm, J.E. 1998. *Public Capital Expenditure in OECD countries: The Causes and Impact of the Decline in Public Capital Spending*. Cheltenham, UK: Edward Elgar Publishing Limited.

Subbarao, D. 1994. 'Calculating the Fiscal Deficit'. *Economic and Political Weekly* 27 August, 29(35): 2311.

Sundararajan, V. and S. Thakur. 1980. 'Public Investment, Crowding Out and Growth: A Dynamic Model applied to India and Korea'. *IMF Staff Papers*, 27(4): 814–55.
Sutherland, A. 1997. 'Fiscal Crises and Aggregate Demand: Can High Public Debt Reverse the Effects of Fiscal Policy'. *Journal of Public Economics*, 65(2): 147–62.
Svensson, L.E.O. 1997. 'Inflation Forecast Targeting: Implementation and Monitoring Inflation Targets'. *European Economic Review*, 41(6): 1111–46.
Svensson, Lars E.O. and Michael Woodford. 2005. 'Implementing Optimal Policy through Inflation Forecast Targeting'. In Ben S. Bernanke and Michael Woodford, (eds.), *The Inflation Targeting Debate*. Chicago: University of Chicago Press, 19–83.
Swanson, N.R. 1998. 'Money and Output Viewed through a Rolling Window'. *Journal of Monetary Economics*, 41(3): 455–74.
Tambakis, D.N. 1999. 'Effective Central Bank Independence and the Inflation-Output Trade-off', *Journal of Macroeconomics*, 21(4): 729–53.
Tanzi, V. 1977. 'Inflation, Lags in Collection and the Real Value of Tax Revenue'. *IMF Staff Papers*, 24(1): 540–607.
———. 1978. 'Inflation, Real Tax Revenue and the Case for Inflationary Finance: Theory with Application to Argentina'. *IMF Staff Papers*, 25(3): 417–51.
———. 1985. 'Fiscal Deficits and Interest Rates in the United States: An Empirical Analysis'. *IMF Staff Papers*, 32(4): 571–72.
Tanzi, Vito and Mario Blejer. 1988. 'Public Debt and Fiscal Policy in Developing Countries'. In *Economics of Public Debt*, edited by Kenneth Arrow and Michael Boskin. New York: Martin's Press.
Tanzi, V. and M. Teijeiro. 1988. 'The effects of inflation on the measurement of fiscal deficits'. In *The Measurement of Fiscal Impact: Methodological Issues*, edited by M. Blejerand C. Ke-young. Washington D.C.: International Monetary Fund.
Taylor, J.B. (ed.). 1999. *Monetary Policy Rules*. Chicago, IL: University of Chicago Press.
Taylor, John B. and John C. Williams. 2010. 'Simple and Robust Rules for Monetary Policy'. In *Handbook of Monetary Economics* (First Edition, Volume 3), edited by Benjamin M. Friedman, B.M. and Michael Woodford, 829–59. New York: Elsevier.
Taylor, L. 1979. *Macromodels for Developing Countries*. New York: McGraw Hill.
———. 1989. *Stabilisation and Growth in Developing Countries: A Structuralist Approach*. New York: Harwood.
Temple, J. 1998. 'Central Bank Independence and Inflation: Good News and Bad News'. *Economic Letters*, 61(2): 215–19.
Thoma, M.A. 1994. 'Subsample Instability and Asymmetries in Money-income Causality'. *Journal of Econometrics*, 64(1–2): 279–306.
Tobin, J. 1965. 'Money and Economic Growth'. *Econometrica*, 33(4): 671–84.
———. 1969. 'A General Equilibrium Approach to Monetary Theory'. *Journal of Money, Credit and Banking*, 1(1): 15–29.
Tun, W.U. and C. Wong. 1982. 'Determinants of Private Investment in Developing Countries'. *Journal of Development Studies*, 19(1): 19–63.
Valila, T.T. 1999. 'Credibility of Central Bank Independence Revisited'. IMF Working Paper No. WP/99/02. Washington, D.C: IMF.
van den Noord, P. 2000. 'The Size and Role of Automatic Fiscal Stabilisers in the 1990s and Beyond'. OECD Economics Department Working Papers No. 230. Paris: OECD.
van Wijnbergen, Sweder. 1989. 'Cash Debt Buybacks and the Insurance Value of Reserves'. Policy Research Working Paper Series No. 256, Washington D.C.: World Bank.

Vickrey, W. 1961. 'The Burden of the Public Debt: Comment'. *The American Economic Review*, 51 (March): 132–37.
Vinod, Hrishikesh D. 2004. 'Ranking Mutual Funds Using Unconventional Utility Theory and Stochastic Dominance'. *Journal of Empirical Finance*, 11(3): 353–77.
———. 2006. 'Maximum Entropy Ensembles for Time Series Inference in Economics'. *Journal of Asian Economics*, 17: 955–78.
———. 2013. 'Maximum Entropy Bootstrap Algorithm Enhancements'. Fordham Economics Discussion Paper Series No. dp2013-04, Fordham University: Department of Economics.
Vinod, H. D., Lekha Chakraborty and Honey Karun. 2014. 'If Deficit not the Culprit, What Determines Interest Rate in India: Evidence from Maximum Entropy Bootstrap for Time Series'. Working Paper No. 811, The Levy Economics Institute, New York.
Vinod, H.D. and J. Lopez-de-Lacalle. 2009. 'Maximum Entropy Bootstrap for Time Series: The Meboot R Package'. *Journal of Statistical Software*, 29(5): 1–19.
Vogel, R.C. 1974. 'The Dynamics of Inflation in Latin America, 1950–69'. *The American Economic Review*, 64(1): 102–14.
Wang, Zijun and Andrew J. Rettenmaier. 2008. 'Deficits, Explicit Debt, Implicit Debt, and Interest Rates: Some Empirical Evidence'. *Southern Economic Journal*, 75 (1, July): 208–22.
Williamsin, J. 1988. 'On McKinnon's Monetary Rule'. *Journal of Economic Perspectives*, 2(1): 113–20.
Winckler, G., H. Eduard and B. Peter. 1998. 'Deficits, Debt and European Monetary Union: Some Unpleasant Fiscal Arithmetic'. In *The Debt Burden and Its Consequences for Monetary Policy*, edited by G. Calvo and M. King; Proceedings of a Conference held by the International Economic Association at the Deutsche Bundesbank, Frankfurt, Germany.
Wolde-Rufael, Yemane. 2008. 'Budget Deficits, Money and Inflation: The Case of Ethiopia'. *The Journal of Developing Areas*, 42 (1, Fall): 183–99.
Wood, John H. 1981. 'Interest Rates and Inflation'. *Federal Reserve Bank of Chicago Economic Perspectives*, 5 (May/June): .
Woodford, Michael. 2003. *Interest and Prices: Foundations of a Theory of Monetary Policy*. Princeton, NJ: Princeton University Press.
Wolf, M. 2013. 'The Case for Helicopter Money'. *The Financial Times*, February 12. Available online at http://www.ft.com/intl/cms/s/0/9bcf0eea-6f98-11e2-b906-00144feab49a.html#axzz421rMvLHJ (accessed on 15 March 2016).
Woodford, M, 1994. 'Monetary Policy and Price Level Determinacy in a Cash-Advance Economy'. *Economic Theory*, 4(3): 345–80.
World Bank. 1996. *India—Five Years of Stabilization and Reform and the Challenges Ahead.* Washington, D.C.: World Bank.
Wray, L.R. 1992. 'Commercial Banks, the Central Bank, and Endogenous Money'. *Journal of Post Keynesian Economics*, 14(3): 297–310.

Index

accelerator principle, 47
accrual deficit, *See also* fiscal deficit, 6
aggregate demand function, 159
amortized debt, 5
analytical framework of deficit, 89

bank credit, 54
bank rate, 24, 92
Barro's model, 137
bond financing of deficit, 44
budget balance, 16
budget deficit, 3, 45, 110
    deficit financing through ad hoc treasury bills by RBI, 14
    depends on Reserve Bank policy, 4
    excess of net external borrowing by government, 4
    high ration impact on, 15
    traditional measure of, 4

Cagen's model, 134
call money market rate, 24, 92
capital flows, 87, 89
causality detection, 150
Central Bank, 128, 134, 170
    balance sheet, 121
    financing deficit, 135
    historical and empirical evidences against independence, 152
    profit transfer, 122
Central Bank Independence (CBI), 128
central government deficits in India, trends in, 19
Chakravarty Committee Report, 110, 155

closed economy, 8
co-movement of fiscal and monetary seigniorage, 124
complementary period, 6
contemporary macroeconomic policy, 105
corporate investment, 48
crowd out private capital accumulation, 8
crowding out,
    empirical evidences on, 79
    in Mexican economy, 53
crowding,
    levels of, 44
    reason for, 45
    study in India, 46
    taxonomy of, 45
cyclical deficit, 16

Debt Control Act, 1
debt servicing, 5
deficit financed tax cut, 8
deficit financing, 110
deficit financing,
    definition of, 110
Deficit Reduction, 1
deficit-money,
    historical and empirical perspectives, 152
deficits induced inflation, 134
deregulated financial regime, 150
deregulation of interest rate in India, 110
Diamond's model, 8
direct crowding, 44
dollar-for-dollar basis, 44, 168

dynastic resources, 9

econometric estimation and results, 68, 145
econometric model, 145
Engle–Granger methodology, 63
error correction model, 63, 67, 70, 75, 120
European Monetary Union, 1
excessive deficit procedures (EDP), 165
external debt financing of fiscal deficit, 60
external financing of deficits, 16
extra taxes, 9

FIML approach, 63
final prediction error (FPE), 66, 70, 99, 160
financial crisis, 163
financial crowding out, 45, 53, 169
financial effect, 88
financial theories, 47
financing of deficits framework, 12
fiscal activism, 163
fiscal austerity, 163
fiscal consolidation, 29, 164, 165
  at subnational level in India, 30
fiscal deficit, 177, 133, 135, 152, 162
fiscal deficit,
  money supply, linkage between, 146
  alternative paradigms on macroeconomic effects of, 10
  and private capital formation, 24
  and rate of interest, 26
  and rate of interest, empirical evidences on link between, 82
  and rate of interest, link in deregulated financial regime, 103
  at subnational governments, 7
  containment, 2165
  creates money creation, 137
  cyclical and structural, derivation of, 18
  definition of, 5

excessive, 166
financing identity, 11
financing pattern of, 60
high frequency data analysis, 149
in 2007–08, 13
investment vacuum, 43
limitations of, 7
macroeconomic impact of, 10
measuring macroeconomic impact, relevance in measurement of, 7
methodological limitation, 6
monetisation of, 133
money supply, effect on, 12
OECD methodology for decomposing, 17
of high income states, 32
of low income states, 36
of middle income states, 36
reduction of, 1
related to monetary base, 142
seigniorage, impact on, 169
fiscal dominance, 134, 164
  hypothesis of UMA, 134
fiscal multiplier, 164
fiscal policy institutions, 105
fiscal reforms,
  principle objectives of, 1
Fiscal Responsibility and Budget Management (FRBM), 28, 30
Fiscal Responsibility and Budget Management Act (FRBM), 1
Fiscal Rules, 13, 108, 110, 119, 120
fiscal seigniorage,
  analytical framework of, 123
  estimation of, 124
  Laffer Curve, estimation, 127
fiscal space, 164
fiscal theory of the price level (FTPL), 104
fiscal-monetary policy linkages, 104
Fisher equation, 24
flexible accelerator models, 47
foreign grants, 5
foreign loan, 4

Index

FOREX assets, 120
forex market, 89
Fourteenth Finance Commission, 29
full information maximum likelihood, 71

Gen-Next rules-based fiscal policy, 120
Goria Plan, Italy, 1
government deficit, 2
government expenditure, 5
Gramm-Rudman-Hollings Act, United States, 1
Granger-causality test, 63, 64, 103
gross fiscal deficit, 13
   definition of, 6
Gross Fixed Capital Formation (GFCF), 23
gross investment in private sector, 54
gross redemption yield of Government of India Securities, 24
gross state domestic product (GSDP), 31

high frequency regime,
   detection of optimal lags and FPE, 103
   test results for real rate of interest and fiscal deficit, 103
high income states, 31
high-powered money, 121, 133
Hodrick-Prescott (HP) filter, 93, 94
Hsiao's asymmetric vector autoregressive framework, 61

IMF, 3, 16
Index of Industrial production (IIP), 148
indirect crowding, 45
inflation, 177, 133
   analytical framework, 160
   conceptual backdrop and empirical literature, 158
   determination models, 153
   tax, 120
   and seigniorage, robustness in, 113

inflation-econometric model, 161
inflationary phenomenon in India, 153
interest rate, 87
   function of fiscal deficits, 87
   targeting, 135
intra public sector transactions, 2, 7
investment,
   analysis of, 46
   related linearly to past changes, 47
   vacuum, 43

Keynesian framework, 153
Keynesian paradigm on fiscal deficit, 9

Laffer Curve, 127
linear regression model for private investment, 57
liquidity effect, 88
loanable funds model, 82
long run rates of interest, 167
low income states, 31

Maastricht Treaty (1992), 130
Macro-Fiscal Rule, 120
macroeconomic imbalances, 10
macroeconomic stabilization, 30
macrovariables movement in high frequency regime, 152
market rate, 92
Masshtrict Treaty, 1
Medium Term Financial Strategy, United Kingdom, 1
Medium Term Fiscal Consolidation Plans, 1
middle income states, 31
Ministry of Finance, 80
monetarist model, 155
monetarist tradition, 153
monetary authority, 104, 134
monetary framework in India, evolution of, 133
monetary policy, 137
monetary seigniorage Laffer Curve,

estimation of, 119
monetary targeting framework, 131
monetised deficit, 4, 15
  definition of, 4
  rise since 2008–09, 15
money multipliers, 133, 168
  descriptive statistics of, 152
  trends in, 152
money supply, 87, 133, 135
  and interest rate, 90
multiple indicator approach, 132

National Commission for Enterprises in the Unorganized Sector (NCEUS) study in 2005, 155
Neoclassical paradigm on fiscal deficit, 8
neoclassical view of deficit, 82
net investment in private sector, 54
net lending, 5
New Consensus Macroeconomics (NCM), 141
New Deal, 163
New Macroeconomic Consensus (NMC), 130, 142, 155, 170
New Monetary Framework, 154
nominal exchange rate, 91
nominal rate of interest, 93
non-homogeneity of public investment, 75
non-special category (NSC) states, 31

Oliveria-Tanzi effect, 134, 135
open economy,
  macroeconomic instability in, 67
open market operations (OMOs), 15, 167
open market purchases of Central Bank, 135
Overlapping Generations Model, 8

pegging interest rate process, 128

Phillips Curve model, 155
price expectation effect, *See* Fisher theory, 88
price vs quantity of credit, 60
primary deficit, 13
prime lending rate, 24, 25, 92, 169
Principles of Political Economy and Taxation (David Ricardo), 7
private capital formation, 24, 44
private corporate investment, 60
  and capital flows, 61
  interest rate sensitivity of, 67
private investment, 43, 44, 52
  and output expectations, 58
  modelling in India, 57
  opportunities in debtor countries, 61
private savings, 8
private spending, 45
public debt illusion, 10
public investment, 43, 44,52
public investment crowds, 47
public sector, 122
Public Sector Borrowing Requirement (PSBR), 2
public sector deficit, 2
public sector transactions, 2
public spending, 45
purpose specific deficit measures, 3
purpose-specific budgetary deficits, 3

quantitative easing (QE),
  vs seigniorage financing, 130
quantity theory-based models, 137, 150

rate of interest, 19, 24, 45
  and CPI rate of inflation, comovement of, 103
  and WPI rate of inflation, comovement of, 103
  econometric estimation of, 96
  links with macrovariables, 91

on assets, 122
real crowding, 44
real long run rate of interest model, 103,
real rates of interest,
   calculation of, 24
redemption yield on dated securities, 92
Reserve Bank of India (RBI), 3, 4, 80, 140
reserve money, 121
   high frequency data analysis and regime, 149, 152
revenue deficit, 13, 19
   of middle income states, 3236
   of special category states, 37
Ricardian Equivalence Theorem (RET), 9, 82, 166
Ricardian paradigm on fiscal deficit, 10
rule based monetary policy, 133

Sargent's model, 85
Say's law for deficits, 9
Seigniorage Laffer Curve, 106
seigniorage, 133, 149, 168
financing, 10
   financing, 130
   monetary, estimation of, 119
   short run rates of interest, 167

single measure of budget deficit, 3
small open economy,
   capital inflow in, 8
special category (SC) states, 31
structural deficit, 16
structuralist model, 155
subnational deficits,
   consolidated scenario of, 42
supply-side model, 155

Taylor Principle, 153
Thirteenth Finance Commission, 29
Tobin's Q theory, 47, 48
trends in deficits, 120
Twelfth Finance Commission, 28

Unpleasant Monetary Arithmetic (UMA), 104, 105, 134, 155, 170
unstable money multipliers, 150

Vector Auto Regression (VAR) methodology, 61
validation hypothesis, 135

Wealth of Nations (Adam Smith), 7
WPI,
   and CPI rates of inflation,
      comovement of, 103
   inflation rate in India, 160

About the Author

Lekha S. Chakraborty is an Associate Professor at National Institute of Public Finance and Policy, New Delhi, and a Research Associate at Levy Economics Institute of Bard College, New York. She has received a number of awards, including Shastri Indo-Canadian Institute (SICI) fellowship from the Department of Foreign Affairs and Trade, Canada, and the national (best) thesis award from Indian Institute of Science (IISc), Bangalore. She worked for International Monetary Fund (IMF), World Bank, United Nations Development Programme (UNDP), UN Women and the Commonwealth Secretariat on short stints. She was also Visiting Professor at Carleton University (Canada) and University of Utah (USA). Dr Chakraborty's cross-country work experiences encompass Canada, Morocco, The Philippines, South Africa, Mexico, India and Sri Lanka. She received PhD from the Centre for Development Studies, Thiruvananthapuram, Kerala, where she had also worked as an Associate Professor for one year. She has published extensively in national and international journals on macroeconomics of public finance and human development.